"Mark Joseph is a conscious writer with a love for music that moves both heaven and earth."

Lonn Friend, rock journalist, former editor, *Spin* magazine

"As Christian artists influence pop culture as never before, leave it to Mark Joseph to not only spot the phenomenon, but document it in painstaking detail. This book picks up where *Rock and Roll Rebellion* left off. A must for brave believers who, in the spirit of Christ, want to understand and engage the wide world rather than shrink from it."

Lou Carlozo, writer, editor, *Chicago Tribune*

"If you have ever wondered about God's concern for the rock and roll industry and the millions of lives it encircles, you cannot find a better resource than Mark Joseph's *Faith, God, and Rock & Roll*. His experience and knowledge are evident in every chapter of this informative and engaging book. I'm greatly encouraged to see the way that God is at work outside the bubble of my own religious subculture. Thank you, Mark."

Chuck Smith Jr., author, *The End of the World . . . As We Know It*

"An intriguing view of a significant and underreported segment of the popular music industry. Mark Joseph writes with the knowledge of an insider but never loses his big picture perspective on values and culture."

Michael Medved, radio talk show host, author, *Hollywood vs. America*

"The ancient question was 'What does Athens have to do with Jerusalem?' Today many are asking What does the cause of Christ have to do with rock & roll? The correct answer, it seems, is plenty! The Christian presence in popular music is now enormous. Mark Joseph knows more than anybody else about the opportunities this unprecedented situation brings and the problems it creates, both for the secular world and Christians. If you want to have a good time learning about how real faith operates in the world of rock music, curl up with this new book by the man who knows the whole story."

Phillip Johnson, author of *Darwin on Trial* and *Reason in the Balance*

"There is an undercurrent of profound spiritual content in popular music. *Faith, God, and Rock & Roll* is a riveting guide through the many spiritual influences of my favorite artists. This is a must read for anyone who is spiritually and culturally aware."

Chris Seay, author of *The Gospel According to Tony Soprano*

Faith, God, and
Rock & Roll

*How People of Faith Are Transforming
American Popular Music*

Mark Joseph

Baker Books

A Division of Baker Book House Co
Grand Rapids, Michigan 49516

Published simultaneously by Baker Books, a division of Baker Book House Company, P.O. Box 6287, Grand Rapids, MI 49516-6287, and Sanctuary Publishing Limited, Sanctuary House, 45-53 Sinclair Road, London W14 0NS, United Kingdom.
www.bakerbooks.com

Portions of this book appeared as essays at Crosswalk.com, Nationalreview.com, and Beliefnet.com.

Printed in the United States of America

Library of Congress Cataloging-in-Publication Data
Joseph, Mark, 1968–
    Faith, God, and rock & roll : how people of faith are transforming American popular music / Mark Joseph.
        p.   cm.
    Includes bibliographical references (p.).
    ISBN 0-8010-6500-3 (pbk.)
        1. Contemporary Christian music—United States—History and criticism. 2. Rock music—Religious aspects. I. Title: Faith, God, and rock and roll. II. Title.
ML3187.5.J66 2004
261.5'78—dc22   2003017274

Photographs courtesy of Redferns Music Picture Library, F Hanson/PA News/ CORBIS KIPA, Steve Azzara/CORBISSYGMA, Karen Mason Blair/CORBIS, Kevin Mazur/CORBISSYGMA, Mitchell Gerber/CORBIS, Frank Trapper/ CORBISSYGMA, Gregory Pace/CORBISSYGMA, Neal Preston/CORBIS

To Anna, Maryn, and Kara—"Wywoo . . . Always"

Contents

Contents

Foreword

"What do you mean I don't believe in God? I talk to him every day."

"Peace Sells . . . But Who's Buying?"—Megadeth, 1985

This is the response of many musicians when asked about their faith. The dude from Creed said something like this too. If you'd asked me in 1985, I would've been afraid to answer any deeper because the vultures are on the bedpost waiting for someone to backslide, to expose them as hypocrites or, as I used to call them, "hypochristians." Sadly, in many cases, as with P.O.D. and Howard Stern, these bands just do what God made them good at and they're attacked. Constantly walking in minefields set to expose someone's faith or lack thereof, this says more of the hunter than the hunted.

Faith, God, and Rock & Roll is about people who may not call themselves Christians, but who love God and try to make a difference in a beautiful world full of ugly people and ugly problems. They've maintained their musical integrity while not turning their backs on their faith. You also get a sense of why so many "believers" are cautious to say what their very behavior confirms.

Mark Joseph references how what the artists write and sing actually witnesses to their fans, laying seeds for people searching for relief to confusion and pain. And while they seemingly reject the Christian music industry, they aren't rejecting Christ.

I also found Dan Haseltine's response about Jars of Clay's name causing their struggle with the Christian-band stigmatism hilarious. He said, "and then there's a band called Ministry."

People, stomp out the stigmatism and let the music do the talking.

Dave Mustaine
Megadeth lead singer

Preface

I've learned that a book seems to have a life of its own—as if it is out there ready to be written but simply needs someone to do the actual work. I had written my first and, I thought, only book on this topic in 1999 and had no plans to revisit the subject. But in the spring of 2002, I received a letter from some colleagues that ended with this: "We are looking forward to reading the sequel to *The Rock & Roll Rebellion.*" I had no plans to write such a book, but something within me stirred and I heard, or rather felt, a voice say "It's time." With that, I began the journey of writing this book on airplanes, in coffee shops, in the desert, in my office, and at my home. While my previous publisher would have been a natural outlet, I felt this book needed to go to a wider audience. That was accomplished when an e-mail appeared in my inbox from Lonn Friend, a respected rock critic and former label head, who told me he had heard from a mutual friend—Tim Cook, manager of the group P.O.D.—that I was working on a book about religion and rock. Lonn and my publisher, Iain MacGregor, may have been looking for a book on P.O.D., but instead they got one on the whole scene. Here it is. *Pro Deo.*

Mark Joseph
March 2003

Acknowledgments

Thanks: Tim Cook, Lonn Friend, Iain MacGregor, Chris Seay, Sean Buell, Kara Joseph, Sean Lawrence, Daryn Gabriel, Erik Thoennes, Lance Cook, Chuck Smith Jr., Shea Ramquist, Evelyn Sen, Alisha Marrell, John Mark Reynolds, Jamie Lim, Micheal Flaherty, Jesus, Michael Guido, William F. Turner, Mark Rodgers, Jackie Marushka, Grace Group, Lou Carlozo, Chris Willman, Jehovah, Michael Medved, Shin Domen, Jody Hassett, Kerrigan, Reid, Jacko, Kitto, Julia, Jamee, Lydia, Sandy Becker, Terry Duffy, Tom Nash, Mitsuharu Tanaka, Daryl and Gail Berg, Dan Haseltine, Matt Slocum, Roberta, Howard, Ken Tamplin, Stephen Prendergast, Terry Mattingly, Robin Parrish, Dave Mustaine, Lila Joseph (the voice inside my head), Holy Spirit, Kenny Joseph, Bobb Joseph, Jim Joseph, Kimbo Joseph, Georgia Joseph, Cindi Joseph, Bob Hosack, John Sawyer, Ron Hardy, Pam Watson, Starbucks La Mirada, Renaissance Esmerelda IndianWells.

1

You Say You Want a Revolution

Almost from the inception of rock music, critics assailed it as the devil's music. But both rock's early detractors and supporters likely never anticipated that people of faith would one day show up en masse and invade mainstream rock & roll. But people of faith *have* showed up, and rock may never be the same again.

When I wrote *The Rock & Roll Rebellion: Why People of Faith Abandoned Rock Music and Why They're Coming Back*, I saw a day in the future—the *distant* future—when people of faith would reenter the popular music culture, not as "Christian artists" playing "Christian music" but as Christian men and women deeply committed to that faith, but who avoided those stigmatizing labels even as they infused their music with their faith. I thought I was being realistic saying it might take perhaps twenty years before the proper divisions were achieved: 80 percent of believers rejoining the mainstream of American pop cultural life and 20 percent continuing to perform in a church-based subculture.

What I didn't anticipate was that the changes would happen so rapidly. During the course of researching that book, I came across an interview with a young group from San Diego named

P.O.D. whose members had been claiming in interviews that they were soon to be signed to Atlantic Records and that they were going to enjoy a huge mainstream push. I confess I was doubtful—so doubtful that I didn't even mention them in the book. But I was wrong, for the band was disciplined and relentless in their quest to break out of the Christian subculture and affect the wider world with their music and their faith.

Another band that wasn't on my radar screen then was a Florida-based rock band named Creed. Still another was an L.A. band named Lifehouse. Kendall Payne was another who showed up on Capitol Records with her critically acclaimed album *Jordan's Sister*. Nickel Creek also appeared and took the alt/country scene by storm. Destiny's Child rocked the pop and R&B charts. Jessica Simpson got out of her deal with a Christian-oriented label and recorded a hit album for Sony.

But there wasn't one decisive moment when it became clear that popular music was in the process of undergoing a significant makeover; there were several—like the appearance of P.O.D. on the *Howard Stern Radio Show*, which showed clearly that there were two markedly different responses toward the shock jock from the faith community.

One was the tried and true approach of boycotting and pressuring advertisers to withdraw their sponsorship of the Stern program. The other was an even older approach first modeled by One who made it His habit to spend time with the spiritually sick, reasoning that it was they, not the spiritually fit, who most needed Him.

The first approach was that of a nationally known minister who used his own program to highlight the continuing campaign to reduce the number of stations carrying the Stern show and inform advertisers of what the self-proclaimed king of all media was up to.

The second was the appearance of P.O.D., whose members were on Stern's program and actually earned grudging respect from him in the process.

The members of P.O.D. may believe in the same God that the minister believed in, but their strategy couldn't have been more different. One was reactionary, demanding that those who offered offensive views be silenced, albeit through the legitimate process of moral peer pressure. The other was rooted in the kind of aggressive and confrontational strategy that found early leaders of the Christian faith repeatedly called to testify and defend their beliefs before the Sanhedrin and other public bodies that were hostile to their faith.

Howard Stern had probably never met the minister protesting against his show. He may never even have heard of him. But it's unlikely that Stern forgot P.O.D. As the members of P.O.D. lumbered into Stern's studio and put on their headphones to begin their session with the shock jock, they were sending an important message to the culture and the old guard of American evangelical Christianity: A culture that is abandoned will, by necessity, no longer feature the ideals that believers are told to infect it with. The tired old idea that withdrawal and separation somehow transform a culture was being frontally challenged by the members of P.O.D. who took their faith into the center of the public square and earned respect.

After asking one of the members of the group to show him his tattoo—one that featured Jesus, no less—Stern began with his guests, noting in a voice filled with incredulity, "You guys don't bang your groupies and stuff. I was reading about you. You're young guys. I would be banging the groupies. But you guys are religious guys."[1]

To be sure, Stern had fun with his guests as well, probably to see if their faith also included the ability to laugh at themselves, when he allowed two callers onto the show. One caller claiming to be Jesus Christ told the members of P.O.D. that they were now free to have sex with their groupies, while another purporting to be Satan told them that *he* was having sex with their wives while they were on the road. The tasteless and blasphemous jokes were vintage Stern, but the members of P.O.D. held their ground and impressed their host with the strength of their convictions.

"You actually respect the chicks in your audience and you will not have sex with them and just do them," repeated Stern incredulously. "Well, that's unusual, that's a new point of view I gotta tell you . . . I respect you if you can do that."[2]

It may have seemed like a new point of view to Stern and millions of Americans, but only because of the cultural disappearing act that too many people of faith had staged over the last fifty years, which had too often resulted in their views not being fully aired in the public square. But as P.O.D. and a new generation came of age and rejected philosophies of cultural separation and withdrawal, they were following in the footsteps of cultural confrontationalists like Daniel, Shadrach, Meshach, and Abednego, Jewish captives in ancient Babylon who stood tall for their faith amidst a culture of degradation and wild excess, and never used their belief in God as an excuse to withdraw from a culture into which they had been divinely placed.

The Stern interview was significant because his show was one that serious Christians typically avoided. On the rare occasion when one did agree to be interviewed on the program, it had turned disastrous. When B. J. Thomas, the devout singer who had once achieved success with the hit song "Raindrops Keep Falling on My Head," showed up, he was harangued by Stern who demanded that his guest sing a song that featured some rather off-color lyrics. When Thomas demurred, Stern grew angry, and the ensuing give-and-take, and Thomas's firm refusal to play along, had resulted in Thomas looking prudish and Stern looking like a bully.

But earning the respect of perhaps one of the coarsest voices in American pop culture was the first of many of the accolades that P.O.D. earned, which would propel them to the top of the rock world. But it was an ascent that was anything if not calculated. The Stern interview itself was no accident, for P.O.D.'s manager Tim Cook had, early on, clearly understood it as one of his missions to get his band on the Stern program. Singer Sonny Sandoval may have instructed Cook to get the band booked on the Stern show, but getting a rookie band on was no easy task and would be virtually impossible to achieve without some divine intervention.

That divine intervention came in the way of Atlantic Records executive Danny Buch who had recently helped Stern by lining up talent for the shock jock's birthday party. At the party, Stern had made Buch a solemn promise: As a thank-you for arranging for bands like Stone Temple Pilots to play his birthday fest, Stern promised that he would give free air time to any band Buch chose. Buch's response: He wanted Stern to feature a recent Atlantic Records signing named P.O.D. Stern obliged, but made it clear that he was only doing so because of his promise to Buch. The band's appearance on the Stern show increased record sales and created momentum for its next single, "Rock the Party."

Another moment that served to confirm that people of faith were escaping out of the basement that they had been kept in for three decades by militant secularists and Christian separatists was when P.O.D. singer Sonny Sandoval appeared on Bill Maher's television program *Politically Incorrect*. Maher, a libertarian who leans left on social issues and is always a tough interviewer of people of faith, almost always had the last word. But faced with Sandoval he melted like butter, much as Stern had in his own encounter with the band.

First Maher used an obscure Old Testament passage to question Sandoval's tattoos. Sandoval didn't bite, but *Happy Days* star Marion Ross took up a matronly defense of the singer, reminding Maher that the dreadlocks and tattoos were tools to help Sandoval's audience identify with him. Stymied, Maher went for the jugular. How could Sandoval believe in God, Maher wanted to know, when things like cancer existed? Maher had no idea of the trap he had walked into. Without missing a beat, Sandoval replied that it was cancer that had driven him to God because it had taken his mother's life and caused him to establish a relationship with Him. Maher appeared stunned at the seemingly effortless rejoinder and was uncharacteristically silent as he begged off of the segment in favor of a commercial break.

Still another moment that indicated that a cultural shift of sorts had taken place was when the pop/rock band Sixpence None The Richer's singer Leigh Nash appeared on the *Late Show with David Letterman*. After a rendition of the band's hit song "Kiss Me," Letterman went to commercial break, but not before motioning to Nash and saying, "I want to talk to you."

When the show came back from the break, Nash sat nervously on the sofa next to Letterman and politely listened to his first question.

"Where are you from?" he asked, to which the singer replied that she was from a small Texas town called New Braunfels.

Then Letterman, perhaps sensing the innocence of his guest, showed a surprisingly coarse side by asking Nash first where she was staying in town and then if he could visit the married singer there. Nash looked back at her band members as if for help and searched for the words to answer Letterman, but her silence spoke volumes as a suddenly chastened Letterman profusely apologized, admitting that he had been "needlessly coarse."

With that Nash proceeded to finish the story she had been trying to tell in response to the host's question about how her band got its name.

"It comes from a book by C. S. Lewis," she replied. "The book is called *Mere Christianity*. A little boy asks his father if he can get a sixpence—which is a very small amount of English currency—for the boy to go and get a gift for his father. The father gladly accepts the gift and he's really happy with it, but he also realizes that he's not any richer for the transaction because he gave his son the money in the first place."

"He bought his own gift," Letterman responded.

"That's right. Pretty much," replied Nash. "I'm sure it meant a whole lot to him, but he's really no richer. C. S. Lewis was comparing that to his belief that God has given him and us the gifts that we possess and to serve Him the way we should, we should do it humbly, with humble hearts realizing how we got the gifts in the first place."

Nash's brave performance elicited from Letterman an uncharacteristically earnest response:

Well, that's beautiful. That's very nice. That makes perfect sense. When you hear something explained that is so obvious but yet we need to be reminded of it almost every minute of every day . . . but if people didn't need to be reminded of that there'd be fewer boobs running around doing boob-like things. If we could just keep that little sliver of enlightenment with us, things would be so much better. Well, nice to see you, God bless you, thank you very much. Leigh Nash, ladies and gentlemen . . . charming.[3]

Yet another clue that people of faith were deeply impacting mainstream music was the curious choice of songs selected for The Rolling Stones frontman Mick Jagger's 2001 solo album *Goddess in the Doorway*. Jagger had been accused for years by fundamentalists of being a Satanist or pervert or both, and he had seemed to sing and act over the years in a way that confirmed his critics' darkest suspicions. Such critics used songs like "Sympathy for the Devil" and album titles like *Goat's Head Soup* to insist that Jagger had a thing for Old Scratch, and Jagger's lifestyle confirmed that he had little regard for conventional social morals on marriage and family.

But when it came time to record *Goddess in the Doorway* Jagger surrounded himself with the talents of artists of faith, and what emerged reflected their influence. The effect that U2's Bono and singer Lenny Kravitz had on Jagger was noted by *Rolling Stone* publisher Jan Wenner who, twenty years after arguing against hope that his *Slow Train Coming* album didn't truly reflect a Christian conversion for Bob Dylan, seemed to concede that Kravitz and Bono had indeed had a significant impact on Jagger's thinking.

"'Joy,' a rocking, gospel-tinged collaboration with Bono of U2—and featuring an indelible guitar hook from Pete Townsend—offers a revealing glimpse of what Jagger is seeking: 'I looked up to the heavens/And a light is on my face/I never never never/Thought I'd find a state of grace,'" noted Wenner. "The mark of U2 is over on 'Joy' but the band's influence subtly courses through the rest of the album."[4]

Of another song, "Hide Away," Wenner astutely observed: "The lyrics portray a guy who's got it all—fame, fortune, and the means to indulge any materialistic and hedonistic impulse he might divine—but is wise enough in his late middle-age to know there's something more out there."[5]

But the biggest surprise was a song Jagger cowrote with Kravitz called "God Gave Me Everything," which found the singer crediting God for every good thing in his life.

"Jagger offers unabashedly human, vulnerable sentiments on 'Brand New Set of Rules,'" noted Wenner of yet another song from the record. "I will be kind, won't be so cruel/I will be sweet, I will be true . . . I got a brand-new set of rules I got to learn."[6]

Jagger's "Brand New Set of Rules" sounded curiously like a line from a song, "Gonna Change My Way of Thinking," from Bob Dylan's 1979 album *Slow Train Coming*, in which Dylan had sung, "Gonna change my way of thinking, make myself a new set of rules."

Whether the influences were Dylan, Bono, Kravitz, or a new generation of faith-rockers, the zeitgeist had caught up with even Mick Jagger who was looking for spiritual meaning and coming up with rather orthodox notions of faith. The influence of a new generation of artists of faith had touched a legend of rock and shown again that the ability to change the topic of cultural discussion was often as simple as just showing up. With the help of Bono, Kravitz, and others, Mick Jagger had finally lived up to the meaning of his last name, "messenger of God."

Still another surprise to the rock music establishment came when Billy Corgan, the former lead singer of the band Smashing Pumpkins, delivered his next band outing Zwan, which included a stunningly worshipful song called "Jesus, I." Corgan, who was never known for being particularly respectful of the Christian faith in his work with the Pumpkins, stunned audiences with this lyric:

> Jesus, I've taken my cross, all to leave and follow thee . . . I'm resolute, reviled, forsaken . . . destitute, despised, forsaken . . . yet how rich is my condition, God and heaven are all my own.

Had Corgan undergone a transformational spiritual experience, merely being an artist and telling stories or simply responding to a market need for songs about divine love? Nobody could be sure of the answer to that question, but the result was still the same: another prominent rock star was singing songs of devotion to God.

Still more clues that religious expression in pop music was quickly changing were the results of the 2002 Grammy Awards. For years Christian expression at the Grammys had mostly consisted of the blurb "in ceremonies held earlier this evening for Best Gospel . . . ," which came up just before the real ceremonies cut to commercial. People of faith had for years chafed at their relegation to the cultural backwater. But that all changed at the 2002 Grammys.

Although the show closed with a presentation of "gospel music," with performances by legends such as Al Green, Michael W. Smith, CeCe Winans, and Andraè Crouch, the truly amazing story of the evening was the explosion of people of faith into all genres of the Grammy Awards, a clear indication that they refused to be sequestered in the "Gospel" category and were instead choosing to be heard and awarded in multiple genres of music.

The most obvious case was that of U2, whose members collected several awards for their record "All That You Can't Leave

Behind." Lead singer Bono credited the band's success to God: "We depend on God walking through the room, more than most. And God has walked through the room on our record and I want to give thanks. Amen."[7]

T-Bone Burnett, whose faith burned brightly mostly on the fringes of popular music, had multiple wins at the Grammys with his *O Brother, Where Art Thou?* project, which also won him acclaim as producer of the year.

Lenny Kravitz won a Grammy for Best Male Rock Performance for his song "Dig In," which included this line:

> When the mountain is high, just look up to the sky, Ask God to teach you, then persevere with a smile.[8]

Best Female Rock Performance went to another spiritually themed song by Lucinda Williams, "Get Right with God," which contained these lines:

> I want to get right with God, yes you know you got to get right with God. I would burn the soles of my feet, burn the palms of both my hands. If I could learn and be complete, if I could walk righteously again. I asked God about his plan, to save us all from Satan's slaughter.[9]

Allison Krauss, another devout artist, equaled the previous record by taking home five Grammys for her work both on the *O Brother* soundtrack and for work with her band Union Station.

Destiny's Child earned a Grammy as well for their song "Survivor," which included the line, "I'm not going to compromise my Christianity."

And then there was bluegrass legend Ralph Stanley, who, thanks to the support of Bob Dylan and T-Bone Burnett, finally enjoyed the acclaim he had long deserved, winning an award in the country category for his song "O Death."

P.O.D. passed up a sure Grammy win in the gospel category and instead chose to be nominated in the rock category where they lost out to rockers Linkin Park.

One of the most poignant moments of the evening was country superstar Alan Jackson's rendition of his hit song "Where Were

You," written in honor of the victims of the September 11th tragedy. The song included the lines:

> But I know Jesus and I talk to God, and I remember this from when I was young, faith, hope and love are some good things He gave us, and the greatest is love.[10]

All in all, it was not a bad evening for those who took their faith and their rock & roll seriously. Although awards were also given out in the traditional gospel category, with dc Talk, CeCe Winans, and others taking the honors, as usual the culture barely noticed. However, the lesson of the evening was clear: Strong and clear expressions of faith no longer disqualified artists from being taken seriously by the culture, and even, on occasion, winning awards.

In 2001 even *Newsweek* magazine picked up on the trend and devoted a cover story to the phenomenon entitled "Jesus Rocks." Every decade or so since 1970 mainstream outlets such as *Newsweek* checked in on the world of "Contemporary Christian Music" to take a pulse and report back to the mainstream culture. CCM, as it was known, was a parallel entertainment universe constructed by Christian businessmen to produce and market music made by former rock stars who converted to Christianity and evangelical Christians who were warned of the evils of secular rock.

The first wave of coverage was in the early 1970s when the newsweeklies reported on the burgeoning "Jesus Music" craze, as it was known in the early days of the movement. In the mid 1980s, reporters returned to cover the antics of the rock band Stryper, known for throwing Bibles into its audiences, and the singer Amy Grant. They revisited the issues in the mid 1990s when artists such as Bob Carlisle and Jars of Clay achieved a degree of success with their singles "Butterfly Kisses" and "Flood."

For "Jesus Rocks," *Newsweek* proved once again that when it came to the complicated and nuanced issues surrounding the Christian music underground, most reporters with no background in the genre would come away with half and sometimes less of the true story. The cover story completely missed what was really percolating in the Christian music subculture and how it was already having an impact on the larger pop music culture. *Newsweek* took the pulse of CCM and found it robust, but in the process missed, as do most mainstream publications, the fact that "Christian music" as a concept was in the middle of a quiet collapse as a new generation of rock stars who were Christians were bypassing the industry altogether and signing with mainstream record companies, having realized that the surest way to not be heard by the mainstream music culture was to allow themselves to be branded "Christian rock."

Perhaps the final straw for artists of faith was being made fun of on the popular TV sitcom *Seinfeld*, where one of the characters, Elaine, discovered to her horror that her boyfriend Puddy listened to "Christian rock." Not to worry, George assured her; Christian rock was nice and safe, not like real rock.

For any rock star, Christian or not, being labeled safe is not a compliment.

Sensing the cultural shift, numerous artists who were in the Christian music industry left, resurfacing at mainstream record labels, sometimes with new names. Other younger artists simply avoided the cultural gulag altogether and signed record deals with mainstream labels from the outset.

Incorrectly labeling mainstream artists like Lifehouse (signed to the Dreamworks label) and P.O.D. (signed to Atlantic Records) as Christian music artists, *Newsweek* lumped them in with an industry that they had only allowed their records to be sold into.

The real story that *Newsweek* missed was the same one they missed in the political world in 1980—that just as serious Christians rejected arguments of separatism and entered the U.S. political world, thereby turning it upside down, so they were in the process of entering the popular music culture with their faith-based ideas in tow, all the while throwing off the yoke of the marginalizing term "Christian music."

That's why artists like Creed, Lifehouse, P.O.D., Collective Soul, Sixpence None The Richer, Chevelle, Burlap to Cashmere, Kendall Payne, Switchfoot, Blindside, Project 86, and others had signed record deals with mainstream labels, in many cases turning down Christian music labels completely, or in others distancing themselves from the CCM market by allowing their mainstream labels to distribute their records to the Christian bookstore market but refusing to identify themselves as "Christian rockers."

P.O.D. was the clearest example of this trend, for they had refused offers from the Christian record labels early on and instead signed with the mainstream label Atlantic. Two hit singles, "Southtown" and "Rock the Party," came quickly, but the band had steadfastly refused the moniker "Christian rock" despite the fact that they were clearly devout believers who allowed their records to be distributed to the Christian bookstore market by Atlantic's Nashville-based "Christian division."

This movement of artists out of the Christian music world and onto the rosters of mainstream record labels presented a clear problem for the CCM industry. After all, it had built a business on disgruntled artists who weren't being given a fair shake at mainstream labels, which were in turn accused of trying to get them to tone down their faith-based lyrics or ignoring them altogether.

But that resistance on the part of mainstream labels had begun to crumble and, as artists such as Lifehouse, Creed, and P.O.D. found out, labels were in fact willing to tolerate explicit statements of faith or unfashionable political statements (Creed's antiabortion stance, for instance) so long as the music was good and the cash registers were humming.

What *Newsweek* mistook for a boom in the CCM industry was actually a massive influx of people of faith into the mainstream entertainment world. From Pax TV to *Touched by an Angel*, from *Veggie Tales* to the feature film *A Walk to Remember*, the formerly alienated Christian subculture was now emerging from an 80-year slumber, shedding the marginalization complex that had enveloped it after the Scopes Trial and had sent it into hiding, and reasserting itself in the mainstream marketplace of ideas.

In the process, artists of faith were boycotting or ignoring altogether companies that had developed over the years by using the term "Christian" as an adjective instead of a noun, realizing that it was the surest way not to be heard by the people they were most intent on reaching: nonbelievers.

The impact of this move will be felt over the course of the next two decades, just as the American political scene was jolted by the move of evangelical Christians into politics two decades ago.

However, it is also true that if this trend in entertainment is to be truly understood, it will have to be pursued more vigorously by reporters at mainstream publications who are willing to look beyond industry cheerleading press releases and examine deeper trends and issues, something *Newsweek* had simply refused to do.

Relying instead on reports from the industry organization, the Gospel Music Association (GMA), and its trade representative, the Christian Music Trade Association (CMTA), *Newsweek's* piece was essentially cheerleading for the industry and repeated the questionable numbers that were released by the group, which hid the decline in sales numbers of "Christian music." The group later rewarded the reporter by giving her an award for her coverage at their Gospel Music Week convention in Nashville.

The reports *Newsweek* relied on were regularly issued by the CMTA and showed that "Christian music" had been experiencing unprecedented growth in recent years. But a closer look at the top-sellers of 2001 showed that the strongest "Christian music" draws were actually the instrumental favorites Mannheim Steamroller, the soundtrack for *O Brother, Where Art Thou?*, and P.O.D. All had become "Christian records" courtesy of SoundScan, the company originally created to clear up confusing and misleading statistics in the music industry.

Here's how it apparently worked. Once the industry decided to distribute an album such as Mannheim Steamroller's *Christmas Extraordinaire*, representatives of the CMTA and *Billboard* magazine then declared it a "Christian record" and announced its findings to "Christian SoundScan." Then every *Christmas Extraordinaire* sale, no matter where it occurred, was credited as another sale of "Christian music." Those numbers were then used to show how much growth had taken place in "Christian music."

The same went for P.O.D. If the rock-rap act sold one million records in mainstream outlets and 100,000 in Christian-oriented bookstores, the Christian music industry was credited with 1.1 million units sold.

But P.O.D. didn't consider itself a "Christian band" making "Christian music." Instead, P.O.D.'s members saw themselves as Christians making music about their lives, including their love for God, in the center of popular culture. By signing directly with Atlantic Records in New York, they had hoped to avoid being saddled with marginalizing terms that ultimately kept their music away from non-Christians.

Lead singer Sonny Sandoval believed that potential fans of the band sometimes didn't buy its CDs when they were stocked by mainstream chains in the same bin as traditional gospel singers like Sandi Patty and George Beverly Shea.

"You go into Sam Goody's and you have these kids that just came back from Ozzfest who [say,] 'I want that new P.O.D. I just heard them and they're awesome,'" said Sandoval. "They're [told,] 'OK, they're over there in the gospel section.' That's ridiculous."[11]

A more accurate picture of the "growth" in Christian music could have been obtained by *Newsweek* and other outlets had they simply taken the figures released by the CMTA and subtracted the sales of artists of faith signed to "secular labels," compilation albums of previously released material, and Christmas (or hymn) records made by non-Christian artists. On Christian music's list of top ten albums of 2001, that would have left only four. So much for the explosive growth in Christian music: the truth was that Christian music wasn't growing, but the idea of Christians playing music was growing exponentially.

The picture that then emerged was that of an exodus of devout young artists who were avoiding signing with CCM labels in favor of "secular" ones. They knew that Christian music as its own unique genre would not affect a post-Christian culture trained to resist such efforts. But people of faith working in every musical style—jazz, pop, rock, R&B, etc.—quite possibly could.

Young and devout artists like Lifehouse, Creed, P.O.D., Mary Mary, Kendall Payne, and others were voting with their feet, taking their music to mainstream labels. There they were finding executives who didn't share their faith but who were still helping them find an audience. In their desire to be understood by the Christian community, some of these artists (such as P.O.D. and Kendall Payne) had allowed their records to be distributed to Christian-owned bookstores. But they probably never dreamed that doing this would give all their albums, no matter where they were sold, credit for growth in Christian music.

In theory, this trick, fully utilized, could have allowed the Christian music business to grow each year at whatever level they chose to grow by. Had they chosen, for instance, to label the entire classical music catalogues of the various labels as "Christian" or various Christian-oriented artists like Johnny Cash, Moby, Lenny Kravitz, or U2 and distributed their records to Bible bookstores, they could have perhaps grown by 2,000 percent each year.

Of course, these musicians' mission would have been much easier had their counterparts on the business side of the Christian music industry reformed their companies. Until these executives learned to function in the culture as ordinary labels (albeit ones with spiritual missions), they would continue to lose talented artists to their secular counterparts. If industry executives were to create safe places for artists to emerge without being labeled "Christian rock," artists would not have to go to mainstream labels to be heard by the wider culture.

Many were doing just that. Warner Brothers executive Barry Landis worked hard to allow artists like Plus One and P.O.D. to have access to both mainstream and Christian-owned bookstore markets, not as religious artists, but as artists who were available and accessible to the entire culture without limiting labels.

Tooth & Nail Records was another record label that had modeled how labels owned and operated by Christians could operate in the future. Though essentially staffed by Christians, and though the label generally signed artists who were also Christians, it still functioned as if it were a regular indie rock label by servicing mainstream retail, radio, and video outlets with its product and refusing to wave the "Christian rock" banner that so stifled mainstream acceptance.

"There is no such thing as a 'Christian record label' any more than there is 'Christian McDonald's' . . . or 'Christian hockey,'" said the label's president Bill Powers. "A company is a business. We sign bands that we like. To call something 'Christian' implies that what that organization has to offer is only for Christians."[12]

The move to label records that had not specifically come out of the Nashville-based CCM industry as "Christian music" ended up perpetuating the sacred/secular split that young artists were trying to overcome. It placed emphasis on growing "Christian music" as a genre and thus reinstituted the labeling that limited influence on the wider culture.

Scholar and author Phillip E. Johnson had warned Christians of the danger of going along with those who sought to label their work as religious.

"Classifying a viewpoint or theory as religious may have the effect of marginalizing it," Johnson wrote in his book, *Reason in the Balance*. "A viewpoint or theory is marginalized when without being refuted it is categorized in such a way that it can be excluded from serious consideration. The technique of marginalizing a viewpoint by labeling it 'religion' is particularly effective in late 20th-century America because there is a general impression, reinforced by Supreme Court decisions, that religion does not belong in public institutions."[13]

Still, some continued to promote CCM as a unique genre that incorporated almost every musical style, sometimes even without lyrics. But they found themselves in a shrinking minority. Ironically enough, while the very notion of "Christian music" was in retreat, people of faith were streaming out of their subcultures and making strong statements of faith in the center of the music culture. And they appeared to be continuing to do so with or without help from their brothers and sisters on the business side of the existing paradigm of Christian music.

2

One Man's Creed

In the aftermath of the terrorist attacks on New York City and Washington, D.C., the Florida-based rock band Creed's album *Weathered* rocketed straight to the top of the *Billboard* album sales chart, selling an astonishing two million copies in its first month of release. The record was propelled by the success of its first single, "My Sacrifice," which also quickly reached the top of the singles chart.

Creed was led by singer Scott Stapp, who was raised by fundamentalist Christians who opposed rock music; the conflict between Stapp and his father had caused the youngster to run away from home. Later, at the Christian-run Lee University, Stapp was expelled when he experimented with marijuana. A girlfriend turned him on to the forbidden fruit of classic rock bands like Led Zeppelin, and before long Stapp had a new career goal: rock star.

Creed was formed in Tallahassee, Florida, in 1995 by high school friends Scott Stapp and Mark Tremonti, who quickly recruited bassist Brian Marshall and drummer Scott Phillips. Recording what would become its debut record, *My Own Prison*, on its own Blue Collar record label, Creed began to shop around for a record deal with a major label.

"With *My Own Prison* I knew we had the talent to get a record deal and I knew we had songs good enough to get played on the radio," said Stapp, "but I never had any expectations of reaching this many people."[1]

The change came about in 1997 when the band signed on with the New York–based start-up label Wind-Up Records, which took the band's record, made for a paltry $6,000, remixed it, and released it with some slight modifications to the album cover art.

One of the inspirations for Stapp in making *My Own Prison* was what was happening in radio at the time.

"I remember talking to Mark [Tremonti] when we first got together around '93," remembered Stapp. "I couldn't stand what was on radio—it made no sense to me. I was like, 'dude, I want this band to mean something.' I wanted people to really understand what I was saying."[2]

Tremonti concurred.

"There were a lot of people who liked '70s rock who had nothing to buy. Maybe they enjoyed some of the early '90s stuff, like Soundgarden and Alice in Chains, but there hadn't been any old-school-style rock 'n roll."[3]

"The day our first album was released, Soundgarden had just broken up," he added, "and in the issue of *Rolling Stone* that was out at the time it said, 'Rock 'n roll is dead.' I remember reading that article and laughing because I thought, 'Not anymore.'"[4]

Success quickly followed the release of *Prison* as the album spawned four number one hit singles on the rock charts and earned the band a Rock Artist of the Year nod at the 1998 Billboard Music Awards. But the band's major breakthrough came in 1999 with the release of the ten million selling *Human Clay*, which spent two weeks at the top of the album charts and spawned the hit songs "Higher" and "With Arms Wide Open."

The reaction to Creed by the religious and irreligious was characteristically polarized, and Creed singer and spokesman Stapp treaded gingerly between both camps. Many Christians criticized the band for not being outspoken enough about their faith while secularists, predictably annoyed by expressions of serious faith in popular music, expressed horror at the marriage of Christianity and hard rock.

Stapp carefully avoided the traps laid out by the embracing of either side's agenda, continuing to allow his music to express a rather orthodox (unorthodox for the rock world) faith through his pounding, grinding music, even as he denied that Creed was a "Christian band."

"Are we a Christian band? This is a question we are asked a lot because of some of the references made in the lyrics of the band," noted Stapp. "A Christian band has agendas to lead others to believe in their specific religious beliefs. We have no such agenda. I wrote the lyrics at a time in my life when I was questioning how I was raised, and searching for where I stood concerning those beliefs. I haven't abandoned those beliefs, [I'm] just searching for where they fit into my life."[5]

The necessity of denying the "Christian band" label while simultaneously writing songs with clear and obvious references to and in support of basic Christian beliefs, though seemingly preposterous, had become a necessity in the modern rock world where being labeled a "Christian band" was a sure ticket to the cultural gulag littered with the corpses of rock bands who had allowed the pejorative label to stick to them. Creed would take no such chances by carefully distancing themselves from the term, though never denying their own faith.

Following the lead of U2 and other bands and the admonition of Teddy Roosevelt to walk softly and carry a big stick, Creed tiptoed past labels designed to silence them and continued to let their music loudly and clearly reflect a Christian worldview. For many people of faith this was a dizzying high wire act, which sometimes caused them to lose faith in the band when public statements seemed to show that the band members were back-pedaling away from their faith.

"We have no agenda to make people believe in Christianity," maintained Stapp, "and God and spirituality have never been our primary focus. When we made *My Own Prison* I was in search of beliefs, just trying to figure things out, and a lot of people in the media and the Christian community didn't understand that . . . but it's not a Christian God or a Buddhist God or a Muslim God. It's the God I see when I look at my little boy . . . the God I see in nature. It's the God I see when I look at the Grand Canyon or at beautiful snow-capped mountains. It's the God that is revealed to me through the world around me."[6]

On the rare occasion when Stapp was interviewed by journalists who weren't hostile to his beliefs, however, he was far more forthright, acknowledging that when speaking to journalists ignorant of the Christian faith and out to marginalize his band, thereby keeping them from the masses of rock fans, he was far more circumspect.

"When the secular media asks me questions, 90 percent of them have no background in religion so they don't even understand some of the answers that I give them or even some of the lyrics,"[7] maintained Stapp, who then added why he has always refused the tag "Christian band":

> I say that we're not. The first thing is, the other three guys in my band, they don't believe the same way I do. I write all the lyrics so they're just kind of thrown into these beliefs. They got in the band to be rock stars in the classic sense of the word. And now all of a sudden they're hit with all of this stuff that they didn't ask for.[8]

When it came to the issue of his own faith, however, Stapp was far clearer, though he still sought to avoid labels.

"I was thinking the other day about when someone asked me if I was a Christian and I looked at him and said, 'I don't know, man. I still have a lot of questions that I wish I had answers to.' That's why I don't want to tell anyone that I'm a Christian, first of all, because I don't know if I am. But second of all, I have a lot of questions about that and I can't sit here and tell you guys that by the letter of the law I'm a Christian or not. I know that I believe in God and I speak with Him every day and I have a relationship with Him and I feel like He speaks with me and I feel like He's very instrumental in everything that I do. Maybe the whole struggle and the whole search and the whole desire to ask questions and find the truth is what makes us Christian."[9]

To those in the religious community who condemned Stapp for not being clear enough, for refusing the label "Christian band," or for making his stand in mainstream music, Stapp had this reply:

> I just really felt that it was important and necessary to be there because I wasn't trying to reach people who had their lives together. . . . I wasn't trying to reach Christians. You've got to think

about whom you're trying to reach. And the people that I'm trying to reach, they'll understand it.[10]

Still, the effect that Stapp's Bible-centered lyrics were having on pop culture were not lost on Stapp or on popular publications like *USA Today*, which clearly understood, the band's denials notwithstanding, where Stapp and Creed were coming from when they labeled the band "Bible thumping rockers."

USA Today critic Edna Gunderson voiced much of the disdain that mainstream rock critics had for Creed in her stunningly bigoted review of *Weathered*. What made Gundersen's criticism especially notable was the vitriol she showered on the very notion, personified in Creed, that devout Christians could marry their spiritual fervor with pounding rock.

"Hard rock and Christianity, one of contemporary music's oddest couples have coexisted comfortably through three Creed albums *and that's the downside,*" wrote Gundersen. "Unfortunately *the cozy dovetailing of gospel and grunge eliminates the crucial hell-raising and devil-may-care abandon that elevates rock to transcendent heights*" (italics added).[11]

Comments like Gundersen's made it abundantly clear why rock stars like Stapp were so careful in speaking with rock journalists to avoid being pigeonholed, for such journalists were often contemptuous of faith and particularly enraged, as in the case of Gundersen, at those who would dare mix faith with rock outside of the much-ridiculed Christian music industry.

But Stapp too knew of the effect his songs were having on the children of America and reveled, when he was free to do so, in front of sympathetic reporters, at the results he was seeing.

"This one guy came up to me and he said, 'I turned your album on and I had just finished writing my suicide letter and I was sitting on my bed with a gun and I was going to blow my head off and I got to "What's This Life For," and I just started crying. Thank you,'" remembered Stapp, adding, "I don't want to be this band or this writer that people don't understand. I want people to understand what we're doing. I think a lot of people say it is really eclectic and great and they will ask, 'what does this mean?' Sometimes very creative and artistic people use that as an excuse for not being able to express themselves properly. I just think you can't run from the truth."[12]

35

From the antiabortion elements in "In America" to a more generalized pro-life message in "With Arms Wide Open" to the overt nods to specifically Christian doctrines of heaven and the central role of Jesus in "Higher" and "Faceless Man," Creed was advancing through its music a generally Judeo-Christian world-view and specifically Christian-centered worldview that had long been kept on the fringes of mainstream American media, and especially in the world of rock music.

As one of the leading voices in this transformation of rock music into the music of the counter–counter culture, Stapp clearly understood his role as a revolutionary who had inadvertently fulfilled his parents' desire that their son be a missionary:

> One of the things I used to tell my Dad was "I'm not going to be a missionary, no way I'm going to some third world country, no way." OK God, did you hear that? I'm not going to be a missionary. And I think I was running. I think that I'm still running to some degree. But the ironic thing is that I'm running and that I ran right into Him. And I'm doing the same thing that I'd be doing—I mean I've affected so many people by accident just like I was a minister with the message of salvation in *My Own Prison*. I didn't even think about it until after it was done. And how many people who have never even stepped in[to] a church hear *My Own Prison* every day?[13]

For Stapp, his effect on pop culture was one he had both sought and avoided and he seemed in awe of the way in which he had been allowed to bring his worldview to millions of fans:

> I would ask God for things when I was young. I would be like "God give me the wisdom of King Solomon and give me the spiritual strength of Samson." I would ask Him for all of these things. I would [say] "Please, help me understand," and "Use me" and all this stuff. And then all of a sudden I didn't want it anymore but He gave it to me anyway. And He's like, "Well, if I gave you all of this stuff you're going to use it, whether you want to or not." I think that's basically how it's developed. My songs on this album were . . . you know, there was a lot of "Listen man I know what's right. I know what I'm supposed to feel is right. I've been told there's still something missing." I didn't know we were going to be on the radio or I didn't know that we were going to sell three million records and I was going to be doing interviews like this.

We didn't know. I wrote them for me. The only answer for the success is the message. I think there's a message in there that needs to get out and that God wanted to get out.[14]

Stapp's mother couldn't have been more proud, recalling the time her young son had come to his parents with a clear knowledge of what God's calling was for him to do with his life: "He said that he knew he had a call on his life that he was to be a singing evangelist," recalled Lynda Stapp. "Can you believe that? Scott is doing truly what God wants him to do. I believe that he is touching more lives as a rock star than most evangelists."[15]

3

Payable on Death

Another band that had a strong impact on the rock world was San Diego–based P.O.D., which formed in 1992 and began releasing records through its label Rescue Records. The band took its name from a banking term, Payable on Death. The band's unique mix of rock and rap immediately garnered attention.

"When we started, everybody compared us to Body Count, because this whole rap-rock thing hadn't happened yet," noted bassist Traa Daniels. "After Rage Against the Machine came out, everybody said we sounded like Rage. But we were still trying to figure this out on our own."[1]

Led by singer Sonny Sandoval, Daniels, guitarist Marcos Curiel, and drummer Noah "Wuv" Bernardo, P.O.D. toiled quietly in the underground music world, playing in both the "Christian" and mainstream music scenes, equally at home playing Christian-oriented music festivals as they were mainstream dates. But P.O.D. wasn't content with playing in and having its records distributed in the Christian bookstore circuit.

P.O.D. was fortunate to find a major music attorney, Owen Sloan, and a manager, Tim Cook, who shared the band's vision and were willing to help them implement that vision. Sloan shopped P.O.D. demos around and eventually found a listening ear in Atlantic Records in New York, which promptly came to watch the band.

But before Atlantic came calling, P.O.D. first garnered strong interest from CCM record labels. One in particular, a Brentwood, Tennessee–based label, even made them an offer. Cook was ready to compromise as any good manager would. After all, one of the members of P.O.D. was living out of his car and another was facing strains in his marriage because of the financial pressures. Cook himself was racking up credit card debts. Cook dutifully approached singer Sonny Sandoval with the tempting offer, but Sandoval was insistent: this was not their vision. Their mission was to take their music and their message to the world, and that was unlikely to happen through the efforts of a CCM label that didn't share that cultural mission.

So the band walked away from a sure paycheck in pursuit of the great unknown, apparently willing to sacrifice their career rather than work with people who didn't share their vision.

Then Atlantic Records came calling.

Manager Cook arranged for the band to play at a club in Hollywood and invited executives from Atlantic to stop by. As Cook and the executive headed toward the club, they looked up at the marquee. To Cook's horror it read: "Christian Rock Night Featuring P.O.D." Cook was mortified and the Atlantic executive was nonplussed. Cook assured the executive that the band was not a "Christian rock band," though its members were devout Christians, and the band proceeded to play one of its worst performances ever. Still, Atlantic saw something special in P.O.D. and soon offered them a generous recording contract and set to work on what would be the group's major label debut record, *The Fundamental Elements of Southtown*.

Southtown caused a small stir with the success of the title track, a gutsy song accompanied by a video that mixed the angst of street life with a dash of hope. A second single, "Rock the Party," took the band to greater heights, and P.O.D. was on its way.

To the casual observer, "Rock the Party" may have seemed like just another teen party anthem, but upon closer inspection, the lyrics had a deeper moral message. "We came here to rock this jam," sang Sandoval. "To spread His love is the master plan." Then in a final flurry, Sandoval and P.O.D. included this zinger:

"Don't wanna be caught messing around 'cause a party ain't a party when it gets shut down."[2]

Supporting the record, P.O.D. went on tour with bands like Korn and joined the legendary Ozzfest tour, but the band also had no hesitation in continuing to play the Christian-themed rock festivals where it had gotten its start years before.

By the autumn of 2001 the times were ready for P.O.D. As fate would have it, its second release on Atlantic Records, *Satellite*, was released on September 11, the very day of the terrorist attacks on the United States. The band's first single off of *Satellite* was the hard charging but hopeful single "Alive," which rose to #2 on the rock charts, soothing the fears of a nation rocked by turmoil.

The *Illinois Entertainer* could barely contain its enthusiasm:

> Filled with even more hard hitting yet equally catchy guitar riffs, thundering drums and a melodic vocal tone . . . during the chorus the group sings "I feel so alive/For the very first time/I can't deny You," an obvious reference to their faith, yet a tactful declaration of strength that could also be interpreted outside the context of religion.[3]

As sales of *Satellite* quickly approached one million units, P.O.D. was now a bona fide cultural phenomenon whose success was only cemented when "Alive" went straight to the top of MTV's influential daily request show *Total Request Live*, or *TRL*, a venue usually dominated by pop stars like Britney Spears and the Backstreet Boys.

Even *Rolling Stone*, which too often seemed to either damn with faint praise or ridicule the efforts of artists of faith, couldn't bring itself to slam *Satellite*. "If P.O.D.'s religious devotion inspired them to turn out the most soulful hard-rock record so far this year, then maybe more new-metal heads should get down with God,"[4] began the magazine's review, which went on to give them four out of five stars. It was grudging praise reminiscent of the magazine's praise for another artist of faith twenty years earlier, Donna Summer, who had also created a masterpiece record called *The Wanderer*, which was praised in spite of, and certainly not because of, its statements of Christian devotion.

P.O.D. was another in what was rapidly becoming a slew of bands that had either avoided the Christian music industry altogether or were in effect refugees from a market that had failed to share the artistic dreams of cultural penetration of the artists in their camp. In the case of P.O.D. it was the latter. And like Creed, Lifehouse, and others, P.O.D. instinctively knew that the price of admission into acceptability in mainstream rock didn't require them to abandon their beliefs or stop singing about them, but to change the packaging and refuse to allow themselves to be labeled with a term that rock fans had become immune to: Christian rock.

"We're not a religious band—we're a spiritual band," observed bassist Traa in what by now had become something of a mantra for rock bands devoted to spreading the message of the Gospel. "Yes, we have a personal relationship with God, but we're not trying to convert anyone to live like us. We're just a rock band."[5]

In a profile in the *Boston Herald,* Traa Daniels amplified those sentiments:

> Daniels would like to point out to those who would label P.O.D. a Christian rock band that the band's themes of love, hope, respect and consideration for others "aren't just Christian things, those are humanity things, that's the way you should feel about people in general whether you're a Christian or not. Everybody is given the right to be respected just by being human. I'm not offended by it by any means," says Daniels of the tag, but he would prefer P.O.D. be known as a "rock band with a spiritual message."[6]

For singer Sonny Sandoval there were practical reasons for wanting to avoid the label:

> I always want to come across by relating to people first and foremost. We just want to talk to people and get their vibe, but at the same time just be people first. I don't want to come off as "Hi, I'm Christian Sonny." It's not like "If you don't believe in the same thing then you can take a walk buddy." That's not me. I'm a real person in everyday life. We just happen to be talking about something positive instead of sex, drugs and rock 'n roll or trying to fit the gimmick of evil.[7]

P.O.D. did, however, allow their hit records for Atlantic to be distributed to Christian-owned bookstores. In the case of Atlantic Records that meant distribution to those bookstores by the label's Nashville-based Squint label, which was headed up by an industry veteran named Barry Landis, who saw the potential for artists like P.O.D. to be presented to the mainstream as a straight rock band but still appreciated by their brothers in arms in the Christian subculture.

Unfortunately, the Christian subculture's embrace of P.O.D. and that distribution through Word Distribution caused the band to officially be saddled with the "Christian artist" tag by SoundScan, which labeled any band distributed to Christian bookstores as "Christian artists."

While supportive of the efforts of Landis and his Nashville staff, which helped sell over 100,000 records of each album in their bookstore distribution channels, Sonny Sandoval had less charitable words for the leadership of the Gospel Music Association, which was often in the awkward position of trying to attach labels to bands that were desperately trying to throw them off.

"That's all the politics," he said. "It's like the same people that banned us, now they're in their little meetings and stuff and they're like 'our goal is to help P.O.D. break into the mainstream.' No, it's not. Let's be honest with ourselves: that's not your heart's intention. You're just selling records. Whatever link you have to P.O.D. it looks good on your plate . . . we're not trying to be a part of this little . . . it's almost like a secret society type thing. It's like 'thank you for anything you might have done in the past, thank you for your support, no disrespect, but we're going to go on and do what we want to do . . . we're not trying to cater to one audience.'"[8]

P.O.D.'s distancing act extended to the Association's annual Dove Awards, which honored the work of the leading gospel and Christian artists of the previous year. When the group nominated P.O.D. and its then president begged them to attend their ceremony, the band demurred.

"You can't stop them from nominating you and we were like 'what are we going to do?'" remembered Sandoval. "We were nominated more than anybody because they saw all the mainstream stats and then they're like 'wow! Look at what we've done. Look at what we've accomplished.'"[9]

As a compromise, P.O.D. decided to skip the show but sent their fans to accept any awards that might be forthcoming, a move that was apparently not appreciated by the GMA's leadership.

"They weren't down with that and were like 'what's the big deal?'" remembered Sandoval. "Again it was politics: 'Oh P.O.D. doesn't want to show up at our little event, well we'll see.' We got feedback from all the kids that we sent and they were like 'so this is what you guys go through all the time.'"[10]

If P.O.D. was in open rebellion against the powers that be that controlled the Christian music industry, it was also the case that P.O.D.'s music was itself a rebellion against the prevailing mind-set that engulfed the hardcore rock-rap scene of which they were a prominent part:

> "I call that stuff whiny rock," noted bassist Traa of fellow artists. "We're from San Diego and people in San Diego don't complain about stuff. I can't relate to any artist who lives in a 4 million [dollar] house and sings about being depressed. That guy should be the happiest person in the world. So many bands just want to stick their middle fingers in the air . . . just because it's an easy way to get the crowd to cheer. Everybody we've ever toured with has done that, and it makes no sense to me."[11]

But P.O.D.'s rebellion, like other bands, was also against a religious subculture that had spawned a $0.5 billion a year industry that effectively made money by separating the Christians from the non-Christians, creating, labeling, and then marketing art in ways that guaranteed that it would go unheard by the unchurched masses.

But P.O.D. refused to go along for the ride and allow their integrity as a band to be compromised or to embrace the term "Christian rock," which would mean that the rest of rock that ignored God was somehow normal:

> "We've been together for ten years and we just want to play music," said Sandoval. "Now with the mainstream and everything, we're just a rock 'n roll band out there. I guess we're just against the norm, not as far as the music but the lyrical content. It's always been our heart's desire to encourage people with our music and with our walk of life. It does get frustrating at times, but no matter what you do they're going to label you."[12]

P.O.D. was out in front of a new movement of people of faith into mainstream rock, away from the wild excess of the founders of rock and the pious escapism of the Christian music industry. And many were taking notice. The *Illinois Entertainer* observed:

> There would appear to be a contradiction between such biblically inspired messages and the fact that P.O.D. remains a perennial favorite on MTV's *Total Request Live* and has hit the road with the likes of Korn, Sevendust and the Ozzfest tour. But it's clear there's an instant appeal and acceptance of the message and corresponding lifestyle P.O.D. members bring to the fold. They represent a certain sense of rebellion against the rock star stereotype and rebellion has certainly fueled music history so far. Although singing about spirituality doesn't have immediate sex appeal, it seems the ladies find the group's honesty and care for others to be extremely valuable qualities. The adage of "sex, drugs and rock 'n roll" is clearly getting old for some music lovers who want to be challenged with a deeper way of thinking. P.O.D. along with Creed and Lifehouse are just the beginning of the trend and as long as all three groups can musically evolve, there's no reason why they can't continue sharing their intriguing thoughts with fans from all walks of life."[13]

4
Building (a) Lifehouse

In late 2001, the Los Angeles–based rock band Lifehouse received the BDS Certified Spin Award, which honored the song that was played the most times on American radio that year. In just the first nine months of the year, its hit single "Hanging by a Moment" had been played 420,000 times.

It was an amazing start for a band led by a then 20-year-old singer/songwriter named Jason Wade, whose first album *No Name Face* had been released just months earlier on the Dreamworks label. Like Creed and P.O.D., Lifehouse was another in what had become by now a long line of post-Christian music rockers who were intent on staying a part of the culture they intended to transform by signing to a mainstream label.

Unlike P.O.D., Lifehouse had no history in the Christian music industry and, unlike Creed, didn't have the additional baggage of a strained relationship with the church. In fact, far from being strained, singer Jason Wade was an active member of the California-based Malibu Vineyard Church and could often be found leading music there. Long before American pop radio discovered the band's hit single "Hanging by a Moment," it had been a staple with the church's youth group, FKA or Formerly Known As, of which Wade was an integral part.

"They wanted it not to be like a typical church youth group which is why they had a rock band," remembered Wade. "The church wasn't really conservative—not like you have to wear a coat and tie or whatever. It was more like a cool hang."[1]

A cool hang indeed, for the Malibu Vineyard, under different leadership some years before, was the famous (to some infamous) scene of Bob Dylan's conversion to Christianity. Dylan's then girlfriend Mary Alice Artes had wandered into the Vineyard asking for prayer for her boyfriend and brought a couple of pastors home to meet the singer. A few days later on his own Dylan discovered his belief in Jesus and prayed a prayer of acceptance. Soon he was enrolled in the church's School of Discipleship, which met in nearby Reseda.

In the cases of both Dylan and Lifehouse, the Vineyard church had handled artists who were believers with deftness rare among Christian churches. Countless artists, upon experiencing conversion experiences like Dylan's, were told to leave the music business and "sing for the Lord." This usually meant recording hymn collections or signing up with the Christian music industry and never being heard by their old fans or others who didn't follow the Christian music industry. Other artists like U2, who were once in a spot similar to Lifehouse's, were told to disband or get out of mainstream rock altogether by their church. But from the outset the Vineyard, a movement started by a pastor named John Wimber who broke away from the Calvary Chapel church movement over doctrinal issues, had a more progressive and confrontational approach to popular culture, encouraging their charges to invade the mainstream instead of escape from it—precisely the formula followed by both Dylan and Lifehouse.

Lifehouse had come together at the Vineyard when Wade met bassist Sergio Andrade. Both were missionary kids whose parents had returned to the Los Angeles area from service overseas. They were soon joined by drummer Rick Woolstenhulme, and Lifehouse quickly went from garage band to major label recording artists under the tutelage of producer Ron Aniello, another attendee of the Vineyard.

Aniello had worked with another young artist of faith who had avoided the Christian music world and signed with Capitol Records, Kendall Payne.

"Jason and Kendall were friends . . . and I brought Jason to my studio and heard some of his songs and I was really blown away,"[2] remembered Aniello. After receiving some early interest from Capitol Records, Aniello successfully guided the band to Dreamworks executive Michael Ostin.

Wade's parents had traveled the globe as missionaries, and young Jason had lived in Japan, Thailand, Singapore, and Hong Kong, among other locales.

"We lived pretty much the same wherever we were," remembered Wade, "but sometimes, like in Hong Kong, we didn't have much money which had a way of changing things. At one time there we had like ten dollars a day for groceries, but then my Dad who's a psychologist got a good job and things got better."[3]

The breakup of Wade's parents' marriage drove the youngster to seek out music and eventually landed him and his band with a record deal.

"That was my initial inspiration," remembers Wade of the divorce. "That whole experience led me to the place where I realized I had a gift in writing songs. I honestly think I wouldn't be doing music if my parents were still together. You should never regret your past, even though some of it's hard. It can open you up to something else that's better."[4]

It was also an experience that taught Wade that disappointment with the church shouldn't lead to giving up on God.

"[It was] a turning point in my life," he remembered. "I really disagree with a lot of things that the church does—the Christian church, just religion in general. I see a lot of things that seem off. I saw firsthand how someone like my Dad—maybe he fell, maybe he made some mistakes—but then people from the church would basically say, 'you're going to hell' and turn their backs on him. To me, God is all about love and mercy and compassion and I don't see a lot of that today."[5]

Unlike Creed and P.O.D., whose members claimed not to have followed the Christian music scene very much, Wade was largely raised on the music of the Christian subculture—including Amy Grant, Sandi Patty, and Michael W. Smith records his mother favored. Yet in spite of those musical influences, Wade never seemed to have a desire to be a part of that scene and Lifehouse chose another path.

"Rock musicians raised by Christians can often go two ways," noted *The Edmonton Sun*'s music critic Mike Ross, "become Christian rock musicians like Audio Adrenaline or rebel to become anti-Christian rock musicians like Marilyn Manson. Wade didn't do either. . . . Lifehouse . . . isn't a Christian band—nor do they engage in any of the immoral excesses of other rock bands whose names we won't mention here."[6]

"There's none of that. . . . I'm still living the way I was raised," confirmed Wade. "It's kind of a clean rock thing."[7]

Still, the significance of Wade's decision to record for Dreamworks should have been a wake-up call, as if another was needed, for the Christian rock industry, which was losing talented young artists like Wade who had realized that signing with them was too often a sure ticket to cultural obscurity.

It was a topic that Wade seemed to have clear opinions on and the reason he was careful to make the distinction between Christian rock and Christians in rock, the latter of which described Lifehouse and a new generation of rock's rebels. Wade believed that musicians should communicate through their craft—music—instead of preaching from the stage.

"The more you talk at a concert, the more you can hinder God from actually moving,"[8] he said, defending his band's preference for speaking through its music.

It was a reasonable enough sounding position, but one that was frowned upon by the Christian community for whom it was important to confirm salvation decisions immediately and because of the example of Christian rock bands like Petra and DeGarmo & Key for whom altar calls, or invitations to accept Christ as Savior, were a staple of the concert experience.

But Lifehouse had a different approach, which, while subtle, seemed to differ little from the ultimate goal of the groups who actively proselytized. Wade explains:

My music is spiritually based, but we don't want to be labeled as a "Christian band" because all of a sudden people's walls come up and they won't listen to your music and what you have to say. I think we have a positive message of hope. We're not trying to blatantly preach. It all comes down to love.[9]

The key word in Wade's response might have been "blatantly," because Lifehouse's music was clearly about its members' specifically Christian-oriented spiritual journey.

Though initially skeptical, the Christian music industry began to warm up to Lifehouse and the band began to receive airplay on Christian-owned stations though the stations hadn't even been sent copies of the band's debut CD.

"None of us got serviced on the CD or single," observed Dave Masters, programmer of a Christian-owned radio station in Spokane, Washington. "Any [Christian] station thinking about playing Lifehouse has to pursue it on their own."[10]

"We broke down the lyrics, took a look at lifestyle, and looked at the 'Hanging by a Moment' video, making sure there were no sexual references," said another program director, Steve Strout. "After spending a lot of time with the complete CD we were pretty convinced."[11]

Such was the rigorous lyrical and character assessment that regularly went on in the Christian music world, and the same process kept many artists like Creed off such play lists. But Lifehouse, led by Wade, seemed to walk the tightrope between two worlds, a mainstream culture where expressions of faith were tolerated at best and a separatist Christian subculture where directness was admired if not a prerequisite. Wade charted his own course, however:

> When you say Christian rock, instant walls go up. I automatically assume I'll hear pretentious lyrics and a preachy tone. I shy away from that. My music is spiritual in a very universal way. I don't want to make people feel unwanted.[12]

What factors were contributing to the success of young artists of faith like Lifehouse? According to Warner Brothers executive Jeff Blue, there were several:

> There are kids moving out of what they're being told to buy into—the mass saturation of the boy bands and teen idols and they're looking for attractive young kids that are speaking to them on a different level. Bands like Lifehouse . . . are introspective and meaningful—they evoke an emotion in a younger act that kids weren't getting out of the pop acts.[13]

Still others saw a different factor at work—the return of people of faith to an industry once off-limits to them.

"What makes Lifehouse particularly interesting is the way its church helped the group take their love of music mainstream bypassing the issues of the CCM (Christian music) market," noted Erin McCormick in a piece that appeared on the web site of former Watergate figure and Christian subculture gatekeeper Chuck Colson. "Popular music is often a wasteland, but it doesn't need to be. Our churches have too often abandoned musicians to make their way alone. It seems that may be starting to change now. In any case, the model of Malibu Vineyard's support for Lifehouse is a worthy one for other churches—and bands—to emulate. Together they are helping to bring new life to rock 'n roll itself—not to mention the wider culture."[14]

The very fact that Colson, who had criticized the mixing of God and rock in a book he coauthored, *How Now Shall We Live?*, was allowing such writing on his web site was a sign that artists of faith had arrived on the mainstream map and that evangelical opposition to the moves was beginning to crumble.

But with or without such support, Lifehouse was clearly on to something—finding that worshipful songs written for their God could be understood and appreciated so long as labels were avoided and the work was done in the mainstream culture by artists who had learned to speak its language and allowed their music to be the primary agent of communicating their faith.

5

Daly Impact

Few nonmusicians have so influenced the buying habits of the music-buying public as MTV VJ Carson Daly. From his daily MTV show *Total Request Live (TRL)* Carson Daly not only took the requests of MTV viewers, but helped to set a tone for what was and wasn't cool in the world of pop music. But long before MTV shot him to the top of the pop music heap, Daly had once seriously considered becoming a Catholic priest.

"When I was a high school senior entering a seminary and serving God full time was definitely on my mind," recalled Daly. "When I was offered a partial scholarship to L.A.'s Loyola Marymount University I decided to go, figuring that I would major in theology . . . By then I'd decided against the seminary figuring I could apply my strong moral beliefs more effectively outside of the priesthood."[1]

"Daly's eventual chosen occupation has also proven to be the salvation for thousands upon thousands of the young and the restless," observed *TV Guide* writer Mark Schwed. "Every day he preaches his particular brand of fire and brimstone from the world's most effective pulpit—television—hosting *TRL*, the most popular show on cable's MTV."[2]

While "salvation for thousands" may be a bit of journalistic hyperbole, Daly has indeed, by his presence and influence, helped

51

to define cool and decide which bands would receive extra attention. One beneficiary of Daly's attention was P.O.D., whose members Daly made no secret of his respect for. After P.O.D. graced the *TRL* set and explained the meaning behind one of its songs, Daly replied that the statement was "about the dopest [coolest] thing I've ever heard on this set."[3]

Such endorsements were not lost on *TRL*'s audience, who hung on every word Daly uttered, and P.O.D., partly because of Daly's attention, made a beeline for the top of the charts and saw its song "Alive" reach #1 on the show.

Though Daly was careful to avoid obvious proselytizing on the set and occasionally used mild profanities on *TRL*, his worldview and his willingness to allow it to color his work, unusual for a media star let alone an MTV personality, did not go unnoticed by critics:

> "My faith, I take it pretty serious[ly]," said Daly. "The sad thing about that is ever since I've been in the public eye and I mention my faith, you know, now all of a sudden Howard Stern is calling me a Jesus Freak. I get letters from crazy people now saying I should burn in hell. . . . I don't want to sound preachy, it's simply what I'm about."[4]

What Daly was apparently about was music, faith, and fun. Born and raised in Santa Monica, California, the future MTV star grew up in the Catholic Church and attended parochial schools. After his father passed away when Daly was a young boy, his mother remarried a golf shop owner. Daly gravitated toward golf, playing both in high school and college, and once played with future superstar Tiger Woods. A strong influence on Daly's life from the start was his mother Pattie.

"It transcends mother–son," said Daly of their relationship. "We're such good friends. She's always been the coolest mom . . . My mom was like one of us. She was into our lives. She'd always ask them [my friends] how they were doing. She'd say, 'Are you in love or like?'"[5]

Pattie Daly Caruso's worldview also had a strong influence on her young son: "My mom's motto was, 'nothing good happens after midnight,' and for a long time I actually believed it,"[6] laughed Daly.

Later, Daly's dreams of being a professional golfer caused him to drop out of Loyola Marymount College in Southern California, but that in turn led him to work spinning records at a radio station in Palm Springs. From there Daly made his way to L.A.'s powerhouse KROQ, where his deft on-air touch made him a local sensation and brought him to the attention of MTV executives who were looking for a VJ to anchor their summer beach house coverage. Daly was just the man.

"They said 'do you want to come down and be a guest VJ, and do basically what you do on the radio?' So I did and by the end of the summer they asked me to come to New York, [then they said] 'we just got this new studio and we'll do the show'. . . and that's how it happened."[7]

The transition from wannabe Catholic priest to MTV star was not an easy or expected one, particularly in an age when people of faith often discouraged the next generation from populating cultural outposts like MTV. For Daly, the catalyst was a dramatic spiritual experience:

> I started to have hot flashes, my eyes began to burn, and I started to sweat. My mind started racing and I thought about how lucky I was to live in California and to have such great friends and supportive parents. Then unbelievably, my brain became awash with even bigger issues, like world poverty. All at once, I realized how much I had and how badly I wanted to share it with others."[8]

Daly didn't know what the experience meant, but he knew he would be misunderstood if he tried to explain it to his friends:

> I could just imagine it: "hey, guys! I just got touched by something, I feel like a new man, and I love my mommy!"[9]

But looking back, Daly had a keen understanding of what it was: "In short, I found God and for a short time, I even considered becoming a Roman Catholic priest."[10]

There was a reason why late-twentieth-century American pop culture had so few people of serious religious faith and devotion, and Daly's alternate life story as a Catholic priest may very well have come to pass had he not thought about what it was

53

he wanted to accomplish and how best that could be achieved. Applying his "strong moral beliefs" at MTV, regarded by some as the sewer of pop culture, would prove to be a difficult task for Daly. It was rocky terrain that had previously been walked on by MTV personalities Peter King and Kennedy. Kennedy, though not apparently particularly religious, was notable for being not only a widely sought-after speaker on the conservative lecture circuit, but for her strong pro-life views. King in particular, who moonlighted as lead singer of the band Dakota Motor Company, got a characteristically angry response from fellow Christian youths who were angered that a professed Christian would work for MTV. But Daly, barely on the radar screen of most serious Christians, had few such difficulties since he wasn't perceived as emerging out of the faith community. Still, he too would be faced with questions about the gulf between the faith he professed and the videos he was obligated to play on his all-request show.

When ABC newsman Sam Donaldson, noted for his dogged pursuit of presidents who didn't want to answer his questions, moved off of the White House beat and began reporting for ABC.com, one of his early subjects was Daly. Donaldson raised the question to Daly that was often a thorn in the side of many people of faith: How could he reconcile his beliefs with the material he was in effect promoting on his show? Donaldson could have been referring to Eminem, Limp Bizkit, or a host of other artists who didn't seem to be in sync philosophically with the host of *TRL*, but on this occasion he raised a video that had been a mainstay on Daly's show, The Bloodhound Gang's "The Bad Touch," a song that featured a boy telling a girl that they should get it on like animals do on the Discovery Channel.

"Everybody has to interpret it their own way," said Daly of the song. "I think the point was, you know, we should be careful. We assume our kids don't know so much; meanwhile they're watching things like the Discovery Channel. He actually says that in the song. And, you know, meanwhile, the parents might be doing something in the bedroom. . . . I think the point was we act like our kids don't know and the ultimate thing to realize is they do."[11]

For many in the faith community, such a defense would have elicited guffaws, but what *was* clear was that Carson Daly and many young artists like him were now treading on ground that had not been anticipated by previous generations, and many young men and women of faith were simply unprepared for it. As such, it was left to the next generation to figure out for itself what it truly means to be obedient to Christ's command to be in the world but not of it, a balancing act to be sure for any generation, but more so for a generation faced with a culture that was so at odds with its beliefs.

Hanging out with and playing videos of controversial artists like Eminem and Marilyn Manson, while at the same time giving a leg up to artists like P.O.D., Daly appeared to be trying to find a way to navigate the "secular" culture and doing what a generation of people of faith had so spectacularly failed to do: occupy.

Still, Daly was skeptical of attempts by religious groups to influence pop culture and believed that authenticity was the key to reaching them with messages of faith:

> You don't come up with catchy slogans, you don't try and attach a moral message to a celebrity. And then we'll have that cool dude give a funky little rap, you know, about don't smoke, or don't do this, or don't do drugs, don't do that. And the people will just sit there and watch, and they're just like "that's fake."[12]

One who wasn't thrilled to have a serious Catholic as gatekeeper for what was cool for teens at MTV was rocker Trent Reznor of Nine Inch Nails who, if not the full-blown Satanist his detractors accused him of being, had a fascination with the dark side. Reznor was reported to have said of *TRL:* "As an artist I don't want to kiss Carson Daly's a— to get played."[13]

Daly was characteristically self-deprecating:

> It's probably my favorite . . . moment of all that I have read about myself in the media. To see in *Rolling Stone,* you know, Trent Reznor, someone I liked, actually knew who I was, like that was a cool moment.[14]

Hundreds of shows had come and gone on MTV in its twenty-plus year history, but for some reason *TRL* had caught on as few others had. Though most observers credited Daly with its success, Daly responded modestly:

I think that's a bit of a misconception. You know, I'm like Gene Wilder in *Willy Wonka*, you know? I'm just the guy who opens the gates to the Wonka factory. . . . In a world where you don't feel like you have control over everything, everybody's telling you what to do, here's your 60 minutes on MTV to tell us what's cool. Tell me what's cool. Play "you pick the videos" and they do.[15]

Daly also seemed wary of excessive introspection as to why success had found him:

What tangible talent do I really have? What do I do? I mean if you think about it I don't sing, or perform, or act. You don't go and see me on the big screen. What is it about me that is propelling me into this success? I really don't know, but I sure as heck am not going to argue with it. . . . I don't work! I've got this gig at MTV where I hang out every day and interview cool people.[16]

Daly seemed to understand one rule of American pop culture: Power can often be accumulated by doing distasteful projects and later expended doing projects that one fully believes in. In Daly's case, gaining a platform and finding his voice in pop culture through MTV put him in a place where he was then able to control the agenda of various projects. In late 2001, Daly was named host of his own late-night major network talk show, but that seemed to be just the beginning of Daly's long-term plans.

"There are so many great bands [that go] unheard," he noted. "I want to provide an outlet for everybody who has a genius idea but is just working at Del Taco. I'd like to have a record company, produce TV shows, direct a video, be in a film."[17]

Part of Daly's appeal was his laid-back, *fait accompli* manner, a curious mix of ambivalence, ambition, and humility.

"I've always done what makes me happy and all of this just kind of came with it," he said. "I haven't tried to analyze where my career's going, I've just tried to keep my priorities in line and not put too much weight on making it. As long as I can pay rent and eat, I'm happy. . . . If I get fired tomorrow, I will not be fazed."[18]

Although Daly was remarkably innocent for a young man who had risen to the top of Gen X Hollywood, he was anything if naïve, and quite aware of the pitfalls that he had to navigate through in the crazy world where God and rock & roll intersected:

> At MTV I've seen the power that fame brings and the mistakes I could easily make with it. Backstage at concerts groupies have offered me drugs and attractive girls have suggested sex. It would be so easy to throw your morals out the window in times like these.[19]

For Carson Daly, television and radio talk show host, record mogul and cultural phenomenon, faith is the most important thing in his life, and he believes his position in pop culture was given to him for a reason:

> My faith keeps my priorities in check. I wasn't put on this planet to look cool on TV. . . . But I've found that if you live the way God wants you to, you'll be rewarded tenfold. As a priest, I might have touched a few hundred people; at MTV I have the potential to reach so many more. God's put me here for a reason.[20]

6

Magnified Plaid

"The last bright fire in the pop-punk pantheon . . . the only punk band left that's doing anything worth caring about."[1]

So raved MTV in its assessment of a Seattle-based rock band named MxPx (short for Magnified Plaid) whose members were as passionate about punk rock as they were about their faith in God.

The band had been discovered in the mid 1990s by a young entrepreneur named Brandon Ebel who had formed Tooth & Nail, a Seattle-based independent label that would spawn dozens of Christian-oriented punk and alternative rock bands like Star-flyer 59, Ghoti Hook, and MxPx. MxPx became the label's most successful rock act, enjoying success that eventually brought them to the attention of A&M Records, which signed the band and picked up distribution of the band's record *Slowly Going the Way of the Buffalo*.

Buffalo contained a single, "Chick Magnet," which climbed the alternative rock charts, garnered airplay on MTV, and showed the mainstream music culture that MxPx was a force to be reckoned with.

Formed in 1992 by friends Mike Herrera and Yuri Riley, and later joined in 1995 by Tom Wisniewski, MxPx was quickly signed by Ebel and distributed by his fledgling operation. The Tooth

& Nail label primarily sold records through Christian-owned bookstores, but had managed to secure distribution to ordinary music retail outlets as well.

"He came out to our garage actually and watched us practice and he was into it," remembered lead singer Herrera of Ebel. "I don't know why 'cause we were really bad, and so he signed us for like a couple of records."[2]

Ebel and his partner Bill Powers had a clear philosophy of what they wanted to do, and the members of MxPx would be their star pupils:

> "What is a Christian label? We have never claimed to be one . . . because we think the term is meaningless," said Powers. "If it means anything, it means that the music is only for Christians. That's not what we're about. Are you committed to the Gospel? Of course you are. Are Brandon and I as people committed to it, yes."[3]

MxPx never shied away from directly mentioning God in its songs, but many in the Christian community were dissatisfied with the band's presentation, either unhappy with the venues they played (opening for Bad Religion and playing on the Warped Tour) or the general lack of more overt proselytizing in their music.

Ironically, rejection was something MxPx had grown accustomed to, for its members had found themselves in a cultural no man's land once described aptly by musician Mark Heard this way: "I'm too sacred for the sinners and the saints wish I would leave."[4]

MxPx had continued to make punk rock informed by faith for over a decade, and much of that time the band was hardly living the glamorous rock lifestyle:

> "Over a quarter of my life I've spent in this band," noted lead singer Herrera. "Right out of high school we went out, and it was just us guys . . . kids. We didn't have a touring manager to take care of us. It was just us driving in the van to each city, playing. Whatever problem we had, we had to figure it out on our own. Every time our van broke down, we had to get it fixed."[5]

Herrera was a Christian long before he started MxPx, a heritage he appreciated but that only took him so far:

> I grew up going to church, I've always pretty much believed in God, but there comes a point in your life where you have to really know what you believe, and it's not just what your parents believe. For me, that was probably in high school. I had a couple of older friends who were really good influences on me. And it all just made sense to me. I think we all went through the rebellious stage, but mine was pretty quick. I was pretty focused on making a difference in my own life, as far as whatever I believed, and what I was going to do with my life. I didn't go to college, but I was pretty focused on being in a band, and playing music.[6]

Indeed, Herrera and MxPx patiently plied their trade, taking time to hone their craft through endless concerts at any venue that would have them.

"We were never really too interested in looking really far ahead," recalled Herrera. "We kind of took each of our goals one step at a time. We'd say 'okay, now that we've got this show, what are we gonna do next? We gotta get a show here.' And that's what we did. We set very small goals for ourselves that were fairly easy to achieve and in that way we became successful. When we put out our first record [we said] 'okay, well, we gotta get more shows, farther away from home.' Finally, we started touring. Everything to us is all about the music. I think a lot of younger bands are focusing less on the quality of the music, their passion for the music, and are focusing more on getting signed, putting out records."[7]

Herrera's focus on getting his music out made him somewhat oblivious to the differences between the mainstream music business and the CCM business where he eventually found a deal for his band. Unlike many young rockers of faith, Herrera seemed to not have been raised on Christian pop music and remained blissfully unaware of the differences between the two markets:

> When we started out, we really didn't know anything about the Christian industry. So we always played local shows, with other local bands, and that's how we've always done our thing. We promoted our own shows and sometimes they were at churches,

sometimes they were at community centers, wherever we could get a show. There really wasn't a whole lot of clubs that were actually made for shows, where we're from. We kind of just had to figure stuff out on our own and we kind of just took that, and we got signed to Tooth & Nail, and they're kind of a Christian label. But we didn't realize there was really a difference between the two markets. Which, there is, there really is. But we didn't really like being in just one or just the other. As we see it, music is music, and everybody, as individuals, stands for something. The only thing that's different about other bands is just what they believe, and who they are and what they stand for, and I don't think it should matter where you're playing, or who you're playing with, because people are people. We just play our shows, and we play the places that are right for us, and it seems to work out really good.[8]

Although widely distributed through Christian-owned bookstore chains to fellow believers, Herrera and MxPx still had grave misgivings about the parallel subculture that had over the course of thirty years become a multimillion-dollar business: Herrera observed:

I think a lot of the people working in the Christian market, don't really know what they're doing, because they're kind of just taking stuff and making up their own rules. The music scene's been around for, how long? At least about a hundred years. Obviously, it's gone through major changes. There are just certain things that have happened over the years that have made music what it is today. With Christian music, it's a reflection of what mainstream music really is, it's just not as good. I don't know why that is, it shouldn't be like that. I personally believe whatever you do, you should do it to the best of your abilities.[9]

Something of a perfectionist, Herrera lamented the lack of professionalism among modern rock artists:

There are tons of bands out there, they don't really care about the music itself, they just want to get signed, they want to put out a record, they want to get famous, whatever they want. I talk to bands all the time, and it's just like, "Oh, we gotta get signed," and they've only been a band for two months.[10]

Like their counterparts Creed, P.O.D., Lifehouse, and others, MxPx seemed to have a view of their work that transcended the old extremes, which saw art as either a tool to convert the masses or as simply a form of art to be enjoyed without regard for the profound life-changing effects it was capable of inspiring. Herrera seemed eager to throw off the constraints of utilitarianism while at the same time insisting that his music would reflect his worldview and ultimately reflect his strong beliefs:

> What I believe definitely is reflected in my music. I don't know if I approach the arts any differently. I respect art for what it is, and I think art is important. I personally don't believe that art and music have to have a utility to them to be important. It can just be something to enjoy, it can just be entertainment, it can be a picture, just something to look at. I don't agree with a lot of the fundamentalists out there that say that, if your art or whatever you're doing isn't working toward their goal, whatever it is, then it's not valid. I don't believe that. I think that if we enjoy what we're doing, and other people enjoy it, then that's just, in itself, worth something to me.[11]

Yet with song titles like "The Downfall of the Western Civilization," MxPx's songs were clearly doing more than simply entertaining; they were bringing a generally Judeo-Christian worldview and specifically a Christian-oriented one to unsuspecting fans who may not have been prepared for a crash course in Christian thought.

Comparing the Christian and secular markets to high school cliques, Herrera and MxPx had no stomach for the cultural divisions that they had inherited from their parents' generation—a division that had prevented previous rock bands with strong Christian beliefs from being given an audience by the mainstream pop culture. MxPx accepted no such limitations, eagerly playing rock festivals populated primarily by Christian kids with the same enthusiasm they showed for their mainstream dates.

Eventually, MxPx left Tooth & Nail for A&M Records and questioned the record deal they had signed as high school students.

"We realized from talking to other people in bands that . . . some things weren't quite right with ours, so we really wanted to see some things change,"[12] remembered Herrera.

One person who was eager to facilitate that change was Larry Weintraub, the then vice president of A&M Records who, as head of A&R, was always on the lookout for solid rock bands.

"I learned about the band because the manager of the band Face to Face, another band that I work with, sent me their CD and said, 'you've got to hear this CD. This band is amazing,'"[13] recalled Weintraub.

By mid 1997, MxPx was an A&M band and the label quickly released the band's previous album *Life in General* as well as the single "Chick Magnet," but as a concession to the label that found them, Tooth & Nail was given rights to distribute future records to the Christian-owned bookstores whose sales had given the band a solid base from which to launch their careers. Still, hard feelings were hard to shake for the upstart Seattle-based indie label. The label's general manager Bill Powers noted:

I'd be lying if I said that things weren't tense and didn't get weird somewhere along the line. There was a certain point where we were told we weren't even allowed to talk to the band anymore, and that obviously strained communications between us and that made things kind of weird.[14]

With the A&M deal, MxPx had its shot and "Chick Magnet" climbed up the rock and alternative charts. Although the band never actually achieved superstardom, they earned something even more tangible and difficult to attain: the respect of critics, punk-rock fans, and fellow artists alike.

Through it all, singer Mike Herrera brought a work ethic to his craft that was unusual for such a young man, and it had clearly paid off dividends in the response to the band's music by a rock music culture that too often seemed inhospitable to young men who were devout Christians.

"It is a job, it's the only thing I do for money. But I can't think of anything I'd rather do," said Herrera. "I love to do it. Even if I didn't get paid, I'd still want to do it. On my days off, I'm still usually working. At home, in the studio, or whatever, if I'm not doing something for MxPx, I'll still go in there and try to record a song I've written. It's definitely what I love to do."[15]

Eventually, as A&M folded into Universal Music, MxPx found itself without a label home and rejoined Tooth & Nail, a label whose growth had now caused its product to be stocked in most mainstream retail outlets. The band continued to tour in both the mainstream and Christian-oriented music circuits and also continued to connect with fans of classic punk rock, all the while maintaining their by now time- and road-tested Christian ideals. As such, MxPx was living proof that rock music played well, combined with lyrics that reflected deep Christian convictions, could indeed win the attention of the culture if it wasn't a gimmick and the passion for faith was matched by a passion for the craft of rock music.

7
The Minister's Daughter

When she emerged on the pop music scene with her debut album *Sweet Kisses* in 1999, as far as the mass pop culture was concerned, Jessica Simpson had come out of nowhere to directly compete against better known pop stars like Britney Spears. But to those involved in the Christian music industry, Simpson was a known commodity who had signed with a gospel label and was about to see her first record release. All of that changed when Sony Music took an interest in the young singer, the daughter of a Baptist youth minister whose stand on sexual morality—clear for some, ambiguous for others—combined with her vocal faith, would send the pop music world a message: more and more performers who were Christians would be joining the pop music mainstream, and correspondingly, social mores would be changing rapidly.

Simpson's public image was sometimes at odds with itself, however. The same artist who extolled the virtues of virginity both in interviews and in her music also posed for provocative photos and seemed to relish being named to the provocative *Stuff* magazine's 100 Sexiest Women in the World list.

Born in Dallas, Texas, to a homemaker mother and a father who served as a youth minister, Simpson always dreamed of being an entertainer:

> I always kind of knew in the back of my mind that . . . I would be a singer and do it professionally. I didn't really tell anybody except for my parents. They encouraged me. They're the ones who helped me to open doors. My mom sings and my dad was very theatrical, he went to school on a drama scholarship.[1]

Simpson got her start singing in church and later auditioned for the Mickey Mouse Club. At a church camp she was discovered by one of the speakers who was launching a label of his own. Simpson's masterful delivery of "Amazing Grace" impressed him.

"I was singing in church," remembered Simpson, "and a man was starting a gospel label and he signed me. I never went out to try to make a deal. It was destiny. It came to me."[2]

But Simpson's destiny apparently didn't include the speaker or his label, for after three years Simpson's album, reportedly financed by her grandmother, had still not been released. Those early experiences taught Simpson how to deal with disappointments in the music business.

"When I was 12 and didn't get the job I'd auditioned for on the Mickey Mouse Club that was a big, big let down for me," she remembered. "Then I worked on a gospel record for two years in my early teens only to have the record company fold right when my album was supposed to come out. So I've spent a lot of time not believing it was going to happen for now. But now I'm glad that's how it went, because I wasn't ready for it then."[3]

Once the Christian-oriented label she had signed with folded, Simpson auditioned for other faith-based labels and was surprised at the negative reaction. She recalled:

> We shopped it to other labels, but they were like, "You're too sexy to be singing Christian music." That really hurt me, because those weren't my intentions at all. I was in overalls and a ponytail, and they were telling me I couldn't go out there and sing because it would make boys lust.[4]

Instead, Simpson and her record came to the attention of Sony Music chief Tommy Mottola, the man responsible for turning Mariah Carey into an international superstar.

For years, devout Christians had been kept from signing with mainstream labels, which they referred to as "secular" labels, for fear of having their spiritual messages stymied by record company impresarios, and Simpson entered negotiations with Sony with that thought in mind.

"I was determined that I would be able to stay who I am if I signed to a non-Christian music label and when I met with Tommy Mottola he was genuinely impressed with my beliefs and was completely supportive," recalled Simpson. "I remember singing for him and he told me, 'you are going to change the world with the power of your heart and your music.' When he said that, I knew that I had a home with Sony."[5]

Mottola signed Simpson to Sony, and the fledgling artist began work on her debut album, *Sweet Kisses*. Public reaction to it was swift and powerful.

"A wholesome but decidedly secular assortment of bouncy dance tunes and wistful romantic ballads that has sold more than 500,000 copies," noted Elysa Gardner of *USA Today*. "The first single, 'I Wanna Love You Forever'—a sweeping ode that Simpson delivers with enough vocal bombast to swallow Mariah Carey whole—reached #1. Its video, in which the voluptuous blonde models' attire is a bit more form-fitting than overalls, is an MTV favorite."[6]

Simpson's sexy debut raised questions both for devout Christians and non-Christians alike about the seeming gulf between the image Simpson was projecting and her beliefs, which included a strong stand for virginity. It was a stand that was rooted in her upbringing, observing young women who were in her father's counseling practice:

> I would sit outside my Dad's door while he was working as a therapist. I would hear these girls weep—girls who were pregnant, or had put themselves in positions where they got raped. And I would promise myself, "Jessica, you will never be sitting in that chair."[7]

Simpson's determination to avoid problems encountered by patients in her father's practice may have contributed to her public stand, but the singer expressed surprise that such an announcement would cause controversy. Simpson had been a toddler in the Madonna era when virgin and pop star were considered oxymorons and seemed to be proud of her commitment:

> When I speak about my abstinence, people are like, "Yeah, right—no 19-year-old girl in the industry can do that." But it's not like I don't have any struggles.[8]

"For years, she even wore a gold ring with a cut-out cross to symbolize her commitment," observed Elysa Gardner. "Then she lost her virginity ring while on tour with Ricky Martin last year. 'It fell off while I was performing,' she explains. 'I was so upset. But for Christmas, my Dad bought me a new one—with a triple-diamond cross.'"[9]

"I'm surprised that people are surprised that I'm not having sex," she observed. "There are so many young girls out there who are huge romantics and want to wait until they're married and believe in Prince Charming like me."[10]

Simpson's vision was not off the mark, but though she would eventually find a man who shared those beliefs, her first experience in love was less than positive: "This guy who I was totally in love with—an actor . . . dumped me because I wouldn't sleep with him, and I was like, 'I'm never dating anybody in the entertainment industry again. All they're out for is sex.'"[11]

Simpson eventually found her soul mate in 98 Degrees singer Nick Lachey, for whom Simpson's beliefs were an asset:

> Nick comes along [and] the first time we ever talked I told him about my abstinence, and he embraced it. I feel like he's saving me from all the other crappy guys I would have been manipulated by. When I met him I told my Mom, "That's the guy I'm gonna marry." And he told the guys in the group, "That's the girl I'm gonna spend the rest of my life with." And we've been together ever since.[12]

"He knew about my values and morals before he met me, and that's what he says he loves the most about me," said Simpson. "I know that one day I will marry him."[13]

Despite her clothing and public image, which in 2001 included cleavage-spilling provocative poses for the men's magazine *Maxim,* Simpson insisted that her faith, not her appearance, was what people were attracted to:

> I believe my soul and my faith are what are sexy about me. It's all about what's inside.[14]
>
> The reason I came out with that when I did was because I'd seen so many young girls who hadn't saved themselves and were getting into trouble. You wanted them to know that I may be a person in the entertainment business but I can still wait to have sex and hopefully that would encourage them.[15]

But such responses didn't satisfy critics, including cultural conservatives who complained that Simpson's statements were out of sync with her public image. Others were more supportive, however. One reporter observed:

> Simpson . . . has been especially open about her decision to delay sex until marriage. Her song "Heart of Innocence" talks about what she plans to bring to her wedding night. Her virginal status has so fascinated *Cosmopolitan* that the magazine has published two articles on the subject in the past year. Miss Simpson told the publication she had received "thousands" of letters from girls desiring to follow her example.[16]

Sweet Kisses eventually sold over two million copies in the U.S. and another million copies overseas, making Simpson a certified international pop star, and things only got bigger from there. Her follow-up album, *Irresistible,* hit the pop charts hard and brought her to a higher level of media exposure.

"The first album established her as a star in the making," observed Columbia Records executive Will Botwin. "I think her personality comes across more on this record as a real singer's singer. That makes her different from the rest of the crowd."[17]

The album's first single, "I Think I'm in Love," was a shimmering pop song that brilliantly referenced '80s rocker John Cougar Mellencamp's megahit "Jack & Diane," winning accolades both from the pop singer's fellow teenyboppers as well as other fans who appreciated the familiar nod to Mellencamp.

Simpson had definite plans that went into *Irresistible*. She said of her follow-up record:

> My goal is to reach more people this time around. With the last album, I attracted a certain number with power ballads and my up-tempo pop songs, but on the new one, there are more R&B-oriented tracks, which I think have a nice edge to them. And there's attitude—something that no one has really seen in me before. Believe me, I'm a woman, so hey, I can have attitude.[18]

She added, "I think I've grown vocally because I've grown up, the music has a little more edge. In this album I tell guys off a little bit. *Sweet Kisses* was all about love and first love which is great but this one has a little more edge. I'm not dealing with just love I'm dealing with heartbreak: the real stuff."[19]

"Among the highlights of *Irresistible* is Simpson's favorite, 'Hot Like Fire,' a funky mid-tempo shuffler that she delivers with blazing vocal grit," observed *Billboard* magazine's Chuck Taylor. "It's certainly not kid stuff while 'What's It Gonna Be' casts the singer in a posturing finger-pointer in which she slyly solicits, 'I wanna know where we stand, are you gonna be a dog or a gentleman, are you coming clean, keep it straight with me? Tell me boy, what's it gonna be?'"[20]

Others were not so enthralled with Simpson's new posture. Bob Waliszewski, the chief music critic for a popular Christian-oriented website, Plugged In, notes:

> Considering that this young lady has garnered a loyal following based on her personal claims of chastity, the imminent sexual compromise on *Irresistible* is disturbing. She knows she shouldn't give in, but seems past the point of return ("I can't stop fanning the fire . . . Now inescapable . . . I just can't stop myself.") Similarly, "Forever in Your Eyes" finds a couple lying together "all through the night" ("This attraction fuels a passion/That's just too strong for us to try and fight"). The same artist who recorded "Heart of Innocence" on her last disk makes no such claims of purity here. If anything, *Irresistible* copes with temptation by yielding to it which in conjunction with Simpson's general immodesty models a dubious sexual ethic. Can't she see that the same Lord she worships with "His Eye Is on the Sparrow," also established the line she's determined to straddle?[21]

In spite of critics like Waliszewski, who was so outraged at Simpson's album cover for *Irresistible*, which featured the singer sporting a somewhat see-through blouse, that he refused to post the cover at his publication's web site, Simpson continued her mix of sexuality and Christianity.

"I wanted to give my audience a piece of my heart and soul," she said of the record's closing number "His Eye Is On The Sparrow." "The message is there's so much in life that can get you discouraged, but if you trust that you're being watched over, you have a reason to live and a sense of freedom. It's different for everyone, but for me, my relationship with God is the way I clear out the shadows that hang in our lives."[22]

In spite of her critics, Simpson was clearly a Christian who had chosen to make her stand for her faith and her music in the public square, refusing to be sequestered in the Christian subculture. Unlike Britney Spears, whose Baptist upbringing appeared to be less and less influential in her life with each passing year, and Christina Aguilera, whose spirituality appeared to be limited to vague spiritual references, Simpson's faith seemed more orthodox, traditional, and serious. She had refused to take the path to the Christian subculture but had also refused to go down the path of other prominent singers raised in the church, like Whitney Houston and Mariah Carey, who seemed to leave their faith out of their music almost entirely and certainly didn't take Bible-inspired public stands on sexual issues. In her own way, albeit imperfectly, she seemed intent on trying to integrate her faith into her music and make that music in the center of popular culture.

When asked if she planned to make a "gospel" record, as hundreds of artists before her had done, Simpson seemed uninterested at the prospect of separating her faith from the rest of her music.

"You know, no," she responded. "Every one of my albums I make I'll always do some kind of a tribute to my spirituality but as far as making a straight religious record, probably not . . ."[23]

Amidst a popular culture where many stars in sports, entertainment, and politics begged off of role model status, Simpson welcomed the role she had found thrust upon her:

My favorite thing is to go on my website and see the lives that
have been inspired by my music or my interviews. My ultimate
goal has always been to be a positive role model; now that goal
is fulfilled for me every day.[24]

Had Simpson's deal with the Christian-oriented label suc-
ceeded, she most likely would have joined dozens of other artists
who were stars in the Christian music industry but unknown to
the larger popular culture audience. As such her impact on pop
culture would have been nearly nonexistent. But as a recording
artist in the Sony stable, Simpson had chosen a path that brought
her music, her image, and her public stands to the attention of
American popular culture and a world audience: "Crossing over
has been the best thing that's ever happened to me," observed
Simpson. "I can reach so many more people than I ever could
have in the Christian industry, and that's a blessing."[25]

8
Rockin' the Sabbath

The invasion of people of serious faith into mainstream rock has not been limited to Christians. Twenty-eight-year-old identical twins Evan and Jaron Lowenstein were aspiring pop rockers who took their orthodox Jewish faith so seriously that they refused to play on the Sabbath.

The Lowensteins had followed an unlikely path to pop stardom. Atlanta natives, the brothers had attended Yeshiva High School in their hometown and dreamed not of being rock stars, but of playing professional baseball. Evan Lowenstein's love of music started in a most unlikely way: "We got Discmans for our bar mitzvah," recalled Evan. "I got into music because I needed something to put in it."[1]

Later, when Evan got interested in music after hearing Elvis Costello's song "Allison," his brother came along for the ride: "As soon as I picked up a guitar, we jumped to the next level immediately," said Jaron. "Evan started this whole thing and I jumped on board to do him a favor. Then I became addicted."[2]

The brothers had dropped out of college, planning for careers in major league baseball, but before long music took over and they were playing nightclubs and other gigs around their hometown of Atlanta. *Rolling Stone* observed:

Call it self-prophecy or just plain arrogance, but Evan and Jaron's early confidence—and hard work—paid off. Cultivating a solid following in the Atlanta area through a regular Tuesday night slot at KaLo's Coffee House, the duo slowly won the hearts of fans and, subsequently, several major record labels. Given the strings attached, the payoff has come surprisingly easy. For starters, Evan and Jaron are identical twins. Somehow, they've managed to squelch the whole Nelson thing before it ever got off the ground.[3]

In 1994, faced with radio stations that refused to play their music because they weren't signed to a major label, the brothers showed their sharp sense of humor by launching A Major Label, their own "independent" record label. Soon their constant gigging brought them to the attention of legendary musician Jimmy Buffet, who in turn took them to Island Records president Chris Blackwell.

If Blackwell didn't realize he was on the brink of signing two young rockers who took their faith as seriously as they took their music, he quickly found out when he met the Lowenstein brothers. Jaron recalled:

The first time we met with Chris Blackwell our manager called him and said, "Listen, the guys would love to meet with you, but they have dietary laws. They eat kosher only." Chris said "Absolutely" and sat down and told us about how he grew up Jewish and his family founded the first synagogue in Jamaica."[4]

"Blackwell told the duo if they were as committed to the music as they were to their faith, Island would be happy to have them," observed music journalist Kevin Raub. "The rest, as they say, is history."[5]

Confident, but just shy of cocky, Evan Lowenstein recalled the events with characteristic nonchalance:

We've always been way ahead of ourselves in our minds. It's just been a matter of catching up to where we were. We've always shot way further ahead.[6]

Although Island eventually dropped Evan and Jaron from the label's roster, Columbia Records quickly picked up the duo and before long the brothers had their first hit single, "Crazy for This Girl," thanks to MTV and *TRL*. The group's success was not something Evan and Jaron entirely appreciated, however, as success on *TRL* caused many to think that the duo was a boy band à la *NSYNC and the Backstreet Boys, something the brothers hotly contested:

> "In a lot of ways, MTV put us a step backward," said Jaron. "Don't get me wrong—we appreciate the exposure—but we are not a boy band. We play our own instruments. We write our own songs. Before *TRL*, most of our fans were more or less our age."[7]

Still, the sudden explosion of *TRL*-inspired fame was sometimes off-putting, and the dramatic change was felt by the band at concerts:

> "It's strange," said Jaron. "Three years ago we played 21-and-over clubs. Maybe there would be a few kids at the shows. Now, we have all these people who are under 20. I don't know what it is with this boy band thing. People look at us now and go 'I get it.' Get what?"[8]

Sometimes the new audience made the band's job of communicating difficult—especially in concert. Jaron commented:

> We find sometimes less people in the audience are understanding what we are talking about than they were five years ago. We're 28-year-old guys talking about things relevant in our lives, and it's definitely not relevant in a 15-year-old's life. We make jokes and there are a couple of adults in the back laughing. We call them the carpool drivers—the baby sitters.[9]

In spite of massive success and constant touring, the Lowenstein brothers found the stigma nearly impossible to shake, short of convincing one fan at a time. Jaron stated:

> If I had a dollar for every single production guy or sound guy or security guy at venues across the country we've played who said, "You know what, I didn't know who you were. I thought

you were some boy band, but you were really good," we wouldn't be sitting in this restaurant. I'd own this place.[10]

Beyond the boy band controversy, another issue that loomed on the horizon for Evan and Jaron that threatened to keep the band from being taken seriously, especially by rock critics, was the fact that they were twins. For the brothers it was yet another obstacle to being taken seriously for their music:

> Back in the early 1970s people liked the music because it was just a . . . good song. No acrobats, no jugglers, no twins, no tight leather pants—just a . . . good song. So we don't like to promote the fact that we're twins. We're not running away from it, we just want the music to speak for itself. We're not out there saying, "Hey, it's Doublemint gum, it's Evan and Jaron, have a stick!" We're not doing that.[11]

And contrary to public opinion about twins in general, Jaron insisted that the brothers did not always get along:

> "We fight about everything," he laughed. "But that's probably because we spend so much time together."[12]
> "People think twins are supposed to be identical in every way," Evan added. "That is so not the case."[13]

Still, ultimately it was the strength of the band's music that caused music critics to focus on the songs the brothers were creating. Journalist Kevin Raub observed:

> While the twin issue may cause a few sniggers in the music industry, the music . . . is making noise as well. Equal parts Simon and Garfunkel and The Rembrandts with a dash of Ben Folds Five, Evan and Jaron . . . have mastered the craft of writing a radio-friendly hook . . . not bad for two guys who were more interested in draft picks and World Series champions growing up than how to write a catchy melody.[14]

Clearly understanding that the twin issue and the brothers' poster-boy good looks brought many people to the band in the first place, Jaron maintained that it was the music that would keep them coming back again:

> We're serious about making music. At the end of the day, if our looks get people to check out our music, that's fine, because ultimately our music speaks for itself.[15]

Still, nothing brought press attention to Evan and Jaron like the issue of religion and the peculiarity (at least for the dominant pop media culture) of rock stars who were serious about their faith commitment—in fact, so serious that they refused to play shows on the Sabbath, an absolutely unheard of and unprecedented stand. Even rock and pop stars who were devout Christians had little or no problem with playing on the Christian Sabbath. In the seventy-nine years since the Olympic hero Eric Liddel, memorialized in the film *Chariots of Fire*, had famously refused to run on Sunday, his fellow Christians, even those who took their faith seriously, had come to an understanding of Sabbath-keeping which allowed them to go about their normal activities with little or no thought for the biblical command to "Remember the Sabbath day to keep it holy."

However, Evan and Jaron were not modern-day evangelical Christians, but rather orthodox Jews, who were reared to obey their laws and traditions and take God's commandments seriously and literally:

> "Evan and Jaron are serious about their Jewish faith and relentlessly observe the Sabbath. From sundown Friday to sundown Saturday," observed *Rolling Stone*, "there are no concerts, no interviews and no meetings. They even turned down the opening slot for Oasis on Rosh Hashanah in 1996."[16]

It was a decision that the band looked back upon with no regret and a strong sense of what was and wasn't important in the grand scheme of things:

> "Automatically we said we can't do it," remembered Evan, "and the day before the show, they canceled. Can you imagine if we had given up everything we believed for that one show? How stupid we would have looked."[17]

77

The band's career definitely slowed a bit after the success of the single "Crazy for This Girl" ebbed, something some attributed to the band's unwillingness to play major tours because of their Sabbath "issues." Confirming that in at least one instance that was indeed the case, Jaron Lowenstein seemed content with the brothers' decisions and focused on what they gained by sticking to their beliefs:

> "It definitely hurts us," he acknowledged. "We had to turn down a tour with Stevie Nicks this summer because we couldn't play Friday nights."[18]
>
> "I look at it as a chance for me to step away from everything else that's going on in my life and focus on other things," added Evan. "It's an opportunity for me to step down off my stage and pay homage to somebody . . . greater than myself."[19]

For some, the spectacle of rock & roll—birthed and reared in a culture that seemed to disdain traditional cultural and religious morals—being taken over by orthodox, Sabbath-observing people of faith, might have been troubling, but for a new generation of faith-rockers like Evan and Jaron, separating their faith from their music was simply not an option. While they seemed to clearly grasp the obvious contradictions that rock and faith seemed to represent, they relished the idea of charting a new course that married the two:

> "The reason the press has grabbed a hold of this religion thing is because rock 'n roll and religion are probably the greatest juxtapositions of all time," observed Jaron. "One is clearly about chaos; the other is clearly about discipline."[20]

As with their Christian counterparts in Creed, Lifehouse, P.O.D., and Jars of Clay, the Lowenstein brothers sought to make the distinction between Jewish rock and Jews making rock, arguing that they were the latter:

> "It's like Seinfeld," said Jaron. "He's Jewish, but it's not a Jewish show. It's the same thing with Evan and Jaron. We don't make any statements. You'll never hear Evan and Jaron say, 'Go to church.' No, we're just two Jewish guys who happen to take it to the next level."[21]

While it had become fashionable for rockers to deny that they were on proselytizing missions, it was clear that, intended or otherwise, Evan and Jaron Lowenstein were making powerful statements about what was and wasn't important in life and who they should be pleasing, and millions of fans were starting to take notice of the continued seismic shift that was quietly taking place in rock music.

9

Manifest Destiny

In 2001 when the *Los Angeles Times* polled record label executives to see which artists they most admired, an R&B trio named Destiny's Child beat out top artists and ranked #6. Unlike many pop vocal groups, which were often loathed by such executives (privately anyway), critics spotted in Destiny's Child something unique.

"'The great pop group of the moment,' gushed *Rolling Stone*, the same publication which had once christened U2 the 'band of the '80s.'"[1]

Like U2, Destiny's Child was comprised of Christians who had navigated past the Christian music subculture and had managed to sign with a major label, but whose faith commitment was constantly questioned by other believers.

For the last thirty years or so, the music world had been neatly divided between the secular and the sacred. "Christian" music focused mainly on religious themes and was released on labels with pseudo-spiritual sounding names like Sparrow, Myrrh, Light, and Maranatha! and distributed through a nationwide network of Christian-owned bookstores. "Secular" music on the other hand focused primarily on earthly themes and was released through ordinary or mainstream retail and distribution routes in the primary entertainment culture.

As such, it was easy for many Christians to tell the truly "saved" artists from the spiritual imposters. In the eyes of many, truly Christian artists recorded for "Christian" record companies, while the unfaithful or pseudo-Christians recorded for "secular" record companies. The label the artists recorded for was in some sense an indication of the artist's spiritual character.

But as more and more artists began to avoid signing with "Christian music" labels and signed instead with mainstream ones, it became harder for fellow true believers to tell which artists were truly devout and which were spiritual poseurs. This was of course a highly subjective judgment call, which involved combining an analysis of the artist's lyrics, public statements, and lifestyle.

In general that formula produced an understanding among Christians that placed artists like Prince, Britney Spears, R Kelly, and others, despite public statements affirming their Christian faith, outside of the realm of Christians. But it also left room for disagreement among Christians about other artists. In the brave new world of Christians rejoining the mainstream music business, it became increasingly difficult to figure out who was and who wasn't a real Christian.

Into this already confusing situation stepped three young black women—Kelly Rowland, Beyoncé Knowles, and Michelle Williams—collectively known as Destiny's Child. All three considered themselves to be Christians and followed a strict code of conduct, which meant no drinking, drug use, or sleeping around. Yet their provocative dress and public persona seemed to many to be out of sync with those ideals.

"Attempting to reconcile the imaging of Destiny's Child with Christian beliefs makes many people uncomfortable," noted *Gospel Today* magazine. "While God judges the heart, man can only judge appearances and actions. All three say that they are Christians and that they pray and read their Bibles together on tour, often opting not to attend various parties. For many young girls, they are role models. For many Christian mothers, they bring mixed emotions."[2]

"So what do we make of Destiny's Child, the popular R&B trio who proclaim their Christianity in nearly every interview, but whose latest single is suggestively titled 'Bootylicious' and whose videos are high in thigh and cleavage content?"[3] asked the *St. Petersburg Times.*

The group was actually the brainchild of group leader Beyoncé Knowles and her father, the group's ubiquitous manager, Matthew Knowles, a driven salesman who decided to help his daughter with her burgeoning career by taking business courses and helping her assemble a singing group.

Knowles remembered thinking to himself: "I've been successful at everything I've done. If I could be the No. 1 sales rep at Xerox, if I could be a specialist in neurosurgical equipment, why would I fail at this?"[4]

Keeping it all in the family, the group's name came from Beyoncé Knowles' mother who happened across the phrase "destiny" as she perused the Scriptures one day. What the Scriptures didn't reveal, however, were the years of turmoil that would precede Destiny's Child's eventual three-girl lineup, for before Rowland and Williams joined the team the band had looked different.

"LaTavia Roberson, LeToya Luckett and Farrah Franklin [were] the unwanted children of Destiny," noted the *Los Angeles Times.* "The first two were original members with Knowles and Rowland, but now their names are tied to the group only by the breach-of-contract lawsuit they filed following their March 2000 firings. In interviews, they have referred to the Knowles patriarch as a suffocating force who did not treat them fairly either personally or financially, and who created a cult-like environment around the group."[5]

Replacing the original two members were Farrah Franklin and Michelle Williams, but when Franklin seemed unable to keep up with the group's hectic pace, she too was asked to leave and the quartet became a trio.

"There has been some damage, I can't deny that," said manager Knowles. "Obviously, we had always marketed Destiny's Child with the individuals. Some groups you don't know their names—can you name the members of Dream, for instance? But with groups like TLC or The Supremes or The Temptations, you know the names and that's how we went. So some of the fans were disheartened when those people changed."[6]

For both Beyoncé Knowles and her parents, Destiny's Child was a family. "Those kids were like family, so it was devastating," said Beyoncé. "It was really hard to separate the love from the other part. But looking back now—it's such a relief. It was not a pleasant situation for the last year . . . now we have peace. We pray together, everyone talks to each other, works hard. It's like night and day. It happened for a reason, and I'm happy that it happened, to be honest. That might sound a little cold but it's the truth."[7]

Eventually, when the lawsuits with the various former members were settled, the group was able to get back to making music, which it did with a vengeance on the album *Survivor*, which promptly debuted at #1 on the pop charts.

The genesis of the album's smash single "Survivor" was a good example of the group's ability to overcome and even harness the power of adversity and turn it into something positive.

"The title of 'Survivor' and its words of empowered endurance come from Beyoncé Knowles . . . but the idea . . . came from a Houston radio DJ who compared the local celebs to the popular television show," observed the *Los Angeles Times*. "With so many members discarded, the DJ said, the group was going to become a game of last singer standing. The comment rankled the group but, with a wink, it instead took the criticism as its new mantra."[8]

"We were like, 'all the songs from this point on are gonna be about surviving something,'"[9] said Beyoncé.

But the song that troubled many in the faith community was a song with the unusual title of "Bootylicious," a term that the members of Destiny's Child actually coined themselves. To be sure, it was often the case that many who objected to songs like "Bootylicious" on moral grounds had never actually heard the song or perused the lyrics, for the song was actually little more than an innocent schoolgirl's tease set to music.

"I don't think you're ready for this jelly, cause my body's too bootylicious for ya, babe," went one line from the song, "jelly" being a term of pride given to the well-rounded backsides of the group's members.

Some critics who found such a song offensive and sexually graphic seemed to lack historical context and an understanding of just where pop music made by women had come from. For from the up-front propositioning of Olivia Newton John in her song "Physical" ("I took you to an intimate restaurant, then to a suggestive movie, there's nothing left to talk about, unless it's horizontally"), to Carole King's "I Feel the Earth Move Under My Feet," to Janet Jackson's pleas to "go deeper" in "That's the Way Love Goes," female pop stars had been singing frankly and sometimes lasciviously about giving it away for years. Destiny's Child's message in "Bootylicious" on the other hand, frank to be sure, was built around the subtext of saving sex, presumably anyway, for a marriage relationship.

But that did little to assuage critics like Bob Smithouser:

> I'm scratching my head just like everybody else. Kelly Rowland, Beyoncé Knowles and Michelle Williams are talented ladies with an obvious interest in spiritual things. But . . . they play up the whole sex symbol bit in some of their lyrics, outfits and dance grooves. While many of *Survivor*'s songs are great, "Sexy Daddy," "Apple Pie A La Mode" and the No. 1 hit single "Bootylicious" worship at a different throne.[10]

Still others like G. Craige Lewis, a minister and popular youth group speaker, was troubled by other aspects, disapproving of the group's tendency to "gyrate and make sexual moves," adding, "it's not anything of God."[11]

In the confused sexual ethos of the post-AIDS era, Destiny's Child seemed to be a perfect reflection of the pop culture zeitgeist that was able to marry a somewhat virginal sexual ethic with an up-front and frank sexual posturing. Translation: showing a lot of skin but not putting out.

However, at least one member of the group, Michelle Williams, seemed uncomfortable when questioned about the group's choice of clothing:

> Lots of times, as far as the outfits of the group are concerned, I've been kind of covered up. That's been by choice. Even when I was in the Church I hardly ever wore a pair of shorts. In the blazing summer I always wanted to put on some jeans and cover my legs. When I got in the group my manager knew our style was sort of uncomfortable for me. He knows that and he does try to abide by that. I'm still saved and there's nobody in this world that can judge me and tell me anything otherwise.[12]

But plenty of people were judging Destiny's Child based on its members' clothing, often ignoring the actual lyrics from songs, including this line from "Survivor": "I'm not going to compromise my Christianity."

Lyrics aside, the three members of Destiny's Child also seemed to be very aware of their role model status, taking care to avoid what were for many Christians social taboos:

> "In *Rolling Stone*, it said that I was at Wyclef's afterparty sipping on champagne," said Beyoncé. "I don't drink."
> "We're role models, so we watch ourselves," added Kelly. "And not just when we go to parties."[13]

And the morality seemed to have a clear and present base in the church and active Christian fellowship according to them, for unlike many public celebrities who claimed church attendance was impossible because of their celebrity, the members of Destiny's Child made such attendance a priority:

> "Beyoncé, Kelly and I go to church every Sunday that we can," said Michelle Williams. "We read our Bibles lots of times instead of going to a party. We get on our tour bus and have church in the back of the bus. We surround ourselves with Christians and people who are Spirit-filled. We trust God and He still speaks to us. We know that He does. I can't let anybody tell me that because I'm in Destiny's Child I'm not saved. We never know why we're placed in this area or why I was placed in this group."[14]

Critics of American Christianity were quick to charge that American believers were high on "easy-believism," that peculiarly Protestant ability to rationalize and justify sinful behaviors because forgiveness was readily available. In cultural figures like Bill Clinton, such critics found large and easy to identify targets. But the story of Destiny's Child was far more complicated, for the girls, with Williams as their spiritual spokesperson, seemed to have a genuine faith:

> "I do know that I probably will get some negative feedback from people, but I can't let them discourage me and try to tell me I'm not a Christian and I'm not saved because they're not God," explained Williams. "I know what God has done in my life and I

know that God is still with me and He still loves me. I'm here to testify about that. We feel God's presence. I still feel His Spirit and His anointing on my life. I can't go far from that . . . Right now there are so many things going on, and young people don't have a lot of people to look up to. I want to be an encouragement to people and let them know that their dreams can come true. I've always been prayerful. Every move that I've made, God has been there. . . . God is soon to come. It's my purpose to tell people that don't know Him to get to know Him and that He can change people's life."[15]

"God has a plan," added Beyoncé Knowles, "and God is in control of everything."[16]

"Yes, he is," Kelly Rowland added. "There is no way in the world that you can tell me that this was not meant to be—three people with the same dreams, the same goals."[17]

Whether combining virginal talk with skimpy outfits and suggestive lyrics was God's plan or the plan of a street-smart manager who understood the confused culture he was trying to sell products to was a matter of debate. Still, Destiny's Child would continue navigating its way through a brave new pop culture which people of faith found themselves thrown into. It was a pop culture whose values were diametrically opposed to theirs, in a world where "Christian" and "secular" were no longer neatly separated, and the resulting confrontation of cultures could sometimes produce messy results. For groups like Destiny's Child, the mission was clear, though the delivery was sometimes muddled and contradictory:

"I know we sing R&B," said Michelle Williams, "but we don't promote premarital sex, drugs and alcohol or do those things. I'm here to help change the world—not have the world change me."[18]

10

Reinventing Alice

Alice Cooper was in many ways an American icon in the modern rock world. Before Gene Simmons discovered grease paint, David Bowie and Michael Jackson discovered gender confusion, and Marilyn Manson discovered the joys of using a female stage name, Alice Cooper had been there and done that.

Cooper was actually born Vincent Furnier, the son of a Phoenix, Arizona, preacher named Ether Moroni Furnier who considered his mission field to be the Native Americans who populated the Indian reservations in Arizona. While Furnier senior was preaching the gospel in Arizona, Furnier junior was touring the world, singing about necrophilia with songs like "I Love the Dead" and "Cold Ethyl," and singing a duet with Satan himself on "Alice Cooper Goes to Hell."

But Cooper's father seemed to never give up on his son, believing that one day he would come back to his faith.

"Cooper's dad . . . wrote the introduction to Cooper's 1976 autobiography, *Me, Alice,*" observed Brian McCollum. "There, he lamented that his son had 'drifted away from church attendance altogether,' before adding hopefully: 'Am I dreaming or suffering from wishful thinking that after all this decadence there will emerge from this dynamic personality a servant of God . . . ?'"[1]

Furnier's fondest wish would come true over a decade later when Cooper underwent an amazing transformation that threatened to destroy the stage personality that he had created with Alice Cooper.

The first clue for Cooper fans might have been the song "Hey Stoopid," a song from the early '90s whose video showed two teenagers about to have sex only to be interrupted by Alice Cooper calling them stupid.

Although Cooper downplayed the transformation publicly, if his music was any indication, there had been a battle raging for his soul. Cooper's transformation apparently had its genesis when he and his wife came into contact with a theologian named R. C. Sproul. Cooper had married his wife Cheryl after the two met when she played a ballerina in his *Welcome to My Nightmare* stage show in the mid 1970s. In the '80s, both became interested in Sproul's teaching tapes, which had reportedly been recommended to the two by Cheryl's father.

While signed to the major label Epic, Cooper had been fairly reticent about proclaiming his newfound faith. Later, however, signed to the independent Spitfire label, he began to grant more interviews and spoke openly about his spiritual transformation. He also set the record straight about his '70s persona, Alice Cooper, and what was and wasn't real:

> You know, everybody has a different story about Alice Cooper. Most of what you've heard about Alice Cooper is urban legend. And it's not just me . . . Ozzy Osbourne, Marilyn Manson; anybody who's in the least bit exotic in the rock 'n roll business gets these incredible rumors going. Granted, I have done some pretty strange things on stage, and in my new show there're even more strange things, but 90 percent of the things I've heard I've done I didn't do.[2]

One of those rumors included an allegation that the singer had bitten the head off of a chicken during a concert, a charge Cooper was eager to clarify:

> Somebody did throw a chicken on stage. I threw it back into the audience. I didn't even throw it, I thought it would fly away. It's a chicken, it has wings! I'm from Detroit, I didn't know anything about chickens. I didn't know they couldn't fly! I tossed it back

into the audience and they tore it apart. And the crazy thing about that is it wasn't the whole audience . . . they put all of the people in wheelchairs in the front row, so it was the handicapped that tore the chicken apart. I didn't do it, the audience did it. But I got blamed for it.[3]

What was true about that period in Cooper's life, however, was that he was an alcoholic living in a continual stupor:

I was a totally functional alcoholic, probably the most functional alcoholic ever. I never missed a show. I never stumbled. I never slurred a word. I was the Dean Martin of rock 'n roll. I was totally just on a nice glow. I never got drunk to get drunk-drunk. I just kept a buzz on, a nice little glow all the time. I'd go to the studio and be the first one there, the last one to leave. I'd sit there and write like a complete professional artist. But I always had a beer with me. Now if somebody took my beer away, then I'd be very unprofessional and I'd throw a fit. So, I did require my little habit . . . every one of those major songs was written while we were deep into a case of beer.[4]

Unlike many alcoholics who recover courtesy of rehab programs like Alcoholics Anonymous, Cooper claimed to have had a miraculous recovery from his addiction:

I've never had to attend an AA meeting for myself. Not one, ever. I honestly think I was simply and completely healed. Like being healed from cancer, it was taken away from me, something I am eternally thankful for because I've never had to go through the torture of being a recovering alcoholic. I went through the torture of being an alcoholic, drinking like an alcoholic, but I never went through the madness of craving it after I came out of the hospital. I guess you can call it a miracle. It's the only way I can explain it. It was absolutely eliminated from my life. There's a difference between beating drinking, being cured and being healed. I think I was healed. I say that only because I don't know any other alcoholics that came out of the hospital and were never even tempted to take another drink. I never once sat around and thought, "That was a rough day yesterday and I really need a drink." When I came out of the hospital, it was over. I could sit in a bar where everyone was drinking and have a Coca Cola and it would never occur to me to have a drink. I know that's not a normal alcoholic position at all but it's the truth.[5]

Cooper had somehow sidestepped the fate that engulfed other rock stars from Hendrix to Joplin, Cobain to Bon Scott. While it's not altogether clear that Cooper's ability to cheat death wasn't because of his father's prayers and his spiritual heritage, Cooper himself believed that what kept him from being swallowed up by his addictions and the music business was his ability to play the Alice character onstage and return to a normal life offstage, something other rock stars seemed incapable of doing.

"It killed them, all of those amazing artists," said Cooper. "I've known a lot of musicians who've had strong images and they didn't quite know how to divorce themselves from what they were onstage to who they were off. Jimi Hendrix and Janis Joplin, I think that they felt they had to be this character for the public all the time or people would be disappointed."[6]

"I thought I had to be Alice in order to be believable," he added. "I thought I had to go out and wear the make-up with a snake around my neck. I lived in Beverly Hills, Hollywood and I'd go out in all black. I thought I had to be this heavy character. You have to remember, I used to drink with Jim Morrison, Janis Joplin, Keith Moon, and Jimi Hendrix. Almost every one of my big brothers died. . . . These are all people who tried to live their image. I learned that you'd better separate that image [from who you really are]."[7]

Ultimately, Cooper credited the literal presence of God with saving his life:

> I had the faith my whole life, but when I got sober, I understood things better. I didn't need another car. I didn't need another mansion. I didn't need another supermodel. That was all viable, that was all get-able. I had a beautiful wife. I had a beautiful family but I should've been dead 20 times being Alice Cooper. And I thought to myself, this goes a lot deeper; there must be another reason why I'm not dead. Faith kept me alive, and being alive, after what I've seen and done, makes me a very unique creature in the rock 'n roll business.[8]

By itself, the spiritual transformation of Alice Cooper was nothing remarkable. For decades, rock stars had enjoyed wild excess at the height of their popularity, then crashed and burned and found God just as their careers were in the toilet. Then, usually urged on by their ministers, these artists would retreat to the Christian music world and record albums of hymns or albums full of gratitude to God for what He had done in their lives. Unfortunately, since these records were usually not available outside of the Christian-owned bookstore circuit, it was, so far as the popular entertainment culture was concerned, as if they had never been made. From Grand Funk lead singer Mark Farner to Wings drummer Joe English, from Earth, Wind & Fire singer Philip Bailey to the Outlaws bassist Rick Cua, artists who found God were relegated to the backwaters of entertainment, never to be heard from again in any serious or substantive way that might have had an impact on their former fans.

But Alice Cooper chose a different path. Rather than moving to a religious label, he stayed at his longtime home, Epic, generally kept his same show intact complete with outlandish makeup and onstage use of snakes, but began to slowly change the content of his songs. It was a brilliant plan that allowed him continued access to his former fans while slowly, step-by-step introducing them to the new beliefs of the new and improved Alice Cooper.

By the turn of the century, Alice Cooper was speaking loudly and clearly from the very public platform that had been built for him through wild excess thirty years earlier. He had earned the respect of his fans over three decades and hence the right to speak forthrightly and clearly to his fans about his newfound faith. Most significantly of all, he refused to do it while sequestered in Christian America, talking to the faithful on the 700 Club and selling his records next to Precious Moments Bibles in religious bookstores. Sitting down with longtime friend and former *Spin* magazine editor Lonn Friend for an interview with the on-line hard rock bible, KNAC.COM, Cooper pulled no punches:

> I was pretty much convinced all my life that there was just one God and there was Jesus Christ and there was the devil. You couldn't believe in God without believing in the devil. I always tell bands that the most dangerous thing you can do is to believe in the concept of the devil or the concept of God, because you're not giving

them full credit. When you believe in God, you've got to believe in the all-powerful God. He's not just God, He's the all-powerful God and He has total control over everyone's life. The devil, on the other hand, is a real character that's trying his hardest to tear your life apart. If you believe that this is just mythology, you're a prime target because you know that's exactly what Satan wants: to be a myth. But he's not a myth, of this I'm totally convinced. More than anything in the world, I'm convinced of that. So, here we are. We have God pulling us one way and the devil pulling us another and we're in the middle. We have to make a choice. And everybody, at some point in their lives, has to make that choice. When people say, "How do you believe this? Why do you believe this?" I just say nothing else speaks to my heart. This doesn't speak to my intellect, it doesn't speak to my logic—it speaks right to my heart and right to my soul, deeper than anything I've ever thought of. And I totally believe it. That being said, I'm not a very good Christian. I mean, none of us are ever good Christians. That's not the point. When you're a Christian, it doesn't mean you're gonna be good, it means you've got a harder road to pull.[9]

The conversion of Alice Cooper coupled with his refusal to move off of the public stage and retreat to the religious world à la Cat Stevens had turned the rock world upside down, for the king of shock rock was making a rational and logical case for traditional morality and orthodox notions of God while wearing heavy makeup and a snake around his neck. It was a "pulpit" that Ether Furnier could never have anticipated and one which his son Alice relished:

I'm politically incoherent. People ask me if I'm politically correct, and I'm like, "I'm Alice Cooper. I should be able to say what I want to say." Just because it doesn't jibe with what the general rock 'n roll public says, that's not my problem. The amazing thing is, if Alice Cooper pisses off the rock 'n roll community, that's the ultimate rebellion![10]

One subject that clearly annoyed Alice Cooper, the original shock rocker, was some of the antics of Marilyn Manson. Cooper cut Manson a certain amount of slack for his act, which he recognized as theater:

You know, he's one of the greatest button pushers I've ever met, and I know that game because I invented that game: how to push buttons and piss people off. Manson clicked because he found a whole new set of buttons to push. He even pushed my buttons, which is pretty impressive since I was pushing buttons before he was born. I'd really love to sit down and talk to Marilyn, not just about religion, but about anything. I've read interviews with him. He's very bright and quite funny, too. I'd probably get along with him very well.[11]

But when Manson's act turned to desecrating Cooper's Holy Book, Cooper failed to see the humor:

I absolutely don't agree with 90 percent of what Marilyn Manson says. I'm diametrically opposed, in fact. He actually made me mad! Tearing up the Bible is certainly an affront to me. Saying "All Christians are jerks" and he wants to kill all Christians; I'm supposed to be his big hero, so he'd better start with me.[12]

Firing a warning shot off to his protégé, Cooper painted a humorous picture, which pointed out the silliness of performers like Manson whose public persona threatened to overtake their lives:

You paint yourself into a corner when you say, "I am Marilyn Manson" or "I am Rob Zombie" or "I am this guy all the time." They're not! You know, how could Manson be Manson when he takes his girlfriend to dinner or goes Christmas shopping for his Mother? The Marilyn Manson rock star dark character doesn't go Christmas shopping and he wouldn't be caught dead in a restaurant, you know what I mean? So you paint yourself in a corner when you say "I'm going to wear this mask all the time."[13]

Cooper's new "act" as a devout man of faith also included what had by now become the obligatory denial that all rock star Christians had to engage in—denying that they were preaching. Cooper too did the dance but hilariously followed the denial with a thundering "sermon" that would rival any coming from a more traditional pulpit:

People often ask, "What are you preaching here?" I'm not preaching anything, except there's good, there's evil. We have a choice. This is Alice's view, not my view. I'm the optimistic one. Alice's view is very pessimistic. Alice sees things going to hell. "Brutal Planet" is 50 years from now, a world without God. It's a horrific place. My stage show is gonna make it entertaining, and Alice the character is gonna make it entertaining, but the main message is "This is a place where we don't wanna be. There's no redeeming value to this place at all."[14]

As the elder statesman of rock & roll, Cooper was an unusual mix of prophet, preacher, and rocker. He had earned a place of trust among a subculture of hard rockers who would never darken the door of a church.

"I think that people fill their lives with other things, whether that be drugs, or cars . . . whatever," said Cooper. "I've filled my life with a sincere, divine love of rock 'n roll. I will never back down in my rock 'n roll attitude because I think rock is great! I'm the first one to turn it up. I'm the first one to rock as loud as I can, but when it comes to what I believe, I'm the first one to defend it too. It has also gotten me in trouble with the staunch Christians who believe that in order to be a Christian you have to be on your knees 24 hours a day in a closet somewhere. Hey, maybe some people can live like that, but I don't think that's the way God expected us to live. When Christ came back, He hung out with the whores, the drunks and miscreants because they were people that needed Him."[15]

11

Cherone's Pulpit

In 1997 the legendary rock group Van Halen announced that it was replacing the group's second lead singer, Sammy Hagar, who himself had replaced the band's original lead singer, David Lee Roth. While there was nothing particularly remarkable about a rock band playing musical chairs with its lead singer, what was shocking to those who knew something about the new recruit was the fact that Van Halen, the renowned party band, was about to be fronted by a serious Christian named Gary Cherone.

Hailing from Boston and reared in a Catholic family, Cherone converted to a more generic form of the Christian faith in the mid 1980s under the influence of a radio pastor named Chuck Swindoll, who later became the president of the Dallas Theological Seminary. Cherone had played in bands for years, but had hit the big time when his band Extreme lit up the charts in the early 1990s with two hits songs, "Hole Hearted" and "More Than Words."

It was likely that many Extreme fans missed Cherone's somewhat obscure references to God on both these songs, for both could easily have been interpreted as songs to a lover, but were actually both written with a more divine love in mind. On "Hole Hearted" in particular, Cherone had lifted verses directly from the Psalms.

"You know where those lyrics are coming from," Cherone once said to a sympathetic reporter, referring to the lyrics of "Hole Hearted." "I wonder if our audience does, because I plagiarized the Bible with some of those lyrics [he laughs], which I think is the only way you can't go wrong."[1]

Being the lead singer of Extreme provided the singer with a powerful pulpit and Cherone didn't hesitate to use it to promote his beliefs. But he rarely spoke candidly in interviews about his faith, agenda, and what he sought to accomplish through his music. On the rare occasions that he did speak, it was usually to Doug Van Pelt, an editor of a rock journal called *HM (Hard Music)*. Van Pelt, in addition to covering the burgeoning religious rock scene, also featured a fascinating monthly column he called "So and So Sez," which contained often hilarious interviews with non-Christian rock stars.

Van Pelt would begin interviews with the likes of Rob Halford of King Diamond by asking innocent enough questions about their music before invariably tossing hand grenades at his guests like, "Who is Jesus Christ to you?" Some tried to beg off politely, but Van Pelt was relentless in getting an answer to that central question and others.

But on occasion Van Pelt would find a kindred soul, drawing out a confession of faith from a fellow traveler on the road of serious Christian faith. Such was the case with Cherone.

Later, when a TV reporter interviewed Cherone about the deeper spiritual meanings of "Hole Hearted" and "More Than Words," Cherone stonewalled, saying that the meanings of each song were up to the individual listener and that he was unwilling to go into his personal thoughts behind the songs. Later, away from publicists and band members, when the reporter told Cherone that he had read Van Pelt's interview, Cherone's cryptic response was "Are you a . . . ?" the clear inference being "did the reporter share Cherone's faith?"

Assured that the reporter wasn't out to attack Cherone's faith, the singer relaxed and told of how difficult it had been to deal with rock reporters who often seemed inhospitable to Cherone's mixing of rock and religion in Extreme's music.

Cherone was no ordinary Christian, the kind found in thousands of churches in strip malls across the country that could sing praise songs with gusto but seemed to have little grasp of theology. A student of philosophers like Francis Beckwith and preachers like Swindoll, Cherone's background in philosophy would be put to the test when, as lead singer of Van Halen, he debated the abortion issue heatedly and publicly.

"He's just amazing," said Cherone of Swindoll. "You can just understand it when he's talking or when you're reading him. He's not like some other writers. I try to read C. S. Lewis and I have to read a page, like, five times and have a dictionary and a thesaurus. Chuck's the man."[2]

From Swindoll, Cherone had apparently learned the importance of a personal and vibrant relationship with Jesus.

"My relationship with Christ . . . is the only thing that keeps me afloat," he said. "I had some problems . . . with depression—the ups and downs of whatever, the business or the highs and lows of your life—and I've come to the conclusion, I don't think it's a great big revelation, but it's not necessary that I'm supposed to be happy all the time. There are these ups and downs. I, for no reason think I'm Job, but he never lost his faith. I think that's the rock—the only thing that can't crumble in your life. It's grown. The more I learn, the more I realize that I don't know. It keeps you humble. I love gaining more knowledge about Him. I'm as strong as I am at this point."[3]

But much like Creed frontman Scott Stapp, who seemed unwilling to reveal the true nature of his faith to rock journalists, Cherone too was hesitant about outing himself too strongly in such interviews, believing that it was essentially an act of, in biblical parlance, casting pearls before swine:

"I think in the past I might've ducked and skirted and avoided the subject," he said in reference to being asked in interviews about the beliefs behind his music. "I used to go home at night and say, 'why should I deny my Savior?' So, I feel a little bit stronger now. The thing that bothers me when you profess your faith is that they put you in a little box and they don't want to hear you. They have their stereotype."[4]

Like Stapp, Cherone was even wary of being identified by the term "Christian" because of what it had come to mean in the post–Jim Bakker/Jimmy Swaggart culture:

I've been asked, "Are you a Christian?" I don't like answering that question, because "Christian" is such a general term. Someone in an interview just the other day said, "Do you believe in God?" I said, "What is that question?" His interpretation of God could be a four-footed monkey man—the same thing with "Christian." You have Jehovah Witnesses and different sects and different factions that proclaim they're Christians, and they're not. Talking in a secular world, how would a sound byte explain your faith? It's a frustrating thing . . . but there are too many things going on in my head when these questions are asked. From a secular standpoint, I just want to shut up, because anything I say they're going to twist and turn or paint me in a little corner and no one's going to want to hear our music.[5]

On rare occasions, however, Cherone was able to get his message out through the media, but it proved to be an exception to the general rule of rock reporters being less than friendly to a man of rock and faith like Cherone:

There was one article that I still have, and it encourages me. It was written by Ann Powers from *The New York Times* who talked about "heavy metal aligning itself up with the devil . . . and these characters from Extreme seemed to be aligning itself up with the other Deity." If you consider the devil a deity, I don't, but . . . that's something I keep to encourage me. When things get down, I read it and I go, "Okay, well someone gets it out there." I don't know if it got the attention I thought it would.[6]

It wasn't just Powers who was being influenced by Cherone's powerful songwriting. While many Extreme and later Van Halen fans simply enjoyed Cherone's music, others like Chris Sernel were actually being influenced by Cherone to make life-changing decisions. Sernel, today the lead singer of the nu-metal band Escape From Earth, traced his conversion to Cherone's songs:

I first got into Gary Cherone and Extreme back in the late '80s and immediately fell in love with the band. I had always believed in God but never really understood who Christ was and in fact thought Born Again Christians were wackos. Then I found out that a friend of mine was a Christian. He engaged me in dialogue about Christianity and I was somewhat open to the concept. I put on the Extreme CD for my friend and placed the lyrics in front of him. He proceeded to go through the lyrics to "Watching, Waiting," "Hole Hearted," "Politicalamity", "Who Cares," "Am I Ever Gonna Change," and "Rise 'N' Shine" and began to cite the Biblical references that Gary was quoting in each song. When my friend left, I yanked out an old Bible I had and began to check all of these references that my friend had made from Extreme songs to the Bible. At first it was merely to see what made Gary tick . . . but as I got into the biblical stories, I started to understand that there were things to be learned in the Bible, things that interested me. After that point, I started reading my Bible every single day. Gary is definitely partially responsible for my becoming a Christian. God knew that it wouldn't be easy to get through to me . . . so He utilized one of my "secular" interests (music) to open my eyes to Christianity.[7]

Like his hero, Sernel and his band sought to bring their faith to those who loved rock music and charted a course similar to Cherone's:

I am a Christian, but I don't write "Christian songs" *per se*. Gary was much the same. I write songs about life and certainly there will be subtle Christian messages in those. I learned from Gary that beating non-believers over the head with Bible verses is not the way to do it . . . but rather to first and foremost, write great songs with great hooks. Put on great live shows and treat everyone with love and respect on and off the stage. Fans will be able to see that as something different from everyone else in music and ultimately God can use that to reach people. Escape from Earth has tried to mirror Gary in how we live as Christians in the rock 'n roll world."[8]

Extreme's third record *III Sides to Every Story* had delved with reckless abandon into issues of faith and had sold moderately well, though not reaching the heights of the second record that had boasted of the twin hits "Hole Hearted" and "More Than Words." But on Extreme's final record, *Waiting for the Punchline*, Cherone had come out again with guns blazing, taking on numerous sacred cows of secularism with gusto.

First, Cherone took aim at secularism with the ironically titled "There Is No God."

I tried to pick apart the lyrics and . . . pitted religion versus science and the parallels that they have and the leap of faith that you have to take with both. I'm glad I have to take this leap of faith of believing in God. I don't think God would have it any other way. You know, you hear that argument, "Well, if there is a God, why doesn't He come on television and show us?" Coincidentally, I just read something in Romans . . . about how men profess to be wise, but are foolish and that God makes Himself known. The creation of God is the evidence of God. If you can't see that, then you're blind and you're letting your intellect be your God—and that's pretty vain—you have to have a pretty big ego. That's "There Is No God." That title . . . I don't know where that came from. Obviously, it probably came from the paraphrase from *Time* magazine's headline—"God Is Dead." In "There Is No God" there's, [the line] "You gather information as much as you can and, if you're humble enough to realize that you don't have all the answers you take the leap of faith," whether it's in God or in science or whatever.[9]

Next, Cherone had the theory of evolution in his crosshairs. "That's one of my pet peeves," he said. "The amount of faith that it takes—the leap of faith you have to take—to believe in an ameba coincidentally evolving into a human being. This Carl Sagan quote: 'billions and billions of years . . .' Does he realize what a billion is?"[10]

Cherone was an aggressive expositor of the Christian faith, but unlike most television evangelists who seemed cocksure of their faith, Cherone believed that in order to win converts to his faith, he must take on the role of the honest seeker who had not yet found the truth:

I'm trying to be honest with myself and my faith and put it up for grabs. I know where I'm coming from with these songs. Throw it out and some people are gonna dive into it; to some people it's just going to be meaningless jargon . . . I could easily say it's devil's advocate [and] I'm playing the role. I don't think it's so much a devil's advocate. It ends up being a question.[11]

People of faith in Cherone's position in the culture were often thrown on the defensive, but Cherone would have none of it, believing that it was up to secularists to defend their lack of belief and not to the man of faith to defend the existence of God:

> "Without being arrogant, I like to turn the question around," he said. "Why should they paint me in a corner? Let me question your faith. Where do you come from?"[12]

Cherone would have plenty of opportunity to preach from an even larger pulpit, when shortly after Extreme disbanded in the mid '90s, Eddie Van Halen asked Cherone to take over most of the lyric-writing chores for Van Halen's first and only record with Cherone. Once again the singer came out swinging.

On the song "Once," Cherone articulated the biblical doctrine of eternal security, a central tenet held by many Christians that faith in God could not be lost, that a soul once in God's hands was eternally secure. On "Fire in the Hole," Cherone again lifted lyrics from Scripture, this time from the Book of James, a passage that described the tongue as a fire, impossible to tame and always ready to spew out poison.

Shortly after the release of *III*, Cherone used his platform as lead singer of Van Halen to bring attention to his other pet peeve: abortion. Penning an open letter to Pearl Jam's lead singer Eddie Vedder, an active and vocal supporter of legalized abortion, Cherone challenged Vedder to define when life began if not at conception. When Vedder failed to respond, Cherone took his challenge to Fox TV's *The O'Reilly Factor* program. Within weeks, Cherone was out of Van Halen, although the exact reason for his dismissal wasn't clear.

It was probably a safe bet to assume that Cherone's pro-life activism had been premature at best, considering the fact that Van Halen's *III* had not sold well and many fans of the band were less than thrilled at the new direction.

Nevertheless, Cherone had proved himself to be a man of courage who cared little, perhaps too little, about public opinion, and used his own bully pulpit to advance his beliefs.

Before long, however, Cherone had reorganized musically and taken the songs he had intended for his second outing with Van Halen and plugged some of them into his next band, Tribe of Judah.

Would Tribe of Judah have the kind of impact on the popular music culture that Cherone had had with Extreme and Van Halen? Would he again find a way to bring his agenda to the fore? Or would he simply be the elder statesman of the faith-rock movement, looking on with satisfaction at Lifehouse, Creed, P.O.D., and Escape from Earth—bands that had picked up his way of articulating faith in pop culture?

Tribe of Judah's debut record, *Exit Elvis,* was released in late 2002 on the independent Spitfire record label, but whatever the ultimate answer to that question, what was clear was that Cherone's faith was strong and would carry on, whatever direction his music took him. Navigating the difficult waters of the mainstream rock culture, a world that had been largely abandoned by devout Christians, was no easy task, with compromise a daily challenge. But for many young people of faith, Cherone was proof positive that standing tall for one's faith in the center of that lion's den must be tried and could, with help from above, be survived:

> There's not a day in my life—whether it's music or walking through the street with a bunch of buddies—that [I'm not] aware of compromise. You don't have to be playing music or singing about Jesus to compromise. You could be hanging out at a cafe with four or five people and things get said and silence is also a compromise. Every day . . . I question if I'm compromising. At the end of the day . . . at the beginning of the day, too, I get on my knees and say, "Do not let me deny my faith." Sometimes I have better days than others. This is the stuff that makes you tick—makes me tick.[13]

12
After the Flood

From the beginning of his career in music, Jars of Clay's lead singer Dan Haseltine seemed to have been on a crusade to have his music heard by the mainstream music culture. Unfortunately, having signed to a Christian-owned, Nashville-based label when he and his bandmates Matt Odmark, Charlie Lowell, and Stephen Mason were just college students often made that a difficult task.

Haseltine and Jars' difficult and sometimes painful journey toward gaining, keeping, and trying to reclaim an audience began when their demo tape was passed around to every Christian-owned label in Nashville in the mid 1990s. The tiny indie label Essential won the bidding war to release the band's self-titled debut, but what happened next was a complete anomaly and largely a result of the work of one obscure radio promotions man named John Butler, who refused to buy into the notion that Christians should make music for Christians and secularists for everybody else.

Butler, an employee of the music giant Zomba that had recently acquired Essential, pitched Jars of Clay to rock radio without mentioning the label they were signed to, the beliefs of its members, or indeed the moniker "Christian rock." The results were astounding: Jars of Clay scored an enormous hit with the song "Flood," crossing over several formats and jetting straight to the top of various charts. Butler's strategy of simply pitching the song to pop and rock radio sans the "Christian rock" moniker had sidestepped the prejudices of radio program directors like Mike Morrison of L.A. radio station KSCA, who candidly admitted why he added the track to his station's playlist:

> "Had I known it was a Christian record when I started hearing about it, I hate to admit it, but I probably wouldn't have been as amenable to the idea," admitted Morrison. "But I started liking it before I realized it had those roots."[1]
>
> "We were dropped from playlists at radio stations when they figured out that we were Christians," recalled guitarist Steve Mason. "There was a perception change, and there still is."[2]

Mason's observation was likely half true, for mainstream radio stations have often played songs by artists who were Christians (Creed, Lifehouse, U2, etc.). What was fully true, however, was that mainstream radio stations did shy away from playing artists who were signed to Christian labels and marketed as "Christian rock bands." Such thinking was at least a defensible position, since the radio stations might correctly argue that as Christian bands had their own radio stations, they should be approaching the stations that already fit their format of music. In addition, the attempts to reach out to mainstream radio, video, and press outlets by Christian-owned labels like the one Jars was on were too often an afterthought, with most of the focus of efforts targeted instead at the Christian music subculture.

Nevertheless, for bands like Jars of Clay, which sought mainstream exposure, the stigma associated with the brand "Christian rock" was an unwelcome one:

> "We carry with us the perception that we are a Christian band," said Haseltine. "On one level, that's a great thing, and, obviously, it holds very true to what we believe. On the other, it has a lot of negative stereotypes attached to it when it comes to people who aren't familiar with what being a Christian is. We've seen the perception of Jars of Clay as a freakish, Bible-throwing, rightwing, overly pious, religious band grow outside of what the reality of the band has been. It's important to us that people know that we are not, necessarily, what the media has created us to be."[3]

Over time many major media outlets came to agree with Haseltine's assessment of his own band. The *New York Post* observed:

> Most Christian rock ranks right up there with the great plagues of the Bible, including rivers turning into blood, frogs raining from the sky, and those nasty angels of death. Jars of Clay are not to be crucified.[4]

Mainstream rock critics have long been critical of the Christian rock movement for several reasons, some of them legitimate, some not. The illegitimate ones centered around the very notion, deeply offensive to militant secularists, that people of faith would have the audacity to show up in the second-to-last bastion of hedonism (the last being porn flicks) and ask for a place at the table.

The more legitimate criticism had to do with the near total lack of context and historical understanding that many in the Christian music world had when it came to the larger rock music world from whence it came. This exhibited itself in an unwillingness to acknowledge, study, and understand rock's past before they invaded it. Just as one wouldn't attempt to run for president and influence the direction of U.S. domestic policies without studying Roosevelt's New Deal, Truman's Fair Deal, or Reagan's New Federalism, so one couldn't be expected to understand popular music without having in some way studied The Beatles, Elvis, Sam Cooke, and The Rolling Stones. And yet that is precisely what Christian rock music had attempted to do. Forbidden from listening to the devil's music, even for purposes of understanding their craft, musicians who were Christians too often appeared to create art in a cultural vacuum. But Jars of Clay had no such inhibitions. On a 2002 swing through Los Angeles, Haseltine and crew packed out the legendary Greek Theater, with a show that *The Hollywood Reporter* likened to a performance by The Beatles.

It was an unusual and remarkable display of religious devotion, rock & roll mastery, and quiet introspection. Jars of Clay was obviously influenced by bands like Toad the Wet Sprocket (two of the members met because of mutual affection for the band), but the Greek show indicated that they were also students of rock history as well and understood keenly that the roots of their music went back at least to Liverpool.

The show opened with the George Harrison tune "Here Comes the Sun" (or was it Son?), which may have gone right over the heads of its audience but showed the band was in touch with that legacy, and they later referenced it again when, in the middle of their latest hit song, the pounding "Revolution," Haseltine briefly sang a few lines from another song of the same title that had the world rocking three decades ago.

Haseltine was an unlikely rock star. Quiet and introspective, seeming to be more at home with a good book than in front of thousands of fans, he nonetheless lived out the role he'd been given in life as the band's frontman.

Jars of Clay had always been known for its activism, and this night was no exception as Haseltine lectured his charges on why HIV in Africa could not be ignored, asking that everybody sign up to sponsor a child in the region.

Haseltine may have lacked Bono's showmanship and Scott Stapp's drama, but he did have the humility and courage to embrace causes that were not establishment approved. Stapp's Arms Wide Open Foundation did good work with children, and Bono jetted around the world for AIDS and debt relief, but Haseltine's most unlikely crusade, in addition to his work on behalf of AIDS babies in Africa, was bringing the plight of persecuted Christian pastors in China to the attention of unlikely allies like Amnesty International.

Conservative Christian types had long railed against groups like Amnesty, but Haseltine had a different idea: co-opt them. Enlisting the group's help in his cause, Haseltine agreed to have his band play an Amnesty benefit show in their adopted hometown of Nashville under one condition: that Amnesty bring public pressure to bear on behalf of the suffering pastors in China. The liberal political action group, which had for years ignored such causes, readily agreed, and an unlikely alliance was formed.

"We really do look at fulfilling tangible needs as a responsibility of humanity in general," said Haseltine. "Given that, we do it without an agenda. Our agenda's not to help humanity so that people will come to know Jesus. We hope that that would happen, but I think we're simply called to love people and to serve people without an end. Maybe that's what separates it from some of the other types of core Christian humanitarian work."[5]

What Haseltine and Jars of Clay still lacked, however, was a solid place in pop culture, earned by strong record sales. While bands like Creed or U2 breezed past the two million mark in records sold in the first few months, after six months, Jars of Clay's *The Eleventh Hour* was closing in on 500,000 units.

Some of that had to do with the fact that they were a rock band on a pop label, with music biz people in charge of their record who knew how to handle Britney Spears and *NSYNC but weren't quite sure what to do with a band like Jars of Clay. It also had to do with the cultural biases that haunted the band because of its members' faith and the fact that their music was sometimes marketed, against the band's wishes, as Christian rock.

Jars of Clay essentially had two label homes: one for the mainstream rock market, Silvertone Records, and one for the industry that was based in Christian-owned bookstores across the country, called Essential Records. Problems arose when one label got in the way of the other. In the case of Jars that meant their CDs ending up in record outlets like Target, Sam Goody, and Waldenbooks in the gospel section instead of the pop/rock section, the unfortunate result of lobbying by their Christian-owned label eager to have their own religious section and thereby make the shopping experience of people of faith easier at a retail store.

In cases like these, the band had to personally go to work, calling retail chains and asking that their music be stocked in the ordinary pop/rock section rather than the religious one.

It also meant, on more than one occasion, Haseltine himself calling rock publications and asking that the band be reviewed in the category that described the band's music, pop/rock, not the category that described their faith, Christian/gospel.

USA Today, for example, was a notorious example of how mainstream outlets, unwittingly perhaps, sentenced rockers who happened to have a deep faith to cultural obscurity by reviewing artists who emerged from the Nashville-based Christian rock industry in the gospel section of the paper instead of the pop/rock section. While any publicity was typically appreciated, such segregation communicated to the rest of the music business that such artists were not a part of the rock music world, but in a separate religious world, and tended to keep them from being taken seriously at places that mattered: MTV, VH-1, and thousands of pop and rock stations around the country.

Understanding this intuitively, Haseltine went to work, personally contacting *USA Today*'s music editor and requesting a review in the pop/rock section. The paper obliged, but the punishment was a frosty review in the pages of *USA Today* and a confrontational interview by the paper's reporter for another publication. Still, Haseltine had accomplished his goal of having his band, its music and message, taken seriously, and before long the pieces began to fall in place when Mel Gibson came calling with a request for a Jars song for his film *We Were Soldiers*. Strong reviews followed from the industry bible, *Billboard* magazine, and other outlets like *The Hollywood Reporter* and the *New York Post*.

Haseltine shrugged off criticism of his hands-on approach to publicity, from the *USA Today* reporter: "I'll send as many emails to editors as I have to," he said with a touch of defiance. "I don't mind doing it."[6]

When the reporter then went on to ask Haseltine if Jars hadn't contributed to the perception by their choice of band name, a reference that was taken from the New Testament, Haseltine offered this terse reply:

"Then there's a band called Ministry."[7]

"That's a fair point," allowed Matt Odmark. "I think what Dan's trying to say is that 'Christian' is definitely a part of our identity. It's who we are; it's what we believe; and it colors our music. Yet the way we understand 'Christian' and the way our culture characterizes 'Christian' feel like two distinctly different things. We don't want to say, 'No, we're not Christian' because we are. Like you said, our name comes from Scripture, and that is something we believe and hold true. We feel like it expresses something very true, not only about the nature of all of us as humans, but it also describes a bit of where our inspiration for music comes from. Where it gets tricky for us, we want to be good stewards of who we are by constantly asking people to define their terms. Don't just carelessly call us a 'Christian' band and allow all these untrue connotations that come along with that be lumped in with us. We do feel like we're distinct from those things."[8]

When the reporter persisted, arguing to the band that many of the group's lyrics couldn't be understood by non-Christians, Haseltine disagreed sharply:

> I would say that it's just higher literary language. It's not necessarily even biblical in that approach. At least, my intentions are not that they are metaphors and things drawn from Scripture, but from other readings. We write songs that are about love and that are about loss, that are about longing. Those are things that transcend religious language.[9]

"We believe that we have something to offer Christians as well as people that don't share that same belief," observed Stephen Mason. "We write from a place less of songs about faith, but more songs because of faith. That's kind of the window through which we see the world."[10]

In the spring of 2002 the band launched its own tour, playing sold-out venues across the country. The band's fourth record, *The Eleventh Hour*, was a strong and steady album, which grew on listeners with each play. Haseltine and Jars of Clay seemed to be in it for the long haul and appeared intent on building their audience, and in some cases rebuilding their audience, one listener at a time.

With *The Eleventh Hour*, the band returned to the roots of the success it had on the first record—sort of—by producing the record themselves—sort of—only because two of the standout tracks on the band's debut record were produced by Adrian Belew, a talented producer who once played guitar in David Bowie's band.

Some industry watchers like Chris Willman of *Entertainment Weekly* and Terry Mattingly of *Scripps Howard News Service*, who had followed the band closely since its debut, held out hope that the band would consider dancing with the one who brought them to stardom by asking Belew to at least produce a few tracks and recapture the magic of "Flood" and the other Belew-produced track, the inspiring "Liquid."

"It was his off the wall touches on the first singles that made them sound like more than just a folk rock band," said Mattingly. "He is a huge and unique talent. They should give credit where credit is due and 'dance with the one who brung 'em.'"[11]

"This is a group that does not benefit from self-production," added Willman of the band's record *The Eleventh Hour.* "It's a slick album in a time when slick music is being eschewed at least outside of teen pop. Ironically, they need to bring someone in who would force them to not be so professional and stuffy."[12]

Still, whatever the future held for Jars of Clay, its four members had conclusively proved, as if it still needed to be proven, that people of faith could indeed make great rock music that could also be enjoyed by people who didn't necessarily share that faith but were still open to hearing about their spiritual journey, especially when that journey was wrapped up in shared experiences, feelings, and appealing music

"I hope you don't hear the noisy vocabulary of religion," said Matt Odmark of his hopes for his band's music. "I hope you hear music that results from faith, not music that is about faith. I hope you hear our lives in each note, sound and lyric. I hope you hear the joy and the heartbreak of friends wrestling to sing in harmony, not perfectly, but believably. I hope the songs remind you how to believe. This is music that is born in the gut and travels through the soul and rings in the ears with echoes of eternity."[13]

So was Jars of Clay's music affecting people and was their music actually getting through to those the band intended to reach with it? While many nonbelievers simply enjoyed the music, some were affected more deeply:

"About a year ago when I was about as far away from God as you can become . . . one of my good friends gave me Jars of Clay['s CD]," said a fan named Amy Morris. "I love music, so I was thrilled. I didn't know it was Christian, all I knew was that it was a CD. I put it in my CD player and I couldn't stop crying. This music had something behind it—it meant something more. I listened to my Jars CD over and over again. With Jars' and [friend] Chris's help, I became a Christian. God showed me everything and the blindness I had felt went away. As Jars' 'Love Song for a Savior' goes, I fell in love with God."[14]

"'I feel like our voice should be heard in that culture,' said Matt Odmark, speaking for the band and a new generation of artists of faith who seek to convey that faith through rock music. 'What we have to say is no less legitimate.'"[15]

13

God's Troubadour

David Wilcox's career in music was one of the best arguments against those in the religious music subculture who fostered a persecution complex that caused them to insist that Christians simply could not survive if they refused to keep their faith out of their music. Wilcox, who reminded many fans of a young James Taylor, combined an unabashed love for his master Jesus with a distaste for many forms of organized religion and an even stronger distaste for the religious music subculture that, he believed, functionally kept music made by the faithful away from the musical mainstream.

Wilcox was reared near Cleveland, Ohio, but didn't get into music until he was in college.

"I would see my friends playing guitar and they were . . . really working hard at it," he remembered. "I heard this woman playing in the stairwell at college, and to me that really made the guitar an amazing instrument because it sounded beautiful on its own. She would show me some songs, and I think I had four lessons that I paid for from this classical player. He taught me some warm-up exercises. . . ."[1]

Wilcox would later come to be admired not only for his songwriting and singing skills, but for his guitar work, which blossomed despite his late start:

"When I first started to play I was in college, so I would comb the dorms for guitars," he remembered. "For the first year I just borrowed and that's how I developed a more refined taste for good guitars."[2]

Strongly influenced not only by artists like Taylor and Joni Mitchell, but also by Motown, Wilcox built up a local following that eventually landed him a major recording contract and his first recording, *Nightshift Watchman*.

"I was a street musician before *Nightshift Watchman* came out and I was making better money than I would have with a minimum wage burger job, and I realized that I was working at what I loved, and I would survive," recalled Wilcox. "I realized that my music would not hurt me. If I trusted my music and followed it I would not starve to death or something."[3]

Wilcox also learned important lessons about music and true wealth in those early days before his major label debut:

I was very wealthy because what wealth is can be defined as getting the time to do what you want, and I realized that with discipline I could do what I loved. The discipline came because you had to lower your spending to match your earnings, you can buy your freedom with the money you don't spend. If I wanted to live the life that felt most true to me I could do it if I would give up all the silly things, and foo foo stuff like having a car that was all one color, and an address, and more than one pair of shoes, which were all unnecessary things compared to working at what I loved.[4]

Throughout the 1990s, Wilcox continued to tour and record nonstop, in the process building a loyal following especially on college campuses. Over time he developed a reputation as an introspective singer/songwriter who managed to outlive '80s metal, '90s grunge, and turn-of-the-century hip-hop. Fads came and went but David Wilcox and his guitar remained in demand around the country.

The *New York Daily News* once said of Wilcox that he had given "sensitive singer-songwriters back their good name," and to hear the singer wax philosophical about his relationship with his guitar was to understand the meaning of that phrase.

"I have come to a kind of a peace with the fact that each guitar has a particular voice—a particular kind of inspiration," said Wilcox. "There are some riffs and some musical voicings that sound really great on one guitar, but another guitar won't bring out the magic. So I've learned to become less attached."[5]

For Wilcox the songwriter, the guitar was more than an instrument, more like an intimate cowriter, leading Wilcox on, developing ideas for songs in a magical quest:

> Mostly songwriting for me is based upon my belief that the guitar knows the song. If I listen to the guitar, put it into some weird tuning and begin to experiment, it will play me some melody. I will say to the guitar "Wow, that's beautiful what's it about?" and the guitar will reply, "How does it make you feel?" and I might say that it makes me think about this or that and the guitar says, "Well that's probably what it's about then." At that point I ask what's next and the guitar will usually respond by saying, "It depends on what the lyrics are about. Why don't you start writing and I'll tell you the rest." So I start writing ideas and the guitar says, "Stop right there, this is the part, you gotta put these words with this phrase," and I say, "Oh guitar, you're killin' me!" So I'm just listening to the guitar.[6]

When asked about his own songwriting skills, Wilcox was characteristically modest:

> If you're writing songs you can have a lot of talent or a lot of time and I choose the time method. If you know what you like and have a way of creating interesting mistakes that will give you new variations . . . then the laws of probability are in your favor. You will have an endless supply of new ideas that if you continue to sort through and store on a tape recorder, you can gather these great musical ideas, as if you had the talent to make them up, when it was really the guitar of course that writes all the songs.[7]

In stark contrast to the guitar heroes of the '80s who gloried in long guitar solos in which the instrument seemed to be obeying the commands of its player, and the grunge rockers of the '90s who relished destroying their instrument onstage, Wilcox's love for his own instrument led him to believe that it was the guitar that played the player and not the other way around:

If I could contribute anything to guitar playing it would be this notion that it's not something you do to the guitar, it's something it does to you. You need to listen to it and give it some leeway and let it play what it wants to play. Get your fingers off those strings and let them ring, don't always be trying to wrestle it to the ground. I love the attitude of "let's hear what the guitar wants to play" and getting into that beginner's mindset again and really enjoy the sound of it. I am so grateful for the enjoyment I've gotten out of the sound of the guitar. It really saved my life.[8]

At first glance, Wilcox's faith seemed to be a curious mix-ture of Christianity and New Age sensibilities, but upon closer inspection it appeared instead to be a traditionalist Christian faith rooted in an understanding of a living Christ that was minimally influenced by the organized religion of his time. It was a faith likely influenced by Wilcox's own lack of religious upbringing:

I grew up with absolutely no tradition whatsoever. Yet I felt a strong presence of guidance that showed up in timing and co-incidence. I've come to understand that I can also describe that with other language. Like, prayers are answered, as in, if you pray for something, you better duck, because it is coming in low and fast behind you. The amazing thing for me was that I was very aware—as hard as I was searching, I was searched for. I was very aware that whatever sort of language I wanted to give it, I could feel the presence of a power that was bigger than just that language, than just those ideas. My path has been proved to me—if all tradition was lost we would have no problem connect-ing with God. If all language was lost about the way people have spoken in the past, we would invent new words. The experience is real. The experience is tangible. The spirit of Jesus is something that can come into your heart and just absolutely prove to you that it is real. Even if you have completely different language, the experience is tangible truth.[9]

Highly skeptical of organized religion, Wilcox's brand of faith had much in common with the historical Quaker and Brethren traditions that strongly deemphasized authoritarian church leadership and urged individual members to assume greater leadership in churches.

The traditions that I have felt most comfortable with are the radical—meaning from the root traditions. Like the Quakers who have the nerve to say that God is willing to speak through you if someone needs the words of God, and you are the only voice around. God will speak through you. There are church elders who are threatened by this, because it is the decentralization of religion. It is the very thing that Jesus was talking about. It's not just following the rules and being a part of the organization. It is a one on one thing, and it has much more to do with where your heart is, not just how people see you.

. . . One of the advantages of moving past the old governmental model of the church is that it is less important for the pastor to have the authority—that powerful words of wisdom from a direct line from God sort of thing. . . . In the Middle Ages, when the Roman Empire crumbled, you had to have somebody step in and say "here is how we are going to run things." It was the church. They fulfilled a great role; they were the governing body. They needed to look like they had the authority. You don't do that by waiting for the Spirit to move. You did that by saying, "I am infallible. I am the Pope."[10]

Wilcox was specifically critical of many modern movements within the church because of the tendency they had to drive away outsiders who were afraid:

It's not natural for the church to try to force people with that governmental model of spiritual leadership. The people who are really wanting spiritual connection are trying their best to find a way to reconcile heart and mind. Because they are so careful about what they believe, which is a spiritual quality, they are very cautious that humans can be duped into belonging to some group. They see these various cults that make people feel welcome. Their sense of truth is more important than their own pleasure. That is a sacred thing. Their doubt is a sacred thing.[11]

For such seekers, many of whom Wilcox regularly played for, his message was to not give up on the quest for God:

The truth will shine clear in their own hearts. It will be obvious to them out of their own empirical experimentation. Just play-fully, try believing this for awhile. See how you feel. See what happens. Even if you can't use the word "believe," you can say, "Imagine, imagine that there is guidance. What would happen, no

115

harm done, act as if there is guidance in a simple thing?" That is a prayer. That is saying, "God, will you meet me here?" And God will say, "Watch out, here I come!"[12]

For American churches, steeped in traditions, some of their own making and some inherited from centuries past, Wilcox offered this challenge:

> How much more powerful would it be for a pastor to have a tear in his eye and say, "I feel a trembling in my heart as I admit to you that I am not moved by the Spirit. I am not confident that my words will serve you. So, I will shut up right now and the Spirit will move."
>
> It's kind of like the Wizard of Oz idea—a mask. Toto pulls back the curtain and finds an old man instead of the Wizard. That could be some of us behind the curtain hiding behind a mask of spirituality. When you are placed into that position, stage or pulpit, there is sort of a hiding.[13]

It wasn't just religious expression as it was organized that Wilcox, though mild in demeanor, had harsh words for. He also seemed keenly disgusted with the whole notion of a Christian rock industry, which he saw as actually getting in the way of music by Christians reaching out to those in the audiences who didn't share that faith. It was a subject that he had thought long and hard about and had much to say about:

> The reason I don't market my music as contemporary Christian music is because I really want people to get the message of Christ. I love that irony. . . . Music can transmit a spiritual message. People can feel something very true in their heart that they don't even understand yet. By following the hole in their heart they can come to their understanding of this faith that their heart has jumped into. Although it is true that music can communicate the Spirit of Christ, . . . when you market something as Christian music, you use the techniques of marketing. The techniques of marketing are to divide each other against each other. That is how you sell Pepsi instead of Coke. You tell people that you'll be part of something. Or, you'll feel different from those people. You'll feel included in these people. You sell a sense of belonging. You especially need to do that when you are selling Pepsi—something that has no intrinsic value compared to Coke. You need to create a sense of belonging. People have learned to market things in that way.[14]

For Wilcox, the tendency to market music made by devout believers as "Christian music" was just another Madison Avenue marketing technique whose greatest sin was excluding people that he believed would otherwise be thirsty for truth:

> The sad truth is that when you market truth that way it loses the message which is inclusiveness. The sad part about that is that what you are marketing to Christian radio, you market the same way you market to country radio. You say to them, "You people are country people. You're not rock and rollers. You are different than that urban stuff. You are different from those black people. You are white people. You drive pick up trucks. You listen to this. You do that. You wear hats. You wear boots. You do line dances. Don't you feel like you belong?" What you are building for them is a fence. What you are building for them is a safe place for them to belong inside a world that confuses them inside a world that they feel scared in.
>
> You say, "We are safe within these walls. This is our kind of music." If you market Christian music, you are marketing safety. That is not the main point of Christianity. Safety is walking by the guy who got beat up, not helping him. Safety is feeling like you belong in this little group of Pharisees or whatever because you follow the rules. You know what your group believes in. The whole message of Jesus is, "Okay, you can have all the groups you want, but you don't get in on somebody's guestpass to heaven. The Kingdom of Heaven has to do with being someone's neighbor. Who is your neighbor?" It's not just someone within your same fence.
>
> The sad thing to me is when Christian music is marketed as safe music and non-threatening music. . . . Yes, we are supposed to comfort the afflicted. Yes, we are supposed to afflict the comfortable. We are supposed to stretch people into daring to believe, not hiding in a belief, daring to believe. Shaking the safe foundations and finding that you have no protection. What you have is a challenge to make yourself vulnerable. What you have is a chance to make yourself of service—not just to protect it.[15]

Wilcox believed that rather than huddling in an artificial genre called "Contemporary Christian Music," artists with a deep Christian faith should consider each musical genre a mission field and, just as missionaries were sent out to foreign countries, take the message of faith in God into each genre:

The beauty and the power of the message is not just to speak it within these safe walls. Go out and trust that if you speak this in the language of whatever country you go into—whether it is the country of urban music or rock and roll music—and you speak the language and you speak the truth, the message will get across."[16]

For years, devout artists were presented by leaders of the Christian subculture with what many considered to be a false alternative—that music must be an evangelistic tool or a matter of expression with no thought of how the art would affect others. As a tool, it lacked artistic expression, since it was designed to accomplish a specific purpose—the conversion of lost souls. As mere expression, there seemed to be no thought to communicating eternal truth—a command that was given to all believers in Christ's Great Commission. But Wilcox seemed to accept neither alternative, believing that art could be both redemptive and artistic, that it might, guided by the mysterious Agent who created the wind and the seas, achieve a tangible and redemptive end, though it was created for the purpose of artistic expression:

I know from my experience that music can change lives. I believe in the power of the humble song to give somebody a vision of what's possible for their life. I know that music is a way to get a feeling really quickly that would ordinarily take years of experience. As an audience member, what I go for is nothing less than healing and salvation, not entertainment at all. It's much bigger than that. It's medicinal music. That's what I aspire to.[17]

David Wilcox was a man with whom the times had finally caught up. For years he had shown that a man of faith and deep convictions could survive in the mainstream music world, but it had taken years for the culture to realize that it wanted more from entertainment than simply being entertained. He was a living example that pop culture wanted, and indeed needed, artists to help lost souls find the way:

What I want people to get from my music is to wake up that place in their heart that's been sleeping, to give them power to change what needs to change in their life, and to help them believe that there is hope.[18]

14

A Creek Runs through It

For most mainstream music fans the name Nickel Creek would have meant little before the 2001 Grammy Awards. Seemingly out of nowhere, the San Diego–based threesome earned two Grammy nominations for their self-titled debut album—Best Country Instrumental Performance and Best Bluegrass Album.

The Nickel Creek story was unusual for a number of reasons. First, although they incorporated strong bluegrass influences into their music, they defied neat categorization in that genre. Second, the group hailed not from the South, but from California. Third, all three members were in their late teens, not a demographic typically thought of as a strong presence in country/bluegrass music. Finally, Nickel Creek's members were all devout Christians who had decided that the mainstream music industry was where they belonged.

The band was formed when guitarist Sean Watkins and his sister, fiddler Sara Watkins, met mandolinist Chris Thile at a local pizza joint in their hometown. Before long, Nickel Creek, with its oldest member being all of ten years old, was formed.

"I was six when we met," recalled Thile. "Sean was ten and Sara was six."[1]

"Chris and I had the same mandolin teacher growing up who was the leader of a band that played at a pizza place that had bluegrass music every Saturday night," remembered Sean Watkins about their unusual meeting place. "We met that way. We started playing backstage, and there was this hallway that went to the bathroom where Chris and I would play. Eventually, Sara started playing violin."[2]

Music had a prominent place in both the Watkins and Thile households, a fact that contributed to the young artists' burgeoning love for music:

"My earliest memory is music actually," remembered Thile. "I can remember, before I was born, it's the only memory I have of that time, hearing Stan Getz and Joao Gilberto, the record that has 'The Girl from Ipanema' on it. It was great to have so many different types of music in the house."[3]

"We grew up listening to the generation of musicians that had learned from some of the old guys—Bill Monroe and Earl Scruggs," added Sara Watkins. "Musically they were not as set by these rules about bluegrass playing. We grew up incorporating a ton of different styles—not consciously, but just because we listened to everything."[4]

"My earliest memories, musically, are of my parents listening to a lot of folk and Celtic music when I was real young,"[5] added Sean Watkins.

"I started singing before I started playing," remembered Sara. "When I was four I made a request and the band asked me to come up and sing the request. I sang the chorus of 'Long Black Veil.' That was my first time on stage, and then I finally got to play when I was six."[6]

That strong love of music at such a precocious age strongly affected the young trio's career plans:

"I wanted to be a musician since I was two," remembered Thile. "Every now and then I've wanted to do something else. I went through a little phase where I thought maybe I could be a musician and a baseball player, just like every little kid wants to be a baseball player at one point. I love the idea of being an author.

I love to write, I love to read. Really, I think this is what I want to do."[7]

"I always tried to think of something else I would want to do, like a backup plan or something when I was in junior high, but there was really nothing else,"[8] added Sarah.

A year into its experience as a "band," the group decided it was time for a name and quickly settled on Nickel Creek:

> "Basically, it's the name of a song that a friend of ours, Byron Berline wrote," remembered Sean. "When we were trying to be more of a bluegrass band, we thought that would be an appropriate name for us."[9]
>
> "We were ready for a grown-up name," recalled Chris. "The names, up until then, had been all these cute, kiddies' band names. Nickel Creek sounded very old."[10]

Although chosen for rather simple reasons, the band's name would take on greater significance years later:

> "We were at the Smithsonian and Sara found out that nickel is the most commonly alloyed of all metals," remembered Chris. "That makes sense when you think about what we do in the band. We're so into all kinds of music that it's just kind of like Nickel Creek is sort of alloying ourselves to other music and hopefully something new comes out of it."[11]

Before long, the burgeoning group was getting noticed on the music festival circuit, making a name for itself as a group of teenage prodigies who were still having fun doing what they enjoyed doing:

> "When we started, really young, there was really not that much to take seriously," remembered Sara. "Somebody asked us to get together for the sake of being a cute kids' band opening a festival. Sean and I knew Chris, so we called Chris. We just started singing together. We never really wanted to be considered a kids' novelty band, but of course we were."[12]

Although they primarily played the bluegrass music circuit, their musical influences and sound was always broader than bluegrass:

"One nice thing about the image of the band is as we got older and were subjected to actual culture, it was kind of fun, because we would go to these bluegrass festivals and right away people were tipped off that it was going to be a little bit weird," recalled Chris. "People were ready for something different [when they saw us]. A lot of people that go to bluegrass festivals, if [the acts are not] bluegrass, they're gonna get slammed. With us, they just realized it was going to be different right away."[13]

Different indeed, for Nickel Creek had been influenced minimally by traditional bluegrass giants and owed more to those who were themselves pushing the boundaries of what had been traditionally labeled "bluegrass."

"We haven't really studied the traditional stuff that much at all," said Thile. "Growing up at the time we did, what was traditional to us is completely progressive to most bluegrass fans. It's mainly that. From there, our influences are all over the deck. Certainly we come from that progressive bluegrass background, but that's only where we start from. Everything spawns from that."[14]

Much like the members of U2, for whom the band had over the course of twenty-five years become a second family, Nickel Creek's members found their lives similarly intertwined:

"Since we've grown up together, it's always been like this," said Chris. "It's like you hardly know any different. It's like being in a family. You might stress each other out sometimes, but you know that the relationship is way more important than any little thing ever is, and that making music together and just being friends is so much more important than anything."[15]

Yet, just as all families eventually see members go different ways, so Nickel Creek's members hope the group continues forever but are prepared for other directions as well:

"I'm ready for it to last forever if it needs to," said Chris. "Nickel Creek is like college. It's not the kind of band where we've found what we want to do and we're just going to do it until nobody wants to listen anymore. Nickel Creek is an adventure. We're all growing and we all want the music to grow with us. It's not like a project that's just getting done on the side and isn't going anywhere. It's just like a course. You're learning all the way through. But when it is done, I would love to go back to school and study composition or musicology."[16]

"Me, too," added Sara. "I'd really love to go back sometime and take all the music classes and learn all the theory that I can. But also, I'd like to take different classes that I would never take the time to read about, like I'd love to take a photography class and auto mechanics and that kind of stuff."[17]

After years of touring music festivals, Nickel Creek was discovered by singer/producer Alison Krauss who quickly signed the threesome to her label, Sugar Hill Records. Krauss also signed on to produce the band's debut record and the band, which had long admired the singer, was thrilled. Krauss had a keen understanding of the sound the band was seeking to achieve and guided them through the process:

"She is amazing, so creative," said Sara. "She's got an incredible ear and she's a perfectionist. It was really great to work with her. We're pretty picky ourselves. She understands that. Vocals were never our strong point, so she really helped us with that, especially our performance in the studio, keeping everything fresh and not drilling it to make sure it was technical and fast and everything. She helped us get things down that would last longer on CD, and not necessarily the way we would play them live, so that they would be easier listening to for a longer time."[18]

"The main thing she really left with us was the difference between a live performance and making a CD," added Sean. "There's a huge difference. Live performance is all about the memory, how you feel as it's going by and how you feel when you leave. A CD is a completely different thing. It's about getting the same emotion every time you listen to that song. That was one of the things that we didn't have when we went into this and that we came away with as a result of getting to work with her."[19]

In addition to the obvious country and bluegrass influences, Nickel Creek's music was strongly influenced, incredibly enough, by Celtic music, something the band readily acknowledged:

"We love Irish music. We love every kind of music. But Irish is probably the most recognizable, aside from bluegrass of course," said Sara. "We got into Irish music about four or five years ago.

For a couple years it was most of what we listened to . . . it's so deep, and all the songs have stories behind them."[20]

"There are tons of fiddle tunes that started out Irish tunes but evolved over the years in the Appalachian Mountains . . . it's really nice to explore those roots—instead of just going back to bluegrass roots, go back to where everything started."[21]

If there was one term to describe Nickel Creek in its totality it would be genre-busting, for the band seemed intent on refusing to have its music or lyrics cause them to be categorized in any way that would keep them from having an impact on the larger pop culture. Understanding intuitively that most Americans weren't naturally attracted to a genre of music called bluegrass, Nickel Creek's members worked hard to keep from being branded:

"We hate genres, really," said Chris. "Not that we don't love music that can be categorized in a genre—and if we're categorized in a genre, that's fine. But as far as our goals and our directions, we don't really sit down and go, 'OK, here's where we're going and here's how we're going to get there.' We just want to grow. Whatever that feels like is what we want to be working on. If that's in a certain area, then so be it, but we really don't like to label that kind of thing."[22]

"It seems hard to plan where you're going to be going as far as your creative outlet," added Sara. "Five years ago we weren't planning on writing these kinds of songs, playing these kinds of songs and arranging them. It's hard to project what we want to be doing and limit it to something."[23]

Nickel Creek's "hatred" of genres extended to the "Christian music" genre and, like many of their contemporaries, the band refused attempts to brand their work in that way, despite the clear spiritual messages that some of their songs contained:

"We're all Christians, although we're not a Christian band, *per se,*" said Chris. "The most important thing to us is that we feel that we've been given a gift from God of being able to perform and to record for people. We basically just want to use that gift as we feel God would have us use it."[24]

124

Disagreeing with secularists who couldn't fathom why young artists would want to write songs about their faith in God, Nickel Creek believed firmly that such songs were a natural outgrowth of an ordinary life of faith, and that writing about one's passions was what music was all about. They also refused to make a distinction between hymns, which were obviously about God and faith, and other songs, which though not explicit, carried a subtle gospel message nonetheless: .

> "Even if a song isn't blatantly Christian or isn't a hymn, it doesn't mean it doesn't have that feeling in it," said Chris. "Some people pick up on that. The people that want to, hopefully, do. The people that don't, maybe they'll get something from it anyway."[25]

Nickel Creek's "blatantly Christian" expressions were most pronounced in a stunner called "The Hand Song," a pop/country ballad that pointed listeners toward salvation.

"'The Hand Song' is such a sweet one," observed critic Shelly Fabian. "It is about a little boy that wanted to give his mom something special so he went out to her garden to pick out some roses. When the boy ran back inside, he had thorns buried deep within the skin of his hands. The mom was not mad at him because she knew he picked the roses out of love; she took the thorns out as the boy cried and afterwards they read from the Bible. Then seeing a picture of Jesus he cried out 'Momma, he's got some scars just like me!'"[26]

Nickel Creek was another band in a long line of artists who had decided to make their music and their stand of faith in the center of the public square for all to hear, refusing to retreat to the cultural backwaters of "Christian music." Rejecting the fundamentalist notions of separatism that had caused so many artists before them to go unheard by the larger music culture, Nickel Creek weaved its faith into its work, and for them it seemed the most natural thing in the world to do:

> "Bands like Rage Against the Machine, they write about what they're passionate about, social issues or whatever," noted Sean. "This is just one thing that we happen to be passionate about. It just kinda comes out naturally, I think."[27]

15

Roxie's Boy

From the biblical character Lot, who allowed his surroundings in Sodom and Gomorrah to shape his lifestyle if not his beliefs, to artists like Sam Cooke, who quit making gospel music, crossed over to pop, and died an unseemly death in an L.A. motel room, the implications for young and devout Christians were fairly clear: The world was a dangerous place and the enemy of man's souls would stop at nothing to corrupt men and women of faith who dared to venture into it. Better to stay put in the safe and tidy "Christian world" where things were safer.

For many devout Christians, Lenny Kravitz was the personification of why Christians shouldn't be in rock music or in the "world" period. The greatest fear of many Christians was that the "world" would have a greater effect on Christians who were "in it" than they would have on it and Kravitz, for some, was exhibit number one of the phenomenon.

The irony was that a look at Kravitz's lyrics revealed that not only did he have a solid grasp of Christian doctrine in his lyrics, but he was unashamed of that faith and never hesitant to express it through his music, sometimes in a way that was more direct than artists who were in the Christian rock industry. The way the Lenny Kravitz story eventually played out would impact how people of faith might look at the very notion of reentering the rock music culture with their faith. Would Kravitz continue to stand tall for his faith in a rock music business mostly populated by people who disagreed with everything he believed in, or would he continue down the path of mixing keen Christian-oriented observations with sleazy videos in a manner that seemed to cause the culture to not take his faith seriously and fellow believers to question the genuineness of that faith?

Kravitz was the only son of TV producer Sy Kravitz and Roxie Roker, who later came to fame as the actress who played Helen Willis who lived upstairs on the hit TV show *The Jeffersons*. While growing up half Jewish, half black with a Christian mother and a Jewish father would be enough to justify years of therapy for some, Kravitz seemed to actually appreciate his diverse upbringing:

> It was really cool because I'd go to church and temple. I'd have Easter, Passover, Christmas, [and] Hanukkah. I'm really lucky. The only thing that was weird was when people asked me if I'd been bar mitzvah'd. I remember once I went to Hebrew school with a friend of mine. I was nine or ten and I had this . . . Michael Jackson Afro. Anytime I went to temple, it was like, "Okay, how am I going to get the yarmulke to stay on?" I had to pin it. I went to Hebrew school and all the kids stared at me because no black kid ever walked into Hebrew school. . . . They weren't vicious. It was just like, "Here's this kid with a big . . . puff on his head with a yarmulke pinned to it, and he's brown. What's going on?" So that was the end of my Hebrew school days.[1]

As she would do many times throughout the course of his life, Kravitz's mother Roxie charted the course of her son by helping him to deal with his identity:

> I remember in first grade some kid saying, "Your dad's white!" which rang out as this major statement. But my Mom sat me down and said, "Look, I'm black. I'm West Indian and African-American. Your father's Jewish and he's white. I want you to be proud of both sides. You're just as much one as the other. But society says you're black." She taught me to be proud of what you are. Know that you are both. Embrace it.[2]

When Kravitz's mom, recently divorced, earned a spot on *The Jeffersons* in the mid '70s, she and her young son moved to Los Angeles to do the show and Kravitz grew up among the offspring of Hollywood royalty. Although Kravitz's mother was also a devout Christian, it was a fellow teenager who first introduced the youngster to faith in Jesus.

"Lenny first met God when he was 13," observed writer William Shaw. "A friend, the son of a pastor converted Lenny after they got into a deep conversation about religion. Lenny is convinced that he felt God enter the room as they were talking. He teared up and started trembling. 'It was an overpowering feeling. I was just losing it.'"[3]

As a student, Kravitz's record was less than stellar, but his heart was already pointing him toward his first love: music.

"I went to school enough to pass, but I knew what I wanted to do from the time I was five," said Kravitz. "I was really into music, and at a certain point I was going to class less and less. I'd just go to friends' houses and jam."[4]

When Kravitz burst onto the music scene with his first album, the rock world didn't quite know what to make of his unfashionably retro '60s look and the specter of a young black man making rock music that referenced The Rolling Stones and Led Zeppelin.

"With the first album, people didn't really listen," said Kravitz. "They were like, 'he sounds like the Beatles and Jimi Hendrix,' and I thought, 'listen to what I'm doing. I am influenced by that kind of music, but I'm mixing it with gospel and blues.' I have a soul voice. I'm not a white singer. I've been compared to hundreds of artists, which just goes to show you that I'm not any one thing at all. Led Zeppelin, who are now considered innovators, were told that they were the most unoriginal thing in the world—that they couldn't write, that they ripped off the blues."[5]

For Kravitz, it was a frustration that continued throughout the course of his career:

> They don't get me. My name's Lenny Kravitz. I'm half Jewish, I'm half black, I look in-between. I dress funny. I play all these different styles of music on one record. It's like, "What is he doing? We don't understand where he comes from." The confusion makes people uncomfortable. They can't put their finger on me. But it

Irish rockers U2 have built a twenty-year career out of mixing faith and rock.

Spiritual rockers Sixpence None The Richer scored big in pop music with the smash hit "Kiss Me."

Rockers POD hit the mainstream music scene after years of playing in the Christian-rock world.

Nickel Creek, pictured here with Lyle Lovett at the Westbury Music Fair, mixed Christian values with alternative country music.

MxPx brought God into punk rock.

R&B stars Mary Mary reflect a new generation of Afro-American artists who refuse to disappear into gospel music or change their Christian beliefs.

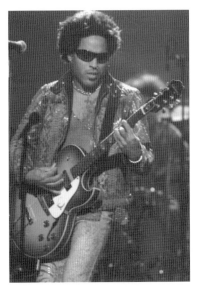

Retro rocker Lenny Kravitz has cultivated a wild image, but his music contains strong Christian statements.

Meltdown or conversion? Lauryn Hill's dramatic change ushered in a new direction for her lyrics.

Pop singer Jessica Simpson has created controversy with her potent mix of sexuality and Christian beliefs.

Former Extreme and Van Halen singer Gary Cherone put Christian doctrines into rock.

Jewish rockers Evan and Jaron take their faith seriously—even refusing to play on the Sabbath.

R&B trio Destiny's Child sends out the sometimes confused message of sexuality mixed with religion.

Dashboard Confessional singer Chris Carrabba got his start on a Christian-oriented label and then moved into the musical mainstream.

Creed, led by singer Scott Stapp, has sold millions of records with songs that reflect his Christian worldview.

MTV VJ Carson Daly once considered becoming a Catholic priest, but chose the music channel instead.

Shock-rocker Alice Cooper got sober and returned to his faith, but refused to leave rock & roll.

doesn't matter. Nine out of ten groups that came out in '89 are gone. I'm still here. There are only so many notes. What makes something original is how you put it together. The funniest review I ever saw about myself was in *The Village Voice*. The first sentence was: "If Lenny Kravitz were white, he'd be the savior of rock 'n roll." I understood what he was saying. If I were white, it would be bigger. I'd get less criticism.[6]

Kravitz also received criticism, surprisingly enough, for his penchant for playing all of the instruments on his records. "Why not?" responded the singer. "I can . . . But more than the fact that I can is just that I get a lot of joy from playing instruments and I have a different personality on each instrument. I like to let that come out. I get kind of selfish. I could give the bass part to somebody else, but I would really enjoy playing that bass part. I could get a drummer to come in, but I would really like to play that groove. And it just goes like that. It's hard to gather people in the studio. I had a lot of practice. I started out with the guitar and got bored and went to the bass, got bored and went to the drums, got bored and went to the keyboard. Not bored with the instrument, 'cause I have so much to learn still. But I always wanted to play other things. I just like playing instruments."[7]

Perhaps due to critics' obsession with Kravitz's ethnicity, retro costuming, and recycled riffs, Kravitz's lyrics seemed to survive what would otherwise have been scrutiny from many rock critics who didn't typically relish the idea of rock stars singing about serious issues of faith. But from the very beginning, Kravitz was doing that in spades. But unlike gooey expressions of non-specific, nonjudgmental faith that tended to waft through the nation's airwaves whenever spirituality was offered up, Kravitz's expressions were specific and the antithesis of New Age religion with its approach of many paths to heaven. Kravitz had no such doctrine, and whenever spirituality surfaced in his music, it was a highly specific brand that described Jesus Christ as the only path to heaven. Critics and fans alike seemed to enjoy Kravitz's first big hit song, "Are You Gonna Go My Way," but few seemed to figure out that the song was actually written from the perspective of Jesus, asking Kravitz and his listeners whom they would choose to follow, something Kravitz confirmed during the taping of his VH-1 *Storytellers* episode.

For his part, Kravitz seemed to understand that many of his messages were not being understood, possibly as a result of the perceived disparity between those messages and the public's perception of who he was. Of his third record *Circus* Kravitz said:

> A lot of people don't listen to the lyrics, really. A lot of my songs deal with spirituality and with God and I guess if you're in tune with that, you'll read into it. A lot of people only listen to the chorus. So when you think of songs like "Rock & Roll Is Dead," which, a lot of people didn't dig or understand, they said, "What are you talking about, 'Rock & Roll Is Dead'? We just made this guy the rock & roll, you know, whatever and now he's saying 'Rock & Roll Is Dead'?" But they didn't listen to the verses to know what I was saying. I was talking about the superficiality of it, the fact that image was taking precedence over music and talent and art. And it's also talking about people that feel they have to live that lifestyle, that stereotypical lifestyle in order to be a rock star. It's like, "Hey, be yourself. You don't have to shoot heroin and act a certain way in order to be a rock & roll musician. It's about the music." We've learned from those that came before us. It's not healthy. You die.[8]

Kravitz's love for his Savior Christ even extended to his choice of tattoos, for around the time of the release of *Circus*, the singer added a piece to his collection that read: "My heart belongs to Jesus Christ."

While references to God and faith were present on his first two records, on that third release Kravitz seemed inspired to lose any ambiguity and boldly declare his faith. Still, the misperceptions persisted, and largely because of the public image that Kravitz himself seemed to cultivate. Outlandish photos featuring Kravitz mostly naked but covered strategically by a tail protruding from his backside no less, graced the *Circus* album. A raucous party complete with topless girls comprised the setting for one of his videos. Though Kravitz appeared to be living something of a chaste life, rarely dating, taking care of his daughter Zoe, whom he had custody of, he was also saddled with an image that seemed at odds with his life and beliefs.

Nevertheless, Kravitz soldiered on, using his music and interviews to advance his orthodox Christian beliefs, beliefs that, album photos aside, doctrinally anyway, were indistinguishable from those shared by Pat Robertson, Jerry Falwell, or Billy Graham:

> "The album's about all kinds of things, the circus of my life in general and also showing that God and spirituality are the things that keep the circus at a level where I can deal with it,"[9] Kravitz said of his third record.
>
> "'Believe' deals with believing in God," he said, "and believing in yourself as well. I was taught by my grandfather that anything that your mind can conceive, you can have it. It's a reality. It begins in your mind."[10]
>
> "That's the beginning of the reality," he added. "You have to work to bring it forth, but, 'Believe' has always been a powerful song. There are so many people that don't believe in themselves and that don't have faith. There've been a lot of people who have said that the song has touched them and caused them to look deeper."[11]

Kravitz's increasing willingness to be bold in his declarations seemed to be a result of what Kravitz was going through at the time as he watched his mother Roxie succumb to cancer on December 2, 1995.

"I'd been caring for her in between tours—I had her all set up at home, with doctors and a live-in nurse," Kravitz recalled. "But when I had to go on the road my family said, 'It's better if you go because if you don't your mom's going to feel even worse.' You know how mothers are. They love you to the end, and she didn't want to hold me back from my livelihood. So I left for a month and called her every couple of days. I came home and she died 24 hours later."[12]

Something of a mama's boy, Kravitz took her death hard:

> After that I really needed to take some time and just chill out and get my head together. So, I spent a little time in the Bahamas and relaxed and thought about life and got comfortable. It was great because I came out of it with a real positive attitude and really had a yearning for life. When you see a close person you know

pass in front of your eyes like that, especially of a sickness, it's hard core, you know?[13]

Taking time off from his busy schedule allowed Kravitz to process his grief and move on:

> It was a distraction, but I was numb at that point. I was so busy that there wasn't much time to get deep into my feelings. So I kept working and then I stopped. I needed to figure out what I wanted out of my life. Witnessing a death will do that to you. All of a sudden you're like, "Man, I may not be here tomorrow." You're never promised your next breath. It really made me think about putting things in an order more conducive to happiness. I spent a lot of time with my family and my kid. And I got to a place where I felt like, "Okay, this is a good starting point." Then I began to work on this record."[14]

Kravitz's grief slowly gave way to joy and that process led to a more upbeat record entitled 5:

> I just realized after all that that I just wanted to enjoy every day. That was my goal: to enjoy something about each day, to give thanks and to live fully. I started feeling good and just went in and started cutting the album and started off with "Live," which was the opening number of that album and the message that I thought was important.[15]

Though she was gone, Roxie lived on through her son, and her ideals and beliefs consistently made their way into Kravitz's music:

> My mother gave lots of good advice and had a lot to say, and maybe at the time you don't realize it or understand everything, or you don't want to listen, but as you get older, you realize everything she said was true.[16]

Through it all, Kravitz soothed the wounds of his earthly sorrows with a heavenly balm, stressing his belief that he and his mother would be reunited as a result of their shared beliefs:

> God is always in my life, and that's the most important thing to me. The last record had a lot of songs that called out to God because

I was in a desperate state. It came out very heavy . . . It's part of life, it's a transition. She has made her transition. I will see her again. I think she is in a much better place.[17]

When Kravitz's grief produced especially direct songs about his faith on *Circus*, songs with lines like "The Son of God is in our face, offering us eternal grace" and "He walked on the narrow path to save us from Satan's wrath, we are not alone and we're going home," not all of Kravitz's fans were thrilled with such explicitness:

"While his first three albums touched on spiritual themes, it appears fans may not share Kravitz's enthusiasm for holy stuff judging by the poorer-than-expected sales for *Circus*,"[18] observed one critic.

"Do you think people resisted *Circus* because of its religious overtones?" asked a reporter in an interview with the singer.

"Oh yeah,"[19] Kravitz replied.

But if fans thought Kravitz was going to give up his faith in order to pad his record sales, they severely underestimated the singer, for 5 again contained numerous references to its creator's faith, depicting spiritual warfare between God and the devil in "Supersoulfighter" and generally continuing to reflect Kravitz's Bible-centered worldview. Kravitz even ventured into the issues surrounding human cloning and sexual perversion in the song "Black Velveteen," another song that seemed to be ripe for being understood by fans and critics alike.

"'Black Velveteen' is about technology and we're getting so pulled in by computers and technology and our kids have their face in the computers all day," said Kravitz. "We have our face in computers all day and the human relationship is being diminished by this, so I figured, well ok, we're so into computers, and we're so into technology and now we're also beginning to play God and get into cloning and all kinds of things, so we don't like to have relationships. We like to have them but we don't like to keep them and we don't know how to keep them. We give up quickly. Divorce is an easy option. So why not just create your own mate and synthesize a human being? You get tired of it, you turn it off and put it in the closet, you know, like the vacuum cleaner. You pull it out when you want it . . . we're going to get to a really sick point of designing fake people."[20]

Although the album was initially met with lukewarm sales, Kravitz's career was saved when he was asked to record the track "American Woman" for the *Austin Powers* soundtrack. Quick-thinking Virgin executives added the track to future editions of 5 and record sales surged.

As Kravitz prepared to release his sixth record of original material, he once again turned to matters of faith on the song "You Were in My Heart," in which he chronicled his struggles against the temptations of the flesh that constantly surrounded him and made clear references to his faith and the One whom he credited with carrying his sins:

> I want to be a better man/Lord knows that I'm trying/I want to keep the Master's plan/But sometimes things get wild/Demons sleep with me in bed/I can feel their fire/When darkness gets around my head/Sometimes I go blind/But You were in my heart . . . Your blood's running through my veins/And I am standing tall.[21]

16
Much the Richer

For all intents and purposes, 1999 was the first time that the world heard of a band with an unusual name—Sixpence None The Richer. Seemingly from out of nowhere the band rocketed to the top of the pop charts with its ode to innocent love, "Kiss Me," which went all the way to #2. But for those who followed the "Christian music" scene, the band's success was no surprise, for they had been pegged by many in the industry as a band that was destined for great things, if they could just get the attention of people in positions of power in the music industry.

The band was formed in the early 1990s by two teenagers who shared a love for music and met at their church. Leigh Bingham (later Nash) was a shy teenager with a silky smooth voice and Matt Slocum was an equally shy son of a bookstore owner who was more at home with books than in large crowds.

For many, both in and out of the Christian music industry where they got their start, Slocum's deft ability to write with Nash's voice in mind, and Nash's equally spectacular ability to make his words her own, were nothing short of remarkable.

"Matt and I grew up in the same town," remembered Nash. "Matt had just written his first song and he heard me sing in church. He liked my voice and he'd written a song, so we started a band."[1]

Slocum's love of reading caused him to develop a love for music at a young age: "I took piano lessons as a child, but my first real musical beginnings were when my dad gave me a guitar for my 15th birthday," he recalled. "I began to write songs shortly thereafter and bought a four-track. When I entered college I began cello lessons as well."[2]

Nash also gravitated toward music at a young age: "I wanted to sing from the age of 12 or so and that's what I did," she remembered. "I sang in the school and church choirs. I also performed in dance halls to gain experience and get rid of stage fright."[3]

Surprisingly, considering her vocal style and taste in music, Nash's early influences were primarily country artists:

> I was listening to old country music. I was inspired by singers like Tammy Wynette, Patsy Kline and Crystal Gayle, singers like that for me. Then, Matt's influences in the beginning when we started Sixpence were the Sundays and 10,000 Maniacs. That's why he wanted to have a band with a female vocalist."[4]

As the band dominated the pop charts, first with "Kiss Me" and later with the song destined to keep them from being one-hit wonders, "There She Goes," many fans and critics alike noticed the unusual chemistry that Nash and Slocum shared.

Nash had a special something that was difficult to describe or quantify, but could only be experienced. Her seemingly effortless ability to breathe life into songs was unusual in itself, but what was also unusual was Slocum's seeming equally effortless ability to write songs that seemed to have come from the depths of Nash's soul.

"Kiss Me," for instance, though written by Slocum, seemed to be written with a distinctively feminine voice, one that was not out for conquest, but rather longs walks on the trail "marked on your father's map."

"He just writes," said Nash of Slocum. "I don't think he has ever said, 'I'm going to sit down and write about this or that.' He is inspired by a book or by something that happens."

"I suppose much of the lyrical content comes from reactions I have to characters in literature or poetry," said Slocum. "I find a lot of my identity in identifying with books and the things they have to say about life. I wouldn't consider myself well read; there is so much out there and I have only delved into a small portion of that vast sea. But most of C. S. Lewis's works; *The Day Boy and the Night Girl*, *The Princess and the Goblin*, both by George MacDonald; Shakespeare's *Hamlet*; *A Consent* by Wendell Berry; *The Happy Prince* by Oscar Wilde; Goethe's *Faust*; the poetry of Rilke and many of Thomas Merton's writings . . . have had a special influence on my life."[5]

In the late '80s a young entrepreneur named Doug Mann launched a label called REX from his New York apartment and quickly signed a slew of death metal and hard rock acts. The slight, balding, softly spoken Mann had soon given up control of REX to a South African expatriate named Gavin Morkel who moved the label first to Chicago and later to Nashville and began to sign dozens of acts to the fledgling label. Among a number of lackluster artists were two standouts: Sixpence None The Richer and Fleming & John. Fleming & John was quickly scooped up and out of the Christian music market by Doug Morris and Universal Records, but Sixpence languished, and when the label was eventually purchased by Platinum Entertainment, the band entered a period of inactivity.

Still, the band's second record for REX, the exquisite masterpiece *This Beautiful Mess*, had caught the attention of many in the industry, including rock impresario Steve Taylor who, with a mainstream record executive named Stephen Prendergast, formed Squint Entertainment, named after a line in a Taylor song. Taylor was a longtime genre-busting CCM artist and Prendergast a journeyman record executive who had managed artists and worked for a number of labels like BMG, Zoo, Om, and Reunion. Together they took Sixpence None The Richer and "Kiss Me" to the top of the charts.

Ironically, "Kiss Me" was a song that Slocum had initially resisted including on the band's self-titled record for Squint, but he agreed to add it at producer Taylor's insistence. From there, magic struck when at a showcase arranged by Prendergast, the song came to the attention of an industry bigwig who had big plans for it:

"We did a showcase in Los Angeles. A man named John Kalodner from Columbia came and heard the showcase and liked that song a lot," remembered Nash. "He knew it was the single and I imagine had heard it before, but he thought it would be perfect for a summer movie. Actually, it wasn't a summer movie, it came out in the end of January, I think. But, he was right. It definitely was a hit with the young folks."[6]

That movie was *She's All That,* the film that introduced actor Freddie Prinze Jr. to filmgoers. The most poignant moment in an otherwise forgettable teen flick, however, was the moment when actress Rachael Leigh Cook came down the stairway dressed in her party dress to Sixpence's "Kiss Me."

Suddenly the song, which had made it as high as #97 on the pop charts before falling back down again, reentered and climbed all the way to #2.

For Sixpence None The Richer, "Kiss Me" was a mixed blessing, as it didn't really reflect the tone of the rest of the album, which was rather dark, nor the depth of the songwriting and emotional depth of most of Sixpence's previous work. Still, the song struck gold in many radio formats including alternative, pop, and adult contemporary.

"There's not really any one song on the album that would have crossed all that territory," observed Nash. "So, yeah, it doesn't represent the band's sound, but hopefully in a career they're the singles that will represent the sound."[7]

As Sixpence enjoyed its "overnight success," few in the mainstream music business seemed to know that the band had been knocking around Christian music circles for years.

"A lot of people think that we have just gotten together and it's sort of an overnight success," noted Nash. "But, there's no way they can know about our past unless we tell them. That's really the most common misconception."[8]

Squint's vice president Prendergast was a canny executive who saw opportunities and turned on a dime to meet a challenge and, realizing that the band lacked a follow-up single to "Kiss Me," hit upon an idea for a follow-up single to offer to radio.

"We were fans of The La's and we liked the song 'There She Goes' a lot," remembered Nash. "We'd been playing it live for about a year and a half. The label encouraged us after a while to go ahead and record it. It was just striking a chord with a lot of people in our live performances. So we went in and recorded it and it came out really well, so we decided it would be our second single."[9]

Not only was it the second single, but Prendergast then stripped the single onto the already year-and-a-half-old record as a bonus track for all future editions of the record. It was a master stroke and the kind of flexibility and forward thinking that had led to Sixpence's big break into the mainstream pop market to begin with.

Slocum and Nash had long hoped to make it out of the cloistered CCM world and now they had finally achieved their goal but had no intention of leaving their faith behind. At the same time, they also actively sought to avoid being labeled a "Christian band."

"We are not ashamed about what we believe in," said Nash. "We're all Christians in the band, but it is really scary to just come out and say we're a Christian band because you are lumped in with all of the other Christian bands, which we are not exactly proud of being lumped in with, sometimes because their music isn't very good or they don't represent themselves the way we want to represent ourselves. It doesn't mean they are wrong, I just think music needs to be lumped into the same pile so everyone can hear it. That is what music is for and we want to be heard by everyone."[10]

Dodging the "Christian band" label was of utmost importance to Sixpence. Once, when asked by a reporter what his favorite part of being in a Christian band was, then drummer Dale Baker tersely replied:

> I don't know. I have never been in one. However, I enjoy being in a band with people who I believe share the same values and beliefs on most things that I do. Some of those things being the validity and truth of the Scriptures and a desire to create excellent art that ultimately brings glory to God.[11]

It was a philosophy shared equally by all members of the band. Nash added:

> Some people might be afraid of the whole idea of Christianity, some might be turned off because everything they've ever heard

about Christian music is bad. A lot of people just don't like the sound of it, or they think it's ripping off of other things. There are a lot of bad connotations, unfortunately, and we didn't create those. We just don't want to have to be kind of lumped in with it. We're never going to deny that we're Christians or sneakily keep it out of anything on purpose. So yeah, it's that we don't want to have people not listen to our music from the get-go just because of something like that. It's music and we're Christians.[12]

Unlike other stealth bands who practically denied their members' faith in order to succeed, Nash had a more forthright policy:

I think it's so much more effective to build a career and not along the way say, "I'm not a Christian," but then you get there and then people find out, "Oh these guys are Christians." We were talking to these young girls last night and this is something I'm really not used to having happen, but they were at a show and they were not Christians and they just asked me, "So are you guys Christians?" They were so cool about it, they were like, "Wow, that's really neat." And I was really happy to kind of show them myself. Or just have them love the song from hearing it on the radio, and then meet me and find that out from me personally and see how that affected them. I thought that was a great thing and that's just going to keep happening more.[13]

Despite their reluctance to be branded "Christian rock," Sixpence's members had a deep faith that permeated everything they did and could hardly have been expected to have been kept out of their music. In an age where rock stars threw around religious terminology but often lived a life at odds with those professed beliefs, Slocum and Nash seemed to have been cut from different cloth. Slocum stated:

Ever since I was a child I've had a strong sense of God's hand on my life and a desire to serve Him. But the actual admitting of my sin and need for a Savior came when I was 14. I felt very close to Christ in the first year after I became a Christian, and it seemed like I was learning so much from the Bible. New ideas and truths from God were almost constantly coming my way. God seemed so close. I guess I admit that need time and time

again and though I know I am eternally cleansed by the blood of
Christ I feel I am at the very beginning stages of the journey to
knowing Him deeply.[14]

Nash too possessed a faith that was strong, vibrant and, above
all else, deeply personal:

The times I feel closest to God are when I wake up in the morning
and my first thoughts are about God. I find myself whispering,
"Good morning, Father! Thank you that I'm alive to live another
day!" It obviously doesn't happen all the time, but it helps if I
go to sleep meditating on God and his Word. You know, the
Bible tells us to think about the things that are good and not
evil (Philippians 4:8). It's hard for bad things to enter your head
if you're keeping your thoughts on God instead of on the things
of this world. In fact, if your first thoughts in the morning are
on God, you'll have a better chance of keeping your thoughts on
God all day long.[15]

Nash's faith, she insisted, was not built on her feelings, but
on something deeper and stronger:

I think God is often hard to "find" because of our humanness.
We depend so much on our feelings: I don't feel God, so he's not
there. But God is as close as our breath. That close. Even if we
don't recognize it, or feel it, he is that close.[16]

Along with dozens of other rock artists who were trying to sort
out what it meant to live a life of faith in the middle of the crazy
business of rock, complete with constant touring and a generally
nomadic lifestyle, the members of Sixpence None The Richer
were in uncharted territory, trying to navigate paths without
maps. Still, they retained a clear vision of what they sought to
achieve with their art and, while some saw art as merely a tool
to be used to coerce people into believing in God, and others
saw it as mere expression, Sixpence believed neither and both.
Slocum said:

There've been many heated and unresolved discussions on this
topic; I'm not sure I really know the answer either. Some say it
must be either/or, but I suppose if you're creating quality art with

the intent of glorifying God, the Lord will use it to achieve both purposes at the same time. Music is robbed of something when it is manipulated for propagandistic purposes. Not that evangelism is propaganda, but Christians are often expected to accept bad art because it embodies a Christian message and reject good art because it embodies a secular message. I think Christian artists should focus on creating works of beauty that will speak for themselves.[17]

While it was unlikely that anybody experienced conversion simply by hearing a simple little love song like "Kiss Me," for many Christians it was nonetheless thrilling to see one of their own, so long closeted in the dungeon of pop culture where their artists rarely made it out, seen and heard in such a high profile way. And whether or not each song mentioned Sixpence's members' faith or not, it was still clear that songs written from a distinctly Christian worldview were floating across the nation's airwaves. The band's path had never been an easy one, and Slocum in particular had never sanitized the struggles he had faced:

You know, the whole Scripture is about people who go through struggles. It's about challenges and painful experiences and the message is to remain strong through prayer and through relying on Christ. What kind of friendship would you have with somebody if you only called him up once every two months? The only way to know someone well is to spend a lot of time with him. When you do, you learn little details about him and his life. You discover what he loves and what he dislikes. You begin to know him so well you can almost know what he's going to say before he says it. It's like you can almost tell what he's thinking. But it takes pursuing this relationship every single day. And that's not easy. As a cellist, I know it takes hours and hours of practice and discipline to be any good at the cello. Mastering that instrument doesn't come easily. But with all the discipline and work comes wonderful music. With disciplined faith comes a rich and close relationship with God.[18]

"The one thing I know for sure today," said Leigh Nash, a young woman who had sung of love and innocence for millions, stood tall for her beliefs on the national and international stage and shown how exquisite art and statements of faith could live in harmony, "is that there is a God and that he loves me."[19]

17

Mary²

In 2000, seemingly from out of nowhere came a song that had the dance floors humming around the country. It was titled "Shackles" and had a good beat, but some may have missed the message of the song, which included lines like "Take the shackles off my feet so I can dance, I just wanna praise you . . . I once was lost, but now am found, I've got my feet on solid ground, thank you Lord."

The song was by a brand-new act that went by the name Mary Mary and significantly it was released not on any of the host of gospel labels that had been set up to market music made by devout Christians, but by Columbia Records. Instead of making its presence known primarily in the gospel music world as polite Christians had done for decades, this duo was from a new era, when people of faith had come to insist that their music be heard everywhere and be marketed to everyone.

Sisters Tina and Erica Atkins grew up in a devout home and had Christian beliefs instilled in them from a very early age.

"We grew up in church with a preacher as a father and a missionary for a mother who was also a missionary/piano player/choir director," remembered Erica. "Big family, whole lot of kids, little bit of money, but we grew up singing. We had a lot of faith and a lot of hope, and we believed that God could supply everything, even though we didn't have much of anything. So our faith kind of infused us, as kids, in that way. As we grew older, we went on to travel in stage plays."[1]

"We're preacher's kids, born and raised in church, basically seven days a week," said Tina. "When we weren't in church we were at school and when we weren't sleeping, we were at church. I think the things instilled in us growing up, they just manifested themselves. They came to fruition when we became adults."[2]

When they were kids, however, all music that was not straight gospel was strictly forbidden, not unlike other future superstars in Creed and Lifehouse:

"Our mom felt that she couldn't buy a record and let us listen to tracks three, five and seven, but tell us not to listen to four, six and eight," remembered Erica. "So in the house we couldn't listen to anything else, but we heard pop music in the neighborhood and at school."[3]

"At school it was Michael Jackson, Stevie Wonder and Whitney Houston,"[4] agreed Tina.

"But as we grew older, mom gave us more slack," added Erica. "When we were 16 we had more freedom to listen to our choice of music in the house. But we still listened to gospel music. Even when we listened to gospel music as kids, we were listening to artists that sounded funky and soulful just as we do now."[5]

Like many R&B superstars before them, Erica and Tina learned their musical chops in church, but those experiences began to open up opportunities outside of church as well:

"I had started singing when I was five," recalled Erica. "Tina could always sing just like I could, but she was a little shy so she didn't start until she was about fifteen. Between singing in choirs and playing a very big part in the music ministry at our church, our talent became more and more of a passion for both of us. Our choir did the *Bobby Jones Gospel Show* and they recorded an album. Later on my family members would sing background for Bobby Jones. I think that's when we caught the bug. From there we started singing with different artists and we realized that we wanted to do this as a career and take it to a more professional level."[6]

"Between Erica and me, we've shared the mic as background singers for artists like Kenny Lattimore, Brian McKnight, Brandy, Eric Bonet, Ray J and Terri Ellis,"[7] remembered Tina.

For many in the African-American church community, the legacy of artists crossing over from gospel to R&B had meant that they left their faith behind to "sing for the world." Tina and Erica's parents feared the worst when their daughters began to express a desire to follow that path:

"At first my parents were strongly against it," remembered Erica of the sisters' forays into mainstream R&B. "The first artist I sang with was Brandy and she was still young with the bubble gum image. But still my mom was like 'Lord Jesus! Those people they be drinkin' and cussin' and sleeping with everybody!' I was like 'Mom, Brandy is 16. Her mom and dad and her little brother [are there.]' She still wasn't comfortable with it. But after awhile she started to pay attention to me. I [asked] my parents one day if they believed they raised me well and taught me what I need to know. And they both said 'yes.' So I said to them, 'Then trust me to make the right decisions. Just know that I'm not going to go and make you look bad and for one, I don't want to go to hell or do anything displeasing to God. Trust that I'm doing the right thing.' After that they started to look at things a little differently."[8]

Having decided to pursue music together, the sisters went looking for a name and a producer suggested Mary Mary:

"He kept saying, 'You guys should really call yourselves "Mary Mary"—I just had that idea,'" recalled Erica of producer Warren Campbell. "Tina was like, 'What did you have that idea for?' But I thought it sounded great because I didn't like 'Erica & Tina' very much. But the reason we kept it is that I did a little study and there's Mary the mother of Christ and then Mary Magdalene the prostitute. When she met Jesus she was moved by his compassion and by his love and she was changed because of that. Not because he judged her or hated her or said, 'Go clean yourself up before you come to me.' So the name represents the fact that no matter who you are or where you come from, He loves us and we can all be changed by His love. Most people feel like, 'I'm way too dirty—I've got to get this stuff straight first and then I'll come to Him.' So when we looked at it in that light, the name stuck."[9]

"They were sisters in Christ and we're blood sisters—we just thought the name would fit,"[10] said Tina, though she was careful to add: "We don't relate to Mary Magdalene! We may be imperfect, but not in the same way as Mary Magdalene!"[11]

"We took that name because it doesn't matter who you are or where you come from, you are still a child of God, whether you are perfect or imperfect,"[12] said Erica.

With the help of their producer, Mary Mary began work on a debut record, though they had no record deal.

"We had been writing for about a year and had about five or six songs written and recorded," recalled Erica. "We weren't really shopping it but our producer, Warren Campbell knows a lot of people in the business and was able to play the music for different people who were interested. A lot of companies were like 'We don't really have a gospel department, and we don't know what to do with it. We wish you the best, but we don't know what to do.'"[13]

But an unexpected break came when a meeting originally scheduled for another purpose quickly turned into Mary Mary's audition that would land them a major label deal:

"C&G Management who later became our management team was having a meeting at Columbia Records with someone else for a totally different reason and someone asked to play the Mary Mary track," recalled Erica. "So, they played the track before the meeting was over and the rest is history. They loved the track and wanted to know who we were. It wasn't as though we sent music to them and they signed us. They just heard our track in a meeting."[14]

In years past a label like Columbia might have blanched at the idea of signing an R&B act with such strong Christian-oriented messages. On the other hand, in a previous time, an act like Mary Mary, devout Christian girls raised in the church, might itself have resisted signing with a "secular" label like Columbia. But in the new dynamic, when mainstream outlets were realizing the financial potential of signing artists of faith and young Christians were eager to hook up with labels that shared a vision for getting their music out of the Christian subculture, Columbia and Mary Mary were a perfect match:

"Columbia has the ability to get our music worldwide, that's what they've done with the artists that they have," observed Erica. "They've built careers with their artists and we felt real comfortable with the whole set up. The message that we have is perfect for the audiences that listen to secular music. So if we can get there and give them the message of Christ, we're doing our job. There really weren't any drawbacks to being on that label."[15]

Still, synthesizing the faith of their upbringing with life in the real world was not an altogether easy task, requiring the sisters to keep their faith but reject the culture of separatism they were raised in:

"From a child we heard that anything that's not talking about Jesus is a sin," remembered Erica. "'If it's not going [on in] church, and all that good stuff, then you're going to hell.' But as you get older you learn that there's no way to get the message to the people if you don't take it there. I think that my purpose for singing with secular artists was not only to work, learn the business and make money, but to also let them see that there are normal people who live for God and serve him with their whole heart. You can do this and stay true to your relationship and morals. Everything is not a sin."[16]

Though their message may have been traditional, rooted in the ancient Negro spirituals that slaves sang to their God in the fields and even further back in a 2,000-year-old message of love, forgiveness, and salvation, the music of Mary Mary was anything but traditional. One thing was clear: This was not your parent's gospel music, and in many ways it wasn't gospel music at all, but rather the gospel in music.

"I think people's presentation has changed, but the word itself, I don't think it has changed," noted Erica. "When you think of gospel music, you think of the same thing from way back in the days. People in 2000 don't do things like people in 1950 did."[17]

"We're a product of music that's current today," Erica added. "High energy, banging tracks . . . that's why our sound has an urban and hip-hop feel. When you're in and around something so much it becomes a part of you . . . when you hear the music it's gonna make you move."[18]

"I think a lot of people have preconceived ideas because gospel music has always been in one vein," continued Tina. "That's something Mary Mary wants to stamp out. I don't think that you should put anything in one box and say that this is the only way it can be done. A lot of people call it R&B, they call it hip-hop, they call it a lot of different things but we call it Mary Mary music."[19]

As Mary Mary's music circulated the globe, the sisters' instinct to take their music and their messages out of the church was sharpened further:

> "Our audience is the world," said Erica. "Anybody who doesn't know God, anybody who knows God, our music is for everyone. It's universal. It crosses age, gender, race lines. We try and tell of experiences that just people in general can relate to. You don't necessarily have to be a Christian or older or younger or whatever. [Even] at our performances we have people of all backgrounds. The message of God is universal. It's worldwide. It's for everybody."[20]

Erica spoke for many in rejecting the paradigm of her parents' generation, which had successfully walled off music made as a result of faith from the "secular" culture:

> There is a great, big God and He can do so many things so why would He put His music in this corner and say, "It belongs over there and if you add this to it then it's not really gospel?" It's just not true![21]

As artists like Mary Mary ventured out of the comfort zones and into a world of drugs, booze, sex, and quiet lives of desperation, the question that would haunt them once again was whether they would be affected by it more than they affected the culture of disbelief around them. It was a question the girls' upbringing had caused them to think long and hard about:

> "We all must remember; whatever you sing, wherever you go, whatever you do, God has guidelines and He has rules," said Erica. "He does not make exceptions. His law is His law, and in the end, I would hate to be one of the ones to find out that I was wrong because I decided to do my own thing. I don't want to find

out the hard way. I'll keep my nose in my Bible and go according to His guidelines and His rules. Because nowadays everybody's making their own rules."²²

She continued, "My mom always said when we were growing up, 'It's better to be saved from than out of.' You don't want to go through hitting rock bottom to realize maybe I should have prayed and maybe I should have thought about letting God be my strength and source. Skip all of the going to the rock bottom and hang in there with God from the start."²³

In the postmodern American pop culture many would-be ministers of the gospel had figured out that the best way to "minister" to their culture was to take off the robes, pull off the collars, and get to work at occupations that impacted the lives of those who lived their lives outside of the church. In Mary Mary's case that was R&B music infused with the sisters' beliefs and they seemed to understand that mission clearly:

> "Right now I know God has placed a calling on my life through my music to touch people," said Erica. "I'm not a preacher but I realize there's a message. My ministry is to make hits. That's my ministry! To make as many hits as possible."²⁴

18
Jordan's Sister

One of the hurdles that had to be jumped before serious Christians could make an impact on pop culture was overcoming the traditional evangelical opposition to being a part of projects that were not in total agreement with their beliefs. Taking a passage from Scriptures that forbade being "unequally yoked" in marriage with a nonbeliever, many Christians had deduced that working in cooperation with non-Christians was also to be strictly avoided. That was what caused many Christian artists to only desire to sign with Christian-run record labels and it also kept many artists from allowing their songs to be used in "secular" outlets like film soundtracks and television shows.

But a new crop of artists like Kendall Payne had no such hang-ups. Payne not only resisted signing with a Christian-oriented music label, she also played on the forbidden and often boycotted Lilith Fair tour, and her signature song "Supermodels" became the theme song for the television show *Popular*.

Payne had grown up in Southern California and through church circles had run into producer Ron Aniello, who would later pluck the modern rock band Lifehouse out of obscurity.

Early exposure to Broadway show tunes gave Payne an early love for music:

"I loved the idea of performing in shows like *Les Miserables* after I heard all that music," observed Payne, "and I joined a local theater troupe because I thought that one day I wanted to be on Broadway myself!"[1]

Another inspiration for the future rocker was her encounter with a pregnant woman who "kicked off her shoes, strapped on her guitar and started playing and singing," recalled Payne. "I got to know her afterwards and I got all her demos, all her songs. She inspired me to want to create my own music, and about two years later I started performing some of the songs I'd written."[2]

If Kendall Payne's music sounded different from the rest of pop music it was probably attributable to her being largely unaware of the scene:

"I didn't listen to pop music almost like a reaction to my sister Jordan," she remembered. "You see, she was always popular and I thought that anything she was into was thought of as cool and I couldn't like anything she liked! Creating my own music was my way of escape, my way of expressing my own individuality."[3]

But it was Payne's brush with Aniello, a producer who appeared to have a vision for taking artists like Payne into mainstream music, that would chart Payne's course for years to come:

"Ron heard my performance and called me the following Wednesday to ask if I minded him playing my material to some music industry executives," recalled the singer.[4]

With Aniello's help, Capitol Records came calling and signed Payne to a multi-album contract. Payne was forthright with the label about her faith and made it clear that she intended to make an album that reflected her beliefs:

I would sit down in their offices, and tell them: "Being a teenager myself, I see firsthand the power that music can have in a young person's life. It is their anthem. It's what they live by and die for. To be honest with you, there's no hope in the music today. I'm all about hope! But the only hope that I have is in God. I haven't always understood Him, but He's never left me and He's never forsaken me. I'm not into beating people over the head with a Bible. I'm just saying God is the only thing I've found worth investing my heart into. Now let me sing you my song."[5]

Before long Payne and Aniello were in the studio recording twelve songs that Payne had written or cowritten and, with the help of Alanis Morissette's producer Glen Ballard on one track, the record began to take shape. According to Payne:

We had no real road map in making the album. We thrashed through a lot of ideas and it was like an organic process. I called this album *Jordan's Sister* because the songs are like a snapshot of a particular time in my life when I felt somewhat insignificant, when I felt like I was nothing more than Jordan's younger sister. She's two years older than me and as with many siblings there was some rivalry, some frustration and tension. We're much better now and she's thrilled that I named the album after her![6]

Payne's music was connecting with fans who didn't necessarily share her faith, the result of a very conscious effort on her part to write songs that were more than praise anthems to God, but rather addressed real-life issues that her peers were facing.

"When I sit down to write a song I'm not trying to write a hit and I'm not trying to write what I think everyone else wants to hear," said Payne. "For me, the process of writing is wrapped up in the challenge of coming before God and saying, 'I'm here to be raw before You, and I'm here for You to change me and use me.' I really think with all my heart that lyrics and music are God-given and that most of the time we're just vessels through which they flow. That's why I'm most affected by a song when the writer has the guts to be real and honest. That quality touches me, and I hope I can reach other people that way too."[7]

From issues of body awareness to insecurities within a family to the plight of the fatherless, Payne's songs had enough hope to keep listeners from despairing but were real enough to acknowledge that pain and suffering were real. One song, "Fatherless at 14," captured the raw emotion of a friend who had just lost her dad:

"A friend of mine was at her younger brother's football game with her family and her father started to feel uncomfortable. The next thing, he had walked away to get out of the sun and he lay down and died. I spent the night with my friend and listened as she cried about how life would never be the same for her. About a month later I wrote this song as a gift to her. I walked upstairs to her bedroom just a few hours after his death,"[8] remembered Payne. "Her eyes welled up with tears and she came and buried her head in my shoulder and started sobbing and she said, 'I'm not my daddy's princess anymore.' Of course I just lost it too and I sat with her all night. A couple of days later I was thinking about what her father would want to say to her if he could. I wrote 'Fatherless At 14' and recorded the demo that same day. My A&R director cried the first time he heard it. He decided it should go on the album exactly the way it was, so we just used the demo."[9]

"Supermodels," the song that brought Payne to a large audience of teenagers courtesy of the TV show Popular, although whimsical, had a serious message: "Barbie's body is melting down, on her face a big fat frown because Mr. Cellulite just moved into town,"[10] sang Payne.

"You look on magazines, TV, anywhere," she added, "and you see everyone aspiring to be this waif-like, drop dead gorgeous supermodel. It's just absurd. When you look at God's word, at His original plan, he speaks of a woman of character, but we've got it so backwards. Consequently, self-image is a struggle for most girls. 'Supermodels' is somewhat tongue-in-cheek and I hope no one tries to interpret it too literally, but at the same time I hope it brings some freedom to girls who are frustrated by that pressure to measure up to something so frivolous and unattainable."[11]

"Many supermodels are on heroin," she added, "seriously addicted to nicotine or doing things to make their bodies look thin. But we think, 'If I just looked like that, so-and-so would like me.' I have to remind myself that it's OK that I'm bigger. And I'm learning that I would rather have someone say about me, 'I love hanging out with her,' than, 'I want to have her in my arms.'"[12]

Payne was especially proud of another song that was in many ways almost an anthem for a new generation of people of faith who saw rock music as a way to communicate with their peers:

> Hollywood is about taking God's hope to the streets. It's almost like a war cry for me. I wrote it on the top floor of the Capitol Records building looking out at the Hollywood sign and at the streets of Hollywood laid out in front of me. I was watching all of the people and just thinking, "Whoever you are, whatever you came here looking for, it's the Truth that will set you free and if you listen, I'm going to tell it to you. I'm going to share my hope."[13]

For Payne, who had grown up listening to music that emanated from the Christian subculture, the decision to go with a mainstream label was a conscious one that was rooted in the Christian rock industry's inability or unwillingness to create paths for artists like her to walk down that would lead them to fans who didn't share her faith:

> "I grew up listening to Christian music and I've always loved it," said the singer. "I'm definitely closer to the Lord because of it. But I was offered an opportunity that a lot of Christian artists don't have, an opportunity to take God's light right into some very dark places. I had to seize the chance."[14]

Although courted by various Christian music labels, including one of the industry's top players, Sparrow Records, Payne firmly rejected their entreaties:

> I met with the people at Sparrow at that time and told them "I love you guys and I love what you're doing, but right now I think God is leading me to be salt and light and I just need to go for it." They said, "This is great, we bless you and support you in what you're trying to do."[15]

Payne's reference to salt and light came from a New Testament passage in which Christ urged his disciples to spread out and affect their world. In the same way that a bit of light could brighten a room and a dash of salt would add a touch of taste and actually preserve meat, so believers were told to spread out and make themselves useful instead of huddling together in areas where salt and light were in overabundance. The clear inference to be taken from Payne's spurning of offers from Sparrow and other labels was an implicit criticism of those labels and their failure to break out of what had often been referred to as the "holy huddle."

Part of breaking out of the holy huddle meant her joining up with the Lilith Fair tour. Lilith had been controversial for several reasons, not the least of which was the association with Lilith, the mythical first wife of Adam who had refused to submit to her husband and abandoned Adam, only to be replaced by Eve, created from Adam's rib.

But many Christian-oriented groups objected to and boycotted Lilith because of a perceived strong lesbian influence and the contention that for many young girls it was an indoctrination center more interested in pushing lesbianism and abortion than in providing great music.

But much like her counterpart Leigh Nash of Sixpence None The Richer, Kendall Payne shrugged off the criticism of her association with Lilith and other mainstream venues and opportunities that came her way, articulating a clear-eyed vision of how people of faith should approach the culture in a post-Christian society:

> I can't just walk up to the front door with my Christian badge and say, "Hi, can I speak with you?" I have to jump over the fence, whip in through the back door, sit down on the couch and start singing before people know what hit them. Yes, I do feel a kindred spirit with women of my own age, but hopefully my music will resonate with everyone.[16]

Payne's music was definitely resonating with Lilith Fair fans, as the singer was often invited back to play before thousands of fans, many of whom were not Christians. For Payne, the experience was unforgettable:

> Being on shows with artists like Sarah McLachlan, Natalie Merchant, The Indigo Girls, Sinead O'Connor and Bonnie Raitt was amazing. I remember one day walking around with my artist's badge and some girl on the other side of the gate was pointing at me, telling her friend, "Look she's an artist!" That's when I pinched myself and said, "Wow, if it hadn't been for the way things have gone in the last couple of years, I'd be there on the other side of the gate too!" But I stay grounded because I still have the same

friends around me that I had before I got my record deal and my parents make sure I still take out the trash every Wednesday night![17]

Payne was an unusual young woman both in terms of her skills as an artist and her sense of calling and mission.

"My greatest fear is of having my life pass me by without doing the things I was sent here to do," she said. "I believe God has placed each of us here with a specific purpose, but so many people walk through lives in a daze never knowing that. I want to be faithful with what's set before me and make a difference in the world. Right now, the doors that have opened for me are through my music. Ultimately, the only real measuring stick for a Christian is the life of Christ. If it's our own life we seek, we're told in scripture that we'll lose it, but in giving it up for His sake, we gain it eternally. When I sing about becoming closer to myself, to who I really am, that really means becoming something closer to Christ. It means being transformed to his image. That's where you find your true life. That's where you find what you're really made of and who you're created to be."[18]

In singer/songwriter Kendall Payne, pop culture had another living, breathing example of how far people of faith had come at bridging the gap between rock and religion. For decades people of faith had struggled to come to terms with rock music and how it could and couldn't be used to communicate eternal truths. In the experiences of artists like Payne and others, a road map was being created for many subsequent artists who shared the passion for the message and the music. That path meant consciously rejecting both the secular culture that had too often sought to keep serious religious impulses out of music and the religious culture that too often ended up keeping expressions of faith in their own bubble. Payne and others seemed intent on creating a new paradigm that would free generations of artists from both extremes:

"I felt like God gave me a choice," said the singer. " 'Do you want to take your bucket of water and pour it back into the ocean or do you want to take it to the people out in the desert?' My response was: 'I want to take my bucket of water to the people who are dying of thirst. I want to give them hope. I want to take my water to the desert.' "[19]

19
Supergirl

Pop singing sensation Krystal Harris, aka Krystal the Supergirl, was another example of the change that had taken place in American pop culture that had resulted in devout young wannabe entertainers moving out of the Christian music subculture and into the mainstream pop music culture.

"She wears a ring in her nose, sports a tattoo on her left shoulder and has triangular tufts cut into her short, jet-black hair (which is naturally blond),"[1] observed reporter David Lindquist.

She was also a devout Christian who declared in interviews that her favorite book was the Bible and that she was sustained on the road by the writings of the preacher Charles Stanley.

Soon after signing her record deal with the Backstreet Boys' own label, KBNHA Records, one of Harris's songs was chosen as the theme song for the WNBA. Still others appeared on the soundtracks for the films *Legally Blonde* and *The Princess Diaries,* and Harris became the opening act for the Backstreet Boys.

Harris grew up in Anderson, Indiana, a conservative enclave that was home to CCM superstar Sandi Patty. Patty's route would have been the natural course for a young artist like Harris to take, but the singer had different plans, signing with a pop label and making a pop record for the mainstream music world that nonetheless reflected her faith. Harris came to the attention of the Backstreet Boys through a friend of the band named Jonathan "Mook" Morant.

"He and I got together just through a guy in Indianapolis who happened to hear about me, and I sang for them," remembered Harris, "and then, however many months later, ended up hooking he and I up for some reason and we sat down and we had a three hour conversation, mostly about Christ and just how our vision for people and what God wanted in us was the same. It blew me away and changed my life. He was really about to leave the music business at that point. I remember him saying, 'I think I've been waiting on this. I think you're what I've been waiting for. So, let's do this thang.' So, that's how it happened."[2]

"I'm always talking about finding a church when I'm going to be in a place," said Morant of his first encounter with Harris in her hometown. "Krystal said, 'Oh, a church? Well, I know plenty.' That led to a whole night of talking about Jesus. That was our bond. There was no music talk at all."[3]

But the music talk was soon to follow as Morant, who had written and produced tracks for the Backstreet Boys, put in a call to one of the group's members.

"He ended up calling Kevin and said 'Hey, Kev, whassup? We've been going around shopping Krystal to all these record companies and everybody's interested and all this, but, we wanna know what your deal is.' So we spewed it out to him. Kevin said, 'Hey, listen Mook, our management company and us, we've been wanting to start a record label. Let's do it. Let's do it with Krystal. We just want her.'"[4]

While Harris had obviously set out to mix her love for music with all things spiritual, it was also part of her heritage because the singer grew up in a household that mixed a love for music with religion. Her father held a master's of divinity degree and a master's degree in Christian counseling.

"Krystal is a feminine way for the name Christian and also it means light and purity," said the singer. "I come from a musical family: my mom plays piano, plays the flute and also sings; my father sings, plays drums and the guitar. My uncle plays bass and sings and all my grandparents play an instrument, so you can only imagine. Also, we're all very involved with church. My father is a Christian counselor. It all started in church. And it still continues to be. When I was seven years old I started working professionally in the studio, singing in choir and doing some jingles."[5]

Harris's lineage included not just great musicians but also the spiritually devout, and the combination of the spiritual and the musical meant hitting the road early:

> On my mom's side of the family, her grandfather [and his family] founded the Church of God in the Midwest and Michigan. So, I had a church background, and when I turned two years old, I went on the road with my family and started singing with them and started ministering with them. I started playing piano when I was three, drums when I was seven, and just continued to learn instruments. In sixth grade I started playing the flute. Around that sixth grade time is when I can remember really . . . you know . . . cuttin' the doo-doo and saying "Okay, this is the time. It's time to leave all of the things behind and start to press on to that higher calling so I can reach people. Take the focus off myself, and go with God."[6]

Still, Harris continued honing her craft and touring the country with her musically inclined family:"We used to go to a lot of different types of places," said the singer. "We'd go to some that you'd call 'tighter' churches, and we'd go to 'looser' ones. All believers are believers."[7]

Two generations ago, when a youngster like Harris felt the call to pursue a "higher calling" it might have meant pursuing missionary service, becoming a pastor's wife, or perhaps becoming a church organist. One generation back it may have meant traveling to Nashville and pursuing a career in Christian music. But for the members of Gen Y who were also Christians, that sometimes meant pursuing a career in the heretofore forbidden environment of "secular" pop music while infusing it with their beliefs. Krystal chose the latter.

In 1999, Krystal entered a contest in Orlando, Florida called Showstoppers, which she subsequently won, performing a Sandi Patty song called "For All the World." Before long, conversations in the family were turning to what Harris should do with her talents:

"Her mission was 'taking light to the darkness,'" said her father. "I think today we have come to the point where many people are saying, 'God help us. I don't care what it takes, we have got to get something to these kids,' . . . hopefully young people will have sort of a mascot in Krystal and maybe a mentor to follow."[8]

Still, Phil Harris was circumspect of his daughter's predicament, perhaps recalling the many artists whose faith had not survived the nasty world of rock & roll:

"That will only be good as long as she continues to follow God," he noted. "I would be inhuman to tell you that it isn't a mother-and-father concern. But we certainly have confidence that this is a good step for her."[9]

Brimming with confidence, Krystal projected an ardent and contagious enthusiasm for her music and her faith, which was reflected in what became her stage persona, "The Supergirl." Harris arrived at the moniker through her love of superheroes:

"I love Superman, and the fascination started when I was writing the song," she remembered. "He's the one I can most relate to, just a normal guy, with normal problems and with all that on top of him, he still has that desire to go help people and just change the world that's around him, and that's exactly what I want to do. Clark Kent was a regular guy who had his regular problems. On the other hand, he was confident enough to help people and changed when he needed to change."[10]

From Superman, Krystal got the idea for The Supergirl:

"I guess I would compare the idea of Supergirl to Superman," said the singer. "The song can be an anthem for people. There's a Supergirl inside you, too. You can conquer what you need to conquer. A Supergirl is a regular chick who lives in regular circumstances, but she has a struggle in life. And through the circumstances, she makes it through and stands out."[11]

Reared in an evangelistic environment that included traveling to churches and prisons with her parents' singing group, Harris never imagined separating her faith from her work as opening act for the Backstreet Boys. Although preaching from the stage was not an option in such a setting, Harris nonetheless used every opportunity she was presented with, including Internet chats with fans and interviews as well as her music, to present a vision of following God that was fun, winsome, and attractive:

"I'm into being myself," said the singer of her spiritual emphasis. "That's such a big part of who I am that there's no way I could deny that. Everybody's got their stuff to deal with. But even in the midst of that, when you see that somebody loves you, you can see something better for yourself."[12]

"She doesn't go up there with a Bible and a pulpit," said her musical mentor/manager Morant. "She just sings and gives her heart and spirit. These kids and parents are really embracing it. They're enjoying it as something new—but it isn't anything new. Maybe it's new as opposed to what's been recent, I don't know. For some reason, it's not threatening and it's cool."[13]

Like many of her contemporaries in the faith community, Harris was intent on breaking out of the Christian music subculture that had started with hopes of making music for the entire world—Christian and secular—but had degenerated into targeted niche marketing to fellow believers:

"Our vision is taking the Gospel to the people," said Krystal. "We've got to break all the labels. We don't want labels on music. We are people in Christ and we do like what He does. He said be like Him. So, we'll do that instead."[14]

It was a conscious and clear rejection of the very notion of creating a genre and calling it "Christian music," and Harris never hesitated about bringing her faith into her songs, eagerly divulging the spiritual content of some of the songs on her debut record:

The title of my album is *Me & My Piano* and it contains songs such as "My Religion," "SuperGirl" and "You're The Reason." "You're The Reason" is basically about my relationship with God, because without him I wouldn't be here and I wouldn't be able to do anything. He's the reason![15]

Krystal was also equally forthright in interviews, making the case for her faith. Asked to name her favorite Bible verse, she characteristically rambled:

> There are so many different ones. It's so hard, and I stink at re-membering. I would say that there are two that are my favorites that I quote to myself a lot. One of them is I Peter 5:6–7, and on through the rest of the chapter, "humble yourselves therefore under the mighty hand of God," which even when I say that, I feel convicted already because that's something we have to strive for every day. "And He may exalt you in due time, casting all your cares on Him, for He cares for you." And, then, there's another one, "There is therefore now no condemnation to those who are in Christ Jesus and are called according to His purposes." It just seems like there's always condemnation, in your brain, even to yourself—self-condemnation. I know I deal with that, because I'm a perfectionist. You have to stop, and go, "I see myself as Christ sees me," and you have to commit so much to Him. Those two verses go together. "Casting your cares, no condemnation, humble yourself." With Christ it's possible.[16]

Responding to a fan's question about what she considered important, Krystal said: "I think about God, and how He loves everyone that's out there watching me and how much I love them too."[17]

To another, searching for advice, she replied: "I pray! I like to thank God for his undying love and presence and I dedicate all my shows to him!"[18]

Asked by still another how she would describe herself, the singer replied, "Geek! Loving, passionate . . . rocker, and, um, Christian!"[19]

One listen to Harris's music made it abundantly clear that she had been listening to more than Sandi Patty or other gospel favorites growing up. Her influences ranged from her "heroes" like Michael Jackson and Prince, to other pop stars like Stevie Wonder, Billy Joel, Elton John, Bon Jovi, and Ray Charles. She dreamed of one day working with Jackson, Music Soulchild, D'Angelo, and another artist to whom her vocals were likened by a reporter—Annie Lenox:

Annie Lenox's voice is so powerful and I love it. Maybe what he sees in her that reminds him of me is that she's a rocker and she's a very strong woman with a rock and punk style. And also, our hair is both very short.[20]

Whatever the future, Harris would always remember the first time her song came on the radio, for most artists an unforgettable experience:

"It was in New Orleans, and we were driving on the road to meet somebody there," she remembered. "The radio came on and they said, 'and now, a new one from Krystal!' We just turned it up and it was cool. You never really expect to hear your songs on the radio, so it was awesome. It was a big thing!"[21]

Looking to the future and sounding more like an evangelist than a pop star, Harris discussed films, soundtracks, and most of all continuing her mission of "still building the Kingdom in whatever way possible. I might still be making music. I'd like to be helping other people do their thing, because that's what it is all about, continuing the rock that rolls down the hill and just gets bigger and bigger as it goes. I don't know what God has in store. I'm unknown to tomorrow. Only He knows. So, we'll see what happens."[22]

"We're everywhere . . . we're in the pit," said Harris, speaking for a new generation of Christians believers who were no longer content to operate in their corner of pop culture, separated from everybody else by an invisible wall of faith. "We're not just in the four walls with the triangle on the top."[23]

20
The Stones

The hard rock band 12 Stones was another in a series of bands that, though still teenagers and devout Christians, had managed to get signed to a mainstream label, an unthinkable proposition for Christian musicians of yesteryear.

If one of the unwritten rules for succeeding as Christians in mainstream rock was to be coy about one's faith at the outset of one's career, the members of the rock band 12 Stones must not have gotten the memo from rock headquarters, for the band's debut record contained many references to the group members' faith and even included "thank-you's" to God and Jesus in the liner notes. In fact, the band's very name had spiritual significance:

> "The name actually is a biblical reference from the Old Testament Book of Joshua," said lead singer Paul McCoy. "It represents the 12 tribes of Israel and their protection."[1]

For the members of 12 Stones, the story of rocks being piled on an altar to remind the ancient Israelites of what God had done for them would be a reminder that their success had come from a higher power.

Though unashamed of their beliefs, 12 Stones' members were also quick to deny the "Christian band" label in one of their earliest interviews promoting their debut record and hit single "Broken."

"No," responded Paul McCoy in response to the now perfunctory question that was posed by non-Christian reporters to nearly all bands composed of Christians that they encountered in interviews. "We each individually have our own personal beliefs and relationships with God and we're not trying to sit here and force our belief on anybody. We're a rock band but we just keep it positive."[2]

Ironically, denying the "Christian band" tag allowed McCoy to be clear about his faith:

> "In this industry and in life in general, whether you hide your faith or show your faith, there are going to be people who disagree with your stand," he said in response to a question about labelmate Creed's sometimes ambiguous spiritual public posture. "A lot of people disagree with Creed for not showing their faith as much, I guess, and there are going to be people who don't like the fact that we show ours as much as we do. We figure if we are not going to be able to please everybody then we might as well stick with what we know."[3]

Signed to Wind-Up, the label that had been put on the map by its first signing, Creed, 12 Stones was, next to Creed, one of the label's few success stories. The fact that the members were only teenagers was amazing enough, but their rise to fame came at an unprecedented fast pace:

> "We were only together I think seven months when we signed, and the funniest thing about it is that we had only known each other for seven months," said McCoy. "We all met through the band. None of us had known each other previously."[4]

Thanks to an aggressive manager with strong connections in the music business, the members of 12 Stones found themselves showcasing for several labels just months after forming, eventually settling on Wind-Up:

> "Wind-Up flew us up to New York, we showcased for seven different labels and got a callback not too long after that they were

interested," recalled McCoy. "Wind-Up has been great, it's like a big family to us. The owner and his wife, they both call us every day and make sure we're OK and they're just great people. It's a really good environment, a great vibe."[5]

"We were strangers when we started, but we've been through a lot. We're like brothers now," guitarist Eric Weaver added. "I think it was an advantage and because we didn't know each other, half of the album was written within a few weeks. From that alone, I was ready to settle in."[6]

The band got together in Mandeville, Louisiana. Weaver was working at a music store where he met McCoy and Dorr.

"We had our drummer at the time and he knew a bunch of people and he was working at this music store alongside Eric our guitar player," said McCoy. "They started talking and I was dating a keyboard player that was in his old band, that he just got out of and we met each other spontaneously like that through the music store. Then our bass player showed up one day looking for some bass strings and we invited him to stay for practice and that's how the original 12 Stones formed."[7]

"There wasn't much of a rock 'n roll scene there when we started," he continued, "just a lot of cover bands. Now there seems to be more rock bands coming out of the area."[8]

Musically, the members were influenced by a variety of sounds: "Silverchair's *Frog Stomp* album, Finger Eleven, who is also a Wind-Up artist," said McCoy of artists he most admired. "They just kind of helped me find my niche of writing."[9]

Within months of signing, the band flew to L.A. to work with famed producer Jay Baumgardner (Papa Roach), and before long the record began to take shape, a decision that both the label and the band concurred on:

> "I researched him really well," said McCoy. "We just saw all of his work . . . I bought all the albums he had done previously. I like his style. We had options of a few, but that was obviously the one they were going to push hardest cause it's Jay Baumgardner. But the label has never been really animated about forcing us to do anything. They've always kind of given us the final decision."[10]

Released in April of 2002, 12 Stones' debut album immediately launched a hit single, "Broken," which rose up the rock charts and saw lots of airtime on MTV and its sister station MTV2. The message of "Broken" was straightforward and earnestly sincere, expressing the members' faith in God:

> I need to be broken, take the pain away, I question why you chose to die when you knew your truth I would deny . . . and all in all faith is blind, but I fail time after time, daily in my sin I take your life.[11]
>
> "'Broken' was a song I wrote at a time I kind of got a little ahead of myself and kind of thought myself to be bigger than what I was,' said McCoy. "Broken" is kind of like my theme song for myself to be humble, appreciate where I am and not forget where I came from. It's basically an anthem of 'I need to be broken back down to my purist form.' It's an anti-egotistical song I guess you could say."[12]

The band also received a boost when one of its songs was included on the soundtrack for the film *The Scorpion King*, joining artists like Godsmack, P.O.D., and Sevendust. The success continued when labelmate Creed asked the band to be their opening act on its world tour:

> "It's just really a big honor for me to go out and open for a band I spend a lot of time listening to and rehearsing to," said McCoy. "We're so stoked and we realize that we're extremely lucky to be here and we try not to take any of that for granted. It's just a blast 'cause I grew up with Creed's first two albums. They were a great influence."[13]

Despite the excitement of touring with an arena rock band like Creed, McCoy expected a time of adjustment to the super-sized crowds he expected to meet up with:

> "Every show we've played I've been able to look everybody in the crowd eye to eye," said McCoy. "I've never been where I can't see the last person's face. I try to be really intimate with the crowd, so that will probably take a little getting used to. I won't say that we're going to be natural at it and nothing will be an issue. I think we'll overcome it and do well. Our biggest crowd to date is like 2,500 and that went really well. We had a lot of fun with that.

We enjoy playing live. We love interacting with the fans and the crowds. I think we'll have the obvious butterflies and nervous tension, but we'll overcome that and make a name for ourselves with that. I think it'll be fun."[14]

Aside from bringing a traditionalist form of spiritual commitment to the rock scene, 12 Stones also packed a more guitar-driven form of rock, which harkened back to great southern rock bands of the past:

"Southern rock and blues do come through," observed *Relevant* magazine of 12 Stones' debut. "Weaver's guitar and McCoy's voice play off each other, almost like the call and response of old time blues. It's not a competition, but rather a completion. Each is made stronger by the presence of the other. It's a balance that is forged in songwriting, and refined throughout the production process."[15]

While not disagreeing with the assessment, guitarist Weaver laughed it off: "I'm not trying to be any kind of legend or anything, but it's cool to bring the guitar back to the forefront. I have a lot of southern rock and blues stuff in me, and that's all guitar based."[16]

"Eric has always said, for him it's been like Jimi Hendrix and Stevie Ray Vaughan," said McCoy of bandmate Weaver's musical influences. "His dad is a huge influence on him, [he's] a great guitar player and kind of taught Eric a lot of stuff."[17]

McCoy and Weaver were talented young songwriters who, because of that youth, obviously had neither the benefit of extensive touring nor training, something the band members considered a plus:

"I don't have any formal training at all," said McCoy. "I don't read music and I don't think the rest of the guys do either, except maybe [bassist] Kevin [Dorr]. I think he had some training on brass instruments in high school—tuba, trombone, stuff like that. Then he picked up the bass and guitar. We all kind of play a little bit of everything, but we really don't know all the technical aspects of anything. I'm excited that I don't have to rely on technically correct musicianship. I like to rely on true feelings and true passions, working things out through my fingers. There are a lot of bands out there that are really good technically, but they have no passion in their music. I take pride in the fact that we have a very emotion-filled style."[18]

McCoy liked to write the music first, followed by the lyrics:

"If somebody comes up with a cool riff or a cool this and that, we turn around and I won't force lyrics," said McCoy. "We could have some lyrics in the works for like three months, we can have just the open music sitting there, like a guitar riff that we really like and it would just be a guitar riff for a few months sometimes until we find the right lyrics to make the song. We just try not to force-write, because we write what we feel and don't fake any emotion,"[19] he said, adding, "I write most of the lyrics, but we all work on the music together."[20]

The members of 12 Stones appeared to have at least two goals in mind with their music:

"I hope that we can be recognized as sort of a break-out, bringing a positive message back in," said McCoy, "and also Eric for bringing back the guitar solo to rock 'n roll, cuz it's been gone for a while and we'd like to be known for bringing that back."[21]

"Of course it's easy to get negative," he added, "that's human nature. We all have our personal relationships with God. You've got to learn to not let that negative stuff destroy you. Why do it? We're not out there to preach to anyone, and we're just hoping they can get something positive in any form that's necessary."[22]

In many ways, the story of 12 Stones was another surprising twist in the upside-down world of rock & roll, which was now filled with dozens of young bands who had divorced themselves from the sex and drugs part of rock's legendary mantra "sex, drugs, and rock & roll." McCoy and company were just one in a long lineup of young rockers who were out to turn back the clock on rock, keeping the essence of rebellion against the status quo, only changing the very definition of what traditionally has been understood as "status quo":

"We have really rockin' kind of hard music," explained McCoy, "but we just really want to emote in the lyrics that you can still have fun and rock out and have good songs and you don't have to be talking about killing people and drugs and all the crap that's been out there. Life is a very valuable thing and to take that for granted is just stupid."[23]

So, what did McCoy want their fans to take away from a 12 Stones performance?

"Just that, there is always another day," responded the singer. "Life's not as bad as it seems sometimes, keep your head up and be positive. Believe in yourself and make things happen."[24]

"I think they are going to walk away feeling better about themselves," he added. "We try to be very positive in our shows. We try to connect with our fans and let them know that we appreciate them. We know that they are the reason that we get to do what we do, and we have a fun show. We like to jump around a lot and make funny faces."[25]

And where did McCoy see 12 Stones in the future?

"Hopefully in a recording studio or on a stage," replied the singer. "God willing, we'll make a career out of this and not disappear into the typical rock band kind of thing. But we've been having fun and we've enjoyed every minute. I hope I can still be doing something that I'm happy with."[26]

"It has been a dream of ours, individually and as a band," he added. "We always wanted to do this, so when the opportunity came along there was no question that we would take it."[27]

Like many other musicians of his generation, guitarist Weaver aimed to make his stand of faith in the center of the rock music culture of his day: "I think our message is for everyone. Our music is from our own personal experiences, but it can be related to by all walks of life."[28]

21

A New Hill

The by now familiar story played out in hundreds of episodes of VH-1's *Behind the Music* and in the lives of thousands of entertainers usually began with an entertainer achieving a dream only to find that a goal attained often led to despair, resentment, and substance abuse.

Other musicians chose a different path, however, turning to God and finding contentment that had eluded them. Lauryn Hill was one such artist. However, unlike many of the new crop of artists of faith who were stepping into the pop cultural limelight with a desire to communicate their passionate love for God, Hill was already an established music icon when her life was revolutionized by what seemed to be a sudden and transformative spiritual experience.

Like Dylan's famed conversion to Christianity in 1978 and Cat Stevens' commitment to Islam in the early '70s, Hill's conversion seemed to be both sudden and gradual. It was gradual because even before it she considered herself to be a Christian and sudden because it seemed to be an all-consuming experience that changed everything in her life, from the composition of her band and entourage to her recording plans. After Lauryn Hill met God nothing was the same.

Hill first entered the spotlight with her band The Fugees, recording a Grammy Award–winning record that included a remake of the classic Roberta Flack song "Killing Me Softly."

If selling 17 million records with The Fugees and acting in the film *Sister Act* weren't enough, Hill was ready for an encore with her solo outing *The Miseducation of Lauryn Hill*, which was a smash hit both critically and commercially. Praise for *Miseducation* and its creator was unequivocal. According to *Horizon* magazine:

> Her voice, husky at some moments, tender and light the next, evokes comparisons to Roberta Flack, Minnie Ripperton, and, yes, even Aretha Franklin. But to limit the analogies to soulful divas would do Lauryn Hill no justice. She possesses the spiritual yearnings of Donny Hathaway, Marvin Gaye's confessional blues, and the womanist assertions of Janis Joplin, Joni Mitchell, and Gloria Gaynor.
>
> *Miseducation* is an R&B album, in fact the best R&B album of the 1990s. But it is also a pop masterpiece because it transcends race, time, and genre. It will be remembered as a classic album, like The Beach Boys' *Pet Sounds* and Marvin Gaye's *What's Going On.*[1]

The Fugees' key players were Hill and Wyclef Jean and from the outset the group decided to defy stereotypes of what hip-hop could and couldn't do, should and shouldn't be:

> "We combined rap with hip-hop and all other musical genres," remembered Hill. "We founded a new musical language, a new universal language, something that everybody everywhere understands. Rap and hip-hop don't belong to the ghetto. We never liked the clichés of gangsta rap; that's sick! Soul never did any harm to any music. It was a time for new inventions. We took a little bit from every genre and invented something new."[2]

The group's members met while still in high school and worked hard to establish their own musical identity:

> "The Fugees were almost an overnight success," said Hill. "We were together at Columbia High School; that was in '88 or so. We changed our name a few times and ended up as The Fugees. Our beginnings were everything else than easy. Clef was our backbone who gave us the courage to pull through. He is very headstrong

and always pushed us in the right direction, made sure that we invested the little bit of money we didn't need for our lives in equipment. Without Clef and our strong belief in God, we would have never gotten that far!"[3]

The group's debut album met with lukewarm reviews, but by the time of the second release, the band was in high gear:

"It was quite a surprise that we got our break with the second album," remembered Hill, "but our first album was a stupid mistake by the record company. They tried to sell us as an alternative act—a big mistake. Unfortunately, they didn't ask us and just went ahead with it. If we would have had a say in it, it wouldn't have happened. We did things the way almost no other band did them, we had no fixed patterns and we avoided getting stuck in our roles in the band. That's one of the reasons why we swapped our instruments. Clef even thought about doing a live performance with an accordion. We wanted to surprise people. That is true hip-hop."[4]

A true genre-busting group, The Fugees not only sought to be liberated from traditional definitions of hip-hop, R&B, and rap, but also from the lyrical limitations that were placed upon artists working within that genre.

"For a while the genre seemed to be just about sex and crime," recalled Hill. "Rappers are storytellers; the stories don't need to be true. Fairy tales are also not true and a lot of rock singers who are happily married sing about broken hearts and love stories. So what? A good rap needs good rhymes and a big mouth. But it's wrong to see rappers just as criminals. A lot of them sing about it, true, but I don't really agree with it. Of course a lot of the guys don't know anything else, but also a lot of people just put it on to cash it in. I don't agree with it; it gives the kids the wrong example."[5]

Although Hill had always been spiritual in a generally Christian way, many Christians would have questioned the true nature of that faith, since it included Hill's living with her boyfriend Rohan Marley, the son of the legendary singer Bob Marley, and giving birth out of wedlock to a child named Zion. For Hill, the pressures that success brought began to catch up with her and she clearly began to feel that she was headed in the wrong direction, away from and not toward God:

> "I was just unhappy with my life," remembered the singer. "I had acquired everything I thought I wanted only to find out, 'this is it.' I ran very fast in the wrong direction."[6]

Hill's desire for truth was met by a mysterious messenger whom the singer refused to identify but who she credited with turning her life around and giving her a deep desire to know God. Hill stated:

> "I met somebody. That person had an understanding of the Bible like no one else I ever met in my life. I just sat at their feet and ingested pure Scripture for about a year. I started to see I was my worst enemy. I was the problem, my own self-image, who I thought I should be, as opposed to who I really was. I just ate it up. I started to see that my concept of spirituality was totally wrong. Real religion is no religion at all. Truth is the true covering and when I started to see that, two things happened. My creativity came back in an overflowing abundance and I got into direct confrontation with everybody I love."[7]

When asked the identity of the mystery man, Hill was cagey:

> It's a brother. I don't speak about him publicly, because he is a good friend of mine. He's not an ambitious person. He just shares and people want truth. I believe God will make a way and He is going to identify [the man].[8]

Hill's encounter with her mysterious spiritual mentor had left the young star sounding more like an evangelist than a rock star and had changed many things in the singer's life, especially the very notion of church and what her responsibilities were to those around her.

"It's like the pulpit. We think that's the church, but that's the wrong concept," said Hill. "Each one is supposed to pull someone else outta the pit. This brother shared with me, and now I share with my husband and he can share with somebody. That is how it is supposed to work. I saw somebody living what he was saying. It wasn't a bunch of jargon. His life was a living testimony of faith and of passion and systematic rebellion. Kind of like a herd of animals. That strong mother doesn't tell her cub, 'Son, stay weak so the wolves can get you.' She says, 'Toughen up, this is reality we are living in.' I went from an emotional, placating environment to 'Toughen up, Lauryn, confront those fears.'"[9]

A dramatic change had occurred in Hill's life, and the singer announced the new changes to her fans via the media in an equally dramatic way. To an MTV reporter she said:

> Now you are meeting another Lauryn, so it's good to be reintroduced. I am not running for social president anymore. I'm just trying to obey God and do my passion and tell everybody else that life is a waste if you ain't doing that. I think the Lauryn Hill of then was looking to be validated, hoping to be accepted. She was looking for acknowledgment from everybody except the One who made me. At this point, the things I am led to do are things that I know He wants me to do. I have inner peace after having done them. It's a different person. Just like everyone else, I wanted to be loved and be liked. So, a lot of my behavior was patterned to be acceptable to whatever the socially acceptable thing at the moment was.[10]

The changes in Hill's life so dramatically affected the rest of her life and career that some speculated that she had some kind of a breakdown, but the singer was defiant in her belief that she had been relieved of a burden that the rest of the world still carried:

> I don't know anybody that's not emotionally unstable or schizophrenic. People wake up, they have one mood, they have another mood. The only reason why it's looked at as crazy is because we have these images, these icons before us that are not reality. I'm saying, "Who told you that was the standard?"[11]

One who didn't share the popular industry perception of Hill as having gone off the deep end in response to the pressures of success was Cameron Strang, a twenty-four-year-old publishing executive who was one of the first to see Hill's new post–spiritual awakening show, which would eventually be released on CD.

Strang was no stranger to rock singers and spirituality, having published two books, *Walk On* and *Restless Pilgrim,* which had examined the spiritual journeys of U2 and Bob Dylan. Strang wrote movingly of his experience in an Orlando club where Hill performed unannounced:

> There she was, 15 feet in front of us, alone on a stage with nothing but a stool and her acoustic guitar. She wouldn't sing any of her old stuff, only new songs from an upcoming album. The music was awe-inspiring. She began the concert by telling the crowd that she chose to have no accompaniment because she wanted us to listen to the lyrics. Listen to what the songs were saying. Truly get them. And they didn't disappoint. The spiritual bent of her previous work pales in comparison to her new stuff. Every song she sung had overtly Christ-centered content. From "Jerusalem," which was nothing but beautifully interwoven Scripture, to songs sung from God to His children, to songs about righteousness, to the river of God, to freedom in Christ, on and on they went. "The road to hell is paved with good intentions," began the first song of the night. To answer her critics: "They don't know me, if they don't know my Father." I heard more truth in that club than I have in church in a long time. Last night I saw in living color what it means to be light in the darkness. Last night I stood within earshot of someone I deeply respect and admire, someone who will touch millions of lives through uncompromised lyrics and amazing music. She will give answers to people asking, 'God, where are you?' She will point people to a relationship with Christ."[12]

By the time the songs from that evening made it to CD, Hill's new material, compiled in *MTV Unplugged 2.0* and featuring thirteen songs interspersed with rambling comments by the singer, had garnered a mixture of cheers, jeers, and bewilderment.

"One incredibly potent albeit perplexing performance," observed *Billboard* magazine.

"This tender renegade purposefully does what she's gotta do to keep her music sacred," observed *Rolling Stone.* "The results are sometimes messy, but more often they're miraculous."[13]

Los Angeles Times reporter Robert Hilburn was predictably not as complimentary:

When Lauryn Hill asks, "What's going on?" during a song on her
new live album, she's trying to draw a parallel between the anxious
social consciousness in her new tunes and the classic strains of
the late Marvin Gaye. Puzzled listeners of Hill's disjointed new
album, however, may be asking themselves, "What's going on?"
in a less flattering way.[14]

"Everything about her current approach contrasts the Lauryn
Hill famous for The Fugees and *Miseducation*," observed *Relevant*
magazine. "She didn't dress up for the MTV special. She flubbed
chords and missed notes. She played without an entourage of
musical accompaniment and sucked on a lozenge to help her
hoarse voice. 'I used to be a performer and I really don't consider myself a performer anymore,' she said before beginning
her first song. Hill's songs tackle huge, universal themes. She
slips an explanation of the fall of humanity into 'Adam Lives in
Theory,' using language accessible to all her listeners, even those
outside the church."[15]

To those pop culture observers still trapped in a 1960s mind-
set of rebellion, which meant young rockers railing against a
conservative establishment, Hill was painting a new portrait of
what rebellion was all about. For her, rebellion was about aligning her desires with God's, her plans with His.

"I didn't understand the difference between rebellion against
God and rebellion against the system that's not God," said Hill.
"I'm a rebel in a sense that nobody's going to force me to do
something against my will. What do I owe anybody that I should
submit my will to them? I mean, I'm not a fool. God teaches me
about reality, so when He tells me to do something, I do something, not because somebody told me to. It's because I'm led to.
I wouldn't try to put myself in a box or put God in a box. I just
know where He has me right now is a brand new and totally
refreshing place. I just feel good about being real. I hope that by
people seeing the result of freedom that they'll want some, too.
It was never about me. It was never about the person."[16]

Hill imagined a new movement of artists, inspired by God,
living healthy lives and sending messages of faith out to a pop
culture in need of faith and inspiration:

"I want to be a part of this new class of artists who don't have to fall apart to be dope," she observed. "I would rather not chronicle my demise. I would like to maintain a healthy, stable lifestyle. When you're young and everything dramatic is exciting, you start to believe that hype that, in order to be an artist, you have to suffer. I've graduated from that school."[17]

Yet, as one who had recently been blinded by the light, Hill still had the wisdom and self-awareness to realize that she could not impose the light on others. Still, the world had only gotten a taste of Hill's new revelations and she seemed unwilling to exit stage right and disappear into Christian America. As the Lauryn Hill story played out, millions of fans would know for sure whether Hill's revelation was a momentary lapse of emotional judgment or a life-changing spiritual revelation:

"Everybody has a choice," said the singer. "There was one song in which I said, 'Choose well.' I am not here to shove my light down everybody's throat. The people who want it are the only people I am concerned about. For those who don't want it, I have nothing to defend."[18]

22
A Lion's Roar

One of the most surprising things quickly learned by many devout young artists who made their way into the mainstream music market was that non-Christians would usually embrace or at least tolerate their music even when it was known that they were devout Christians and that their music was not going to ignore that faith.

Such was the case with a young artist named David Bazan, who recorded with his band under the name Pedro the Lion—a name that Bazan first thought up when he was thinking of writing a children's book of the same name. Despite being known as a Christian, Bazan and his band developed a strong following among people who liked his music but didn't necessarily share his faith—not yet anyway.

"Whenever I mention my new passion for Pedro to people, they frequently say, You know they're Christian, don't you? And so they are," noted one such fan. "Me, I can count the times I went to church in my life on one, maybe two hands. But I don't really care. I like the music, and that's what matters. Perhaps if Bazan was writing songs that were blatantly evangelical, it might not do it for me, but apart from some of his earlier stuff, the songs are more morality tales than they are attempts to convert. But at the same time, I feel a strong sense of spirit communicated through the music. And I like that. In fact, I would postulate that spirit and mystery in music is truly what separates good music from bad. It makes the music transcend and if that spirit is in the music, it is that much more universal."[1]

This was exactly what, for years, leaders of the Christian music industry and Christian separatists in general had maintained could never happen. Taking Jesus' words geared toward those who would suffer persecution for their faith out of context, many leaders told young Christians that their work would simply never be accepted outside of the Christian world because of their embrace of Christ as the only path to salvation. But what artists like Bazan were learning was that persecution was not inevitable, especially when it came to art—and that depended a great deal on the manner in which the work was presented.

Bazan signed early on with the Christian-owned indie label Tooth & Nail where he released an EP before signing with several other indies and releasing more albums. Eventually, Pedro made a strong impression on the indie scene with its record *Winners Never Quit,* released on the Jade label. Bazan grew up in a musically inclined family and his love for music extended to school as well:

> My family is extremely musical. I have been singing and playing some instrument since I was five or six. It was a pretty natural thing, recalled the singer. In high school, I tried to play as much music as possible. Junior and senior years I was in at least four music classes every day. That laid a good foundation for what I am doing now and proved to me that I enjoy it.[2]

Faith was also an important part of Bazan's early years:

> "I grew up in a Protestant home. My Dad was a music pastor at the church," recalled Bazan. "Until sixth grade I went to a Christian school that was part of the church we went to. My Dad being a music pastor, we were most definitely lower middle-class, maybe on the edge of upper lower-class. I liked a lot of what the other kids liked—riding bikes, building, digging, transformers and Lego's."[3]

Like many children of devout Christians who were trying to come to terms with rock music, young Bazan's listening habits were strictly monitored and led to a worldview that saw music as strictly utilitarian, that is valued only for what it could accomplish:

> I grew up only being allowed to listen to Christian music. I think 1991 was the first time that I really owned records that weren't specifically Christian. That's when I started owning Fugazi records and U2 and things. So I grew up with this really weird view of art. I was always hearing comments like, "It sounds to me like the message is getting lost in the music." It was something that was really hard for me to shake for a number of years. Not to mention that it was confused with my own understanding of faith. I often got confused by the fact that I felt a really strong belief in God and Jesus and I would often confuse that with the pressure to include evangelical material in the lyrics. Since then I've been able to realize the true nature of art and where it's at its best and I think that I'm now able to just shoot for that. Not really having tipped the iceberg yet, but I feel that I'm more satisfied with the process of writing and I don't feel encumbered by that old view.[4]

Bazan's art was also influenced not just by his upbringing but also by his personality, something that came through when he was young:

> Ever since I was a little kid, I have been very social. If I felt like I was connected to and approved by a group of friends then I felt good. On the other hand if I felt alienated from whoever it was, then I was bummed. Since I was always pretty well liked it was never that big of a problem. But there was always that fear of disapproval. As an artist who exists first and foremost within a small community of people, my music is affected more than I would like to admit by what certain people think. I am uncomfortable with that and it is a struggle. Dealing with that has been tricky.[5]

As Bazan and Pedro the Lion began to gain a following in mainstream music circles, Bazan was faced with the inevitable questions that most bands like his faced. In Bazan's case, perhaps seeing all the denials of being a "Christian band" by so many other bands, he seemed to give up on the idea of fighting the labeling that so many in mainstream circles sought to do.

181

"I am born again, but I think that that sort of pretense is very destructive to art," said Bazan. "People often call us a Christian band though and I don't argue with them because it seems just as pretentious to insist on not being called Christian as it is to insist on being called Christian. I hope that by maintaining this stance on this and other labeling issues that true creativity will thrive."[6]

Still, there were pockets of extreme secularists who simply could not stomach the fact that bands like Pedro the Lion were being "allowed" to record for mainstream labels.

"The label that distributes Made in Mexico distributes some records through K records," observed Bazan. "One of the guys in Behead the Prophet works at K records. When he found out that we were on the label that they distributed, he called up Ben [Swanson] and just ripped him a new one for an hour. He was just like . . . 'I can't believe you have this F-ing Christian band on your thing' and he just went off on him. . . . I just think there are those people who are prejudiced and ignorant and I'm not really playing to them anyway. I think that art is best realized when it's consumed by thinking people and not by prejudiced people, although we are all prejudiced, but when the prejudice doesn't come in as heavily in a negative sense to appreciating the art."[7]

Bazan's other encounter with intolerance, a trait usually attributed by the mainstream culture to Christians, was related to the abortion issue and the perception on the part of some that Bazan and Pedro were linked to anti-abortion groups. Although Bazan was opposed to abortion (though perhaps unwilling to regulate it by government decree), he was more concerned that in the minds of many in the mainstream culture the basic gospel message was being subordinated to a political agenda instead of the core doctrines of the faith:

> "I think it's totally tragic and wrong, but people need to be convinced of that themselves," said Bazan of abortion. "Legislation convinces no one. People have associated us with things . . . baggage that goes along with Christianity. I'm not ashamed of Jesus in that way, but I am ashamed of Christianity sometimes and Christians. So that's the only time that it ever really comes up."[8]

In Bazan's view, one articulated more fully by the late philosopher C. S. Lewis, there was great danger in Christians linking too closely with any worldly causes since doing so would take the focus off of the central tenet of the Christian faith—God's plan to bring redemption to the human race through His Son, Jesus, and instead cause people to turn away from that to collateral ones:

"It seems from what my understandings were growing up, that a lot of people are missing the Gospel and it's having an effect on things in a negative way," said Bazan. "The Gospel not being: if you ask Jesus into your heart then you're going to heaven, but God's plan of redemption being what the whole Bible is about from cover to cover. When Adam and Eve sinned He began putting the plan into motion. He knew what He was going to do, it was the longing of His heart from the beginning to send His Son back for us and what that means after the Gospels themselves and Paul's writings and in John's writings. That's the Gospel that we are saved by grace alone through faith alone. It's real simple, I mean a lot of people would assent to it, but then they live their lives differently. That's the only thing that I would really be able to say for sure . . . is that I think a lot of people are missing the Gospel. I grew up having missed the Gospel and it caused some problems, but it took me a while of digging on my own. I didn't hear about it in church the first time. I heard about it through God's word, reading it, and through some books I found in a bookstore. From what I see and what I read and what I hear of the state of Christian culture at large, it seems like a lot of people are missing the Gospel."[9]

Whether they realized it or not, by enjoying Bazan's music, his fans were also getting a glimpse of that gospel:

"Call them parables, if you will," noted one reviewer of Bazan's work with Pedro. "The first song on the CD, 'Slow And Steady Wins The Race,' directly addresses faith and its rewards, as the narrator sings about his devotion to all that is good, while his brother takes a darker path through life. Thanks to his good deeds, he believes that he'll be greeted warmly in heaven with the rest of the deserved few."[10]

Bazan then threw his listeners an unexpected curveball:

"The guy who stays on the straight and narrow represents the typical Christian viewpoint," he noted. "Do what's right at all costs. It produces people who think they're righteous and are going to heaven and the Bible's very clear that no one is good or can earn their way because our hearts are dark. The only hope we have is in the record and performance of a different person who's willing to let us take it all on ourselves."[11]

Although a product of evangelical Christianity, Bazan was critical of elements of that subculture and more specifically of its reactions to popular culture:

"Everyone is so closed to everything," he said of fellow Christians. "If He's real and is a real force in my heart or life, I don't have to be closed to anything. I would be the first in line to watch *The Last Temptation of Christ*. It was an utterly boring movie, but it wasn't offensive. If He's God, why would He care about a movie? It's absurd, but that's the way a lot of Christians think. They try to close themselves off to experience. If they're that easily contaminated, then He isn't real to them anyway, He's removed and aloof. If He were real to you, there would be nothing to be afraid of."[12]

Bazan's objections to some of the practices of modern Christendom extend to unlikely issues like a lack of forgiveness among churchgoers, citing the experience of a fellow church member who wasn't allowed to care for children because of molestation in his past, before he had a spiritual transformation:

Freely forgiving doesn't really achieve control the same way that holding it against somebody else does. You lose a lot of control over people when you forgive them. I think that's part of the reason why people are still committed to certain religions. It offers a person an element of control in their life that they wouldn't have over people otherwise. That's human nature. It's sick and unfortunate. But, I think we all have a tendency toward that. . . . Actually it's pretty clear in the Bible that those sort of people, which we are all susceptible to, but those people will spend eternity in hell, contrary to what they think, so that's what it's about.[13]

Bazan's distrust of things Christian extended to the Christian music industry, which he had already expressed his feelings for by signing with mainstream indie labels:

> "Christian rock turns the music and the message into crap," he explained. "The message is degraded when it's made into slogans and low-level propaganda. They're attempting to reach a certain audience just like advertisers do—and that, ultimately, degrades the art."[14]

Still, despite attempts to distance himself from all that he perceived to be wrong with modern American expressions of the Christian faith, it was clear from Bazan's words and from Pedro the Lion's music, that Bazan was a believer who sought to communicate his faith to his fans. As such, he was part of a larger movement that was often made up of the children of serious Christians who refused to reject their parents' faith, yet sought to "evangelize" in a way that would not force them from the marketplace of ideas. Rather than shouting from a street corner, these artists sought to be a part of Mars Hill, a safe place akin to the one visited by the apostle Paul, where many voices were heard from, including the Christian voice of Paul. Bazan observed:

> We get to play for a lot of non-Christian people. They're hurting . . . and we don't want to preach at them or anything but we just want them to know that there's a way not to be full of pain all the time. And there is a way and it's really simple. It's interesting because there is no one that's as blatant as we sometimes are about the Gospel, but we've tried to do it in a palatable way that's not offensive, but it's still kind of offensive to some people, even some Christians that are kind of halfway.[15]

Ultimately, Bazan credited God with moving in ways unforeseen, in and through his music:

> If there's anything that's moving about the band, then it's Jesus and it's not us. Our responsibility is to do our best with what we have and then let Him move through us. It's really cool when it's like that because then the pressure is off you. It's not our responsibility to move people but He does it, every show that we play.[16]

To a confused and mixed up Gen X and Y culture seeking love and truth, Bazan and Pedro the Lion's message was clear and concise: "If you think you're good and you're proud of it you will be very, very sorry one day," he said. "If you're a total mess and you're sorry and you don't know what to do about it, then there's hope."[17]

Although he believed that he had the ultimate answer to life's problems, Bazan knew the importance of first asking the questions. Asked what motivated him to create music, the singer replied: "This overwhelming sense that something is missing."[18]

Church Boy

In the mid '90s singer Kirk Franklin rocked the music business when from seemingly out of nowhere he emerged on the charts with his debut record. Recorded for the tiny Inglewood, California-based label Gospocentric, Franklin's unexpected success catapulted him to the top of the gospel/R&B scene. But Franklin's music was tough to categorize. It sounded like R&B, and Franklin had the sex appeal of Teddy Pendergrass and Al Green, but the lyrics were focused on spiritual messages, and rather orthodox biblical ones at that.

Of course the combination of R&B and gospel was not Franklin's invention at all. Numerous artists like Andraè Crouch had married biblically based messages with hot R&B grooves for years, although mostly within the Christian music industry. But Franklin's rocket-like debut and Gospocentric's determination to get him heard by the mainstream music industry *was* something new, and fans flocked to pick up Franklin's records and see his shows.

Franklin got his start early in the church:

> My first job was a minister of music at a church when I was 11 and what I learned from it was they had no business putting an 11-year-old in the position of minister of music. I was teaching

senior choirs and youth choirs. Can you imagine at 11 years old
telling a 65-year-old woman she's singing wrong?[1]

Such responsibility at a young age did not keep the future
superstar out of trouble, however. Franklin admits:

> I was doing wrong while I was in church. I was in church all my
> life, but that didn't keep me away from drugs, alcohol, sex, just
> whatever you want to name.[2]
>
> I tried to smoke and drink and do all those things. But I was
> still weird with it, it was like trying to wear some shoes that didn't
> fit. I was trying hard to wear them.[3]

What turned Franklin's life around, however, was the realization that life was short and fragile.

"I had a friend get killed when I was 15," recalled Franklin.
"He got shot in a strange way. He wasn't doing anything wrong.
He was just digging in his mother's closet and a gun fell out and
shot him and killed him. I'd been in church all my life, I'd been
hearing about heaven and hell all my life—and when you're
young you never had anyone close to your age die, especially
get killed. It does something to you. That was when I made that
choice that summer in my Momma's den; I accepted Jesus as
my personal Savior."[4]

Though reared in the church, Franklin's musical tastes weren't
strictly limited to gospel. Unlike previous generations of black
artists reared in the church, Franklin seemed to recognize gospel not as a musical genre, but rather as a topic that could be
married with any type of music. He also spent most of his time
listening to R&B instead of gospel:

> "I really wasn't influenced by gospel music," the singer candidly
> admitted. "I've always had an urban ear, because that's what I
> was listening to. I really didn't get involved in gospel music until I
> became a teenager. I will never forget playing at this white church,
> I was about ten, and will never forget this program they were
> having. This lady that my mother used to clean house for, she
> was a Christian and when the white lady knew I could play, she
> wanted me to be on this program they were having at this huge
> white church. I was the special guest. I will never forget people
> saying, 'Boy, you are going to be the next Andraè Crouch,' and I

didn't even know who that was! I was ten years old and I didn't even know who they were talking about!"[5]

Franklin may have been unaware of legends like Crouch, but plenty of people were taking notice of Franklin and his penchant for marrying R&B rhythms with spiritually informed lyrics.

"When I started doing gospel music secular people would come to the concerts and say, 'man the kind of music that you're doing is the kind of music I wanted to do but the church wouldn't let me do it.' For me, it wasn't a thought-out plan 'you know what? I'm going to take urban styles and put Jesus on it!' It wasn't that."[6]

But that's exactly what the budding artist began to do, mixing R&B sensibilities and orthodox Christian-themed lyrics. In so doing, Franklin managed to pull off what Al Green had only hinted at in his post-conversion albums. After Green's dramatic conversion to Christianity in 1973, he had tried to continue to produce R&B albums but with Christian-themed lyrics instead of the sexy lyrics his fans had become accustomed to. While stellar albums like *The Belle Album* and *Full of Fire* were strong musically, they seemed to fall into a no man's land in between the traditional gospel world, which wanted more explicit gospel-oriented songs, and the R&B world, which didn't want sermonizing of any kind. Unsure of which direction to go, Green settled in for nearly a decade-long run of making hymn records.

But Franklin wasn't about to go that route. Part of the new course he would chart, making music that reflected his faith but relevant enough for teenagers raised in the inner city, grew out of his own childhood when he remembered it being very uncool to be a follower of Christ:

"As a young black ghetto boy, brought up in the '70s and '80s, being a Christian wasn't 'in', like being a Christian is in now," remembered the singer. "You know what I'm saying? I mean, you've got the WWJD bracelets, the fish and the cool T-shirts now, but in the '70s and '80s we didn't have all that. There was nothing cool about being a Christian. It was very whack."[7]

Eventually Franklin's music came to the attention of an entrepreneurial couple named Claude and Vicki Latillade who believed in the young singer enough to launch their own label and release Franklin's first record. As Franklin's music connected with more and more fans, the couple launched another label, B-Rite, and signed a distribution agreement with Interscope Records president Jimmy Iovine. Iovine had garnered his share of critics for launching the careers of some of the most offensive acts in rock and rap history, but with Franklin he saw a way to make money and spread positive messages throughout the culture, beginning with a record by a new group that Franklin had assembled—the record was called *God's Property*.

Franklin and Iovine hit pure gold with the smash single "Stomp," a song that channeled R&B and hip-hop grooves into praise to God but did it in a way that would also sustain the attention of the most prolific sinner. It seemed that in Franklin, the potential that many had seen in Al Green, Andraè Crouch, and BeBe Winans had all been realized, for the singer refused to compromise either his beliefs or his commitment to creating funky R&B that would attract nonbelievers.

On the song "Lean on Me" Franklin enlisted the help of U2 frontman Bono, a move arranged courtesy of Iovine. Franklin had first heard U2's landmark *The Joshua Tree* album when he was sixteen and had long admired the singer.

"I asked Jimmy Iovine if I could sing with Bono, and he said 'Yeah,'" Franklin explained. "I said, 'Are you serious? Can you hook me up?' So he called Bono and Bono said he'd love to do it. So I flew over to Ireland. I don't even remember what studio it was. I didn't sleep. But it was quick. I tracked him and we shot some video footage. Then I left. And I was back home the next day for my daughter's birthday. Bono's a nice guy, a very spiritual guy. I asked him how things were going, and he talked to me about the 'Pop Mart' tour. He said one of the shows didn't turn out as big as they wanted it to, and I'm lookin' at him and goin,' 'You're kidding!' And then he mentioned something about *Pop* only selling seven or nine million units! I thought, 'man!'"[8]

With the collaboration with Bono and several hit records under his belt, Franklin seemed to be sitting on top of the world, but part of that world would come crashing down when the singer found himself embroiled in a series of lawsuits—both

190

with distribution companies and fellow group members who thought they deserved a bigger share of the collective pie.

"With the first lawsuit, it was easy for the public to say 'aw, Kirk helped those kids and now those kids are trippin' because of the money,'" he recalled. "But when the second lawsuit hit, the people began to say, 'Now wait a minute. What's going on with Kirk?' In the eyes of many I was guilty. You start doubting yourself in every area."[9]

Although both lawsuits were eventually settled, the experience was a humbling one for Franklin and would be followed by more setbacks, including the failure of a planned sitcom.

"I shot a pilot and it was a real painful experience and I just kind of left it alone," remembered Franklin. "I was out of my element, people kind of hyped me up and made some promises and blew things up real big—and you look and it's over. They've dropped you and nobody calls to see if you hurt yourself when you fell. The whole business of Hollywood and my faith are built on totally different principles. It really knocked me on my knees. There I was, a church boy who got a chance to be in Hollywood. The church didn't prepare me. You know, what we do is supposed to be for the glory of God, and when you get in that world and your flesh is like [turned] on ten, that world is a flesh feeder."[10]

The experiences humbled Franklin and reminded him of the travails of the biblical figure Job: "I like Job's story because of how God broke him down, and there were times that he probably didn't even know if he was gonna get out of that struggle," recalled the singer. "It was crazy what he had to go through, but to still be able to bless God and to be able to say, 'though He slay me, yet will I trust Him.'"[11]

He added, "This season of testing has shown me a God that I never knew just like Job says in that last chapter when God gave him everything he lost back and even more, Job, who had been a servant of God all his life, said, 'before this, my ears had only heard of You, but now my eyes have seen You.'"[12]

Franklin's career in music had stalled a bit and his television career had hit the skids when he decided to take a personal inventory. What he discovered was an addiction to pornography that had followed him throughout his life, a pattern that hadn't been taken seriously even by religious leaders throughout his life. As a teenager, Franklin had gone for help only to be waved off:

> "The pastor said, 'Ah, boy, you're young. You'll grow out of it,'" remembered Franklin. "But I never grew out of it. I grew into it. When I was 17 I had a child out of wedlock. After I got married, I told my wife. I sat her down one day and I shared with her my struggle with pornography. For years I'd go to great pastors that I really looked up to, even after I'd done an album, going to them crying, letting them know that I had this problem. But all I'd get was some oil, somebody laying hands on me, trying to lay me out on the floor, and that's not going to fix that problem."[13]

Meeting a pastor who understood Franklin's problems began to turn the singer's life around:

> "God started really giving me victory in the area of pornography," he said. "I began to be discipled, and my pastor started talking about how we have the mind of Christ and those [impure] thoughts are not my thoughts. I said, 'What?' It was Greek to me—Tony Evans talking about how it's not me, but Christ living in me. I had read that Scripture before, but I had never had anyone tell me that before, that I'm a dead man walking."[14]

Although addictions like Franklin's weren't always cured overnight, Franklin found in his mentors a way out of the porn trap:

> "What I try to do more than anything is be very honest and very transparent, whether it's about the pornography or girls or whatever because I came from a very promiscuous lifestyle, just trying to find love the sex way. So I try to talk about those things and be open about the mistakes I've made."[15]

A truth that seemed to liberate Franklin was the realization that came upon him (one which seemed to elude many performers) that his self-worth needed to be rooted not in what he did but rather in who he was:

> "For the first time I know who I am and it's not who I always thought," confessed the singer. "Music is not who I am; music is what I do. I am a fully loved child of God not because of what I

do but because of what Jesus did and I am who I am in Him by nothing I could ever do. It's a revolutionary truth to know that God wants me more than He wants my gift. I've learned to understand that it was all part of a bigger plan—the plan was God breaking me. I couldn't have made it through this season if not for the discipleship, the teaching and the humbleness, what God has allowed me to go through."[16]

For Christians like Franklin who believed that a war was constantly being waged between forces of good and evil, constant vigilance and reliance on God's power were of the utmost importance:

"Total dependence on Christ, just total, total, total dependence on Christ," said Franklin when asked his secret for living, "because I know, like Jesus told Peter, 'the devil would desire to sift you as wheat.' I know that the devil is not happy with Christ still being preached, whoever He's being preached by. Whatever messenger, he's going to have tribulation. Because of that, the need is Christ. If you go buy a car to satisfy a certain need or you go buy certain clothes, or go outside your marital covenant or whatever it is, [you] will always come to a point of emptiness. Always. And you will always come to a point of total dependency on Christ."[17]

It was a mind-set that continually reminded Franklin how he got where he was and kept him humble and grateful:

"The Lord reminds me that when I try to be self-sufficient," said Franklin. "He lets me know that 'where you're at, I did it. I put you there! I don't need your help.' I have been guilty of that. But I have to constantly die to myself so I can look at the truth that it's God that opens up doors and does this and does that and I just try to make it happen on my own."[18]

In 2002 Franklin released *The Rebirth of Kirk Franklin*, another smash hit record that, while not containing a smash single à la "Stomp," nonetheless debuted at #4 on *Billboard*'s pop album chart and saw success in multiple formats. A few months later Franklin received a vivid reminder of the dangerous path he had once walked when his friend R Kelly, who had once sung a duet with Franklin on one of his hit songs, was arrested on charges of sex with a minor.

The world of popular music had often proved to be an inhospitable place for devout young men and women of faith, and the temptations of the flesh had dragged many down. But the response of many believers, to leave the world behind and record and tour in a parallel religious universe, though perhaps a comforting and comfortable choice, had left pop culture devoid of their values. Artists like Franklin had begun to reverse that trend, to stand tall for their faith in the midst of pop culture. Still, having tasted a bit of that success, Franklin seemed to be on guard, eager for more exposure because of the impact it allowed him to have, but wary of its trappings:

"Success can be such a tool *for* ministry, but yet it can be a trap *from* ministry," he said. "It can be painful. It can make you lose focus. It can become another god. It has so many challenges. At the same time, it can put you up in front of thousands of people to be a witness, but then you walk off the stage and there are some people in the audience that are trying to create another Baal. And you're the one."[19]

24

Carrabba's Confession

In 2002 from seemingly out of nowhere came a young, Florida-based artist named Chris Carrabba who went by the moniker Dashboard Confessional, showing up on MTV2 and playing for thousands of fans across the country. But as with most stories of "overnight successes," Carrabba was no overnight success. His previous band, Further Seems Forever had garnered international attention when it signed to the Tooth & Nail label. When the mainstream indie label Vagrant signed Dashboard Confessional, Carrabba's career was off and running. Carrabba was another in a series of young, new artists of faith who were finding mainstream success. Although Dashboard's music rarely referenced spiritual issues directly, the music was nonetheless always colored by Carrabba's Christian-oriented worldview. The singer, who later made Florida his home, had roots in other parts:

> "I grew up in the Northeast. I lived in Connecticut until I was 16 and then my Mom, my brother and my step-Dad moved to Florida," recalled Carrabba. "That's where I've been ever since. I've got an older stepbrother who might as well be my real brother, a younger brother, and a much younger sister. We are all really close. I'm really proud of them. They're really good people."[1]

Reflecting on his childhood, Carrabba remembered the early influences on his life:

"It was a lot of skateboarding, and a lot of time imitating my brother and stepbrother," he remembered. "I suppose it was pretty cool. I went through some rough times in high school so I sort of lashed out one year. I skipped a lot and went skateboarding. I suppose that's my big 'checkered past'—skipping school to go skateboarding. That's a testament though, it was a lot better than skipping school to do drugs. For a while I wasn't doing that hot in school, then my family life started straightening out and I realized it was sort of silly to be doing so bad."[2]

Carrabba grew up in a musical home that encouraged him in the direction that would eventually lead him to the music business. In particular, Carrabba's mother played a strong role in her son's future career:

"She is a musician herself, not professional, but she's very talented," said Carrabba. "She recognized whatever gifts I was given and encouraged them—not only just music, but especially when it came to music. I remember when we were kids, my little brother and I would collect the popcorn buckets and we'd have popcorn bucket drum sets. Most kids were playing cops and robbers, but I was playing 'band,' so I was kind of a geek I guess. I was sort of singing as long as I can remember. I was in chorus growing up, mostly because I thought it would be easy and I could get a good grade. But I really didn't learn anything, which is a shame, because I could have used a lot of what was there for free—an expert to learn from. I did pay attention, but I just kind of goofed off a lot. I was the class idiot."[3]

But a present from a relative caused Carrabba to think more seriously about music . . . eventually:

"My uncle gave me an acoustic guitar when I was 15, which I was pretty stoked about," remembered Carrabba, "but I was busy skateboarding so it wasn't until years later that I really focused on it."[4]

Still, Carrabba's fledgling career wasn't enough to keep him from going on to college at Florida Atlantic University where he majored in education and eventually went to work as an elementary school administrator.

But music was never far from Carrabba's mind, and before long he was involved with a local group, which led to working with several other bands:

> "I used to be in a band called The Vacant Andy's and I used to play guitar and sing, so that's second nature to me," remembered the singer. "So it took me awhile with Further Seems Forever to figure out how to just sing. I was missing guitar and I went and played in this band called The Agency for a record just to help them out and I got the bug back. Also, the reason I got into Further Seems Forever was because when I was in The Vacant Andy's and we went on tour with A Newfound Glory; right before we left I had these three acoustic songs I had taped and I gave them to Chad [of Further Seems Forever] and he was way into it and that's how I got the Further Seems Forever gig."[5]

After one record with Further Seems Forever, Carrabba decided to strike out on his own with his own band and Dashboard Confessional was born.

"I was talked into it," recalled Carrabba. "That tape I made I did in one night in the studio when I had two free hours and I wrote the songs in a half hour and recorded three songs that night. I made one tape, but somehow hundreds of kids have copies and they always wrote asking when was I going to put something else out."[6]

But before he could sign a record deal, Carrabba needed a name and his first stab at the band name game was "Four-Thirty Airborne":

> "Steve, our drummer, worked at Airborne which is a courier service," recalled Carrabba, "and he had to wake up every morning at 4:30 and so we couldn't practice past 7 P.M. at night, but none of us got out of work until 6:15, so we were racing to practice for 15 minutes so we were going to call ourselves Four-Thirty Airborne at first. But then there are so many 'plane' bands out now and we never really loved the name."[7]

Looking for a name that would explain in a stronger way the music he intended to create, Carrabba came up with Dashboard Confessional:

"The name was born out of one of the songs I had written," recalled Carrabba. "I knew I didn't want to call it Chris Carrabba because it felt a little exclusive. I was leaving out all of the kids I knew were going to be a part of the show, although at that point I didn't think it was going to be more than my few friends that would come. Basically, I wrote a song that turned out to be 'The Sharp Hint of New Tears,' and there's a line that says 'On the way home this car hears my confessions' and Dashboard Confessional just popped up in my head and I thought 'Wow. What a great name for a band that would be, maybe I should start another band.'"[8]

For Carrabba, forming a new band was almost like therapy, for the writing of the songs that would comprise the record essentially came to him as a result of observing things around him:

"Essentially what Dashboard Confessional started out as, for me, was a diary," he recalled. "I don't really keep a diary, I write songs. Had I something to get out of my system—that's what I'd do. I'd write a song about it. So, if there's some passion in there, it's because those are things that I have dealt with or am dealing with and I have strong feelings about. I'm glad people are noticing it's honest, 'cause it is."[9]

When Carrabba first contemplated starting a new band, his plan was to have a band that followed an open-door policy for band members:

"The plan when I did Dashboard was, okay, I'm with this band Further that I love and creativity-wise it's the most original thing I've been involved with," he remembered, "but I missed playing with my friends. That's why I didn't call it Chris Carrabba. I called it Dashboard Confessional so I could keep a revolving door policy. I always planned it to change and change and change and I do think it's going to be a band at some point."[10]

Signing with Vagrant, Dashboard's album *The Places You Have Come to Fear the Most* was released in 2001 and quickly sold 50,000 units. In many circles, Dashboard Confessional had become the band to watch.

Carrabba's faith, though not necessarily front and center in his music, was something that he came to later in life and was, ironically enough, something he was attracted to because of many friends who strongly opposed the Christian faith:

> "I wasn't raised that way. I'm a fairly new Christian," he said. "I went through some personal family tragedy and I started getting interested because I had some friends that were so against it. I didn't really know anybody, except for the guys in Strong Arm, but I wasn't really close to them. With some of my friends being so against it, it made me curious about it and it just all made so much sense to me from the beginning. Then I started to kind of fall away from it for a little bit. Then there was a family tragedy and after it was over I realized that I hadn't killed myself, or lost my mind and no one in my family had either. There was no gigantic backlash from this, even though to me logically, there should have been some sort of fall out. I just attributed that all to God."[11]

To an interviewer wondering about Carrabba's spiritual orientation, who asked "are you Christian?" the singer was forthright: "I am." Although he was quick to add: "I'm not a minister—my music's not a ministry, because that's not my calling."[12]

Carrabba's calling was, in fact, not necessarily writing about his faith, but writing about life that included aspects of his faith and how it colored everything else when the world was viewed through his lens:

> "I don't really have an agenda when I write, I just write," said Carrabba. "I don't think too much about where it's coming from. There are a few songs that are definitely my personal experiences, but one other song for instance, is written about a friend's situation. It was an experiment—can I do this, can I write through someone else's eyes? The funny part is that there are a lot of songs on there not about girls at all and have nothing to do with romantic relationships, but I guess it's my writing style. There's one song that everybody is like 'That's so romantic, what girl is it about?' And I'm like, 'Man, that song is about the worst day of my life and it has nothing to do with a girl at all.'"[13]
>
> "It's a therapeutic process," he added, "a diary, and that is different than Further, because I could write songs that weren't so

literally from a feeling I had directly. But it seems like that's how all this started. I've felt better than ever since I've started all this. I think I'd be a miserable person if I didn't have all this. I think I would never be fun, or funny, or good company."[14]

Whether he had an explicit agenda or not, Carrabba's lyrics were colored by his increasingly strong convictions, especially on the issue of peer pressure:

"Kids think of what's true to them last," said Carrabba. "Even if you're young at 21 or 25 or 15, you do grow out of that and you get to look back on your past and say 'I knew that wasn't true to me,' or 'It wasn't what I should have been doing, but I did it anyway.' I'm not saying to do what I'm doing, or what your Mom or Dad are, but I just feel you should be true to yourself. You have to face yourself. At the end of the day, you've got to look in the mirror and say, 'Did I succumb to this peer pressure or did I do what I believe was right?'"[15]

Carrabba seemed to be overflowing with love for his craft and, unlike some artists who took their audiences and their jobs for granted, seemed genuinely grateful for the chance to make a living playing music:

"I love music, and I do love playing it," he observed. "I love it enough to get up there in spite of the fact that it scares me so badly—and it does scare me so badly. I don't think it's getting any less scary, but I'm so used to feeling scared that at least the shock part of it is wearing off. I still feel scared, but just not quite as in shock."[16]

While some artists record songs written by others or seek to distance themselves from the songs they've written, Carrabba's emotions were front and center in his music and he made no attempts to distance himself from his work.

"Some days it's easier than others [to share private emotions]," said Carrabba, "but mostly, it's pretty hard to get to that place and let that out, so seemingly carelessly, but that's what I do."[17]

Of his frame of mind while he was writing his last album, Carrabba observed:

I don't think it's much different. I think I was still in the same place; I am still in the same place. It was a different time, so I was feeling a little differently about things and that came out in my writing. I was feeling a little more introspective, self-critical. I like to think my writing matures as it goes along.[18]

More than anything else, Carrabba seemed to trust his music to go where it needed to go and do what it needed to do. As such, he was hesitant about giving away the meanings he personally held for songs that he wrote, hoping that the music itself would be used to move each individual in unique ways:

"I'm not going to say, because I'd rather let people hear whatever they need to hear out of the tunes," he said when asked about specific meanings for his songs. "Whatever it means to them is more important than what it means to me."[19]

Carrabba was, in the parlance of the faithful, a "baby Christian," that is, a young man in need of seasoning and growth in his faith, and, it might be argued, the life of a rock star was not the best place to begin a life of discipline that the Christian faith demanded. Nevertheless, Carrabba, through the influence of friends and mentors, seemed intent on standing tall as a man of faith and rock & roll:

"I had never really realized that before, how much you need other Christians," said the singer. "I'm kind of a loner by nature, so that was a lesson I needed to learn. This past year and a half, God taught me that."[20]

25
Under the Radar

No serious look at the intersection of rock music and religious devotion would be complete without a look at the band that in many ways pioneered the idea that rock music that glorified God could be done for a mainstream audience. For two decades U2 had quietly done what bands like Creed, P.O.D., and others had begun to do only recently. Yet it was an arduous and tortured journey that found the band alienating many fellow Christians, especially in the United States.

Although U2 had successfully survived and indeed thrived in the mainstream entertainment industry, many believed they did so only because they were willing to submerge strong and devout statements of faith and devotion and instead write songs that were vague at best, avoiding whenever possible direct references to God that would alienate non-Christian fans. Were they a band to be emulated by a new crop of devout artists, or were they the example to be avoided? Those were the questions for many.

If Bono, The Edge, and Larry Mullen Jr. (the three Christian members of U2) were undercover agents in God's army, it would be argued by critics that they were so successful that few of their fans really knew where they stood when it came to their faith.

Just as Bruce Springsteen's epic song "Born in the USA" was hijacked by Republicans and turned into a jingoistic song that hardly represented Springsteen's intentions when he wrote it, so U2 was often misinterpreted and misunderstood.

This was best illustrated by a story recounted in Steve Stockman's book *Walk On: The Spiritual Journey of U2*. A fan who was called up to dance with the band during Bono's Macphisto period (when he wore devil horns) commented to the singer that she couldn't figure out why he as a Christian was putting on such an act. Bono was said to have asked her if she had read C. S. Lewis's *Screwtape Letters*, indicating that the show and his costume were an elaborate attempt to ridicule the devil.

It's doubtful that more than a handful of the attendees that night knew what Bono was up to, but that seemed to be the way it went for a good part of U2's career.

The title *The Joshua Tree*, for instance, could reasonably be deduced to have been a reference to Christ's cross, Joshua being another rendering of Jesus and the tree another name for the cross, but it's unlikely that very many of U2's fans, much less the wider culture, understood the title as such.

Critics aside, it didn't alter the fact that in some way U2 managed to stand in the center of pop culture and continue to turn out music that was inspired by its members' faith and referenced, however vaguely, the members' deeply held Christian beliefs.

By now the band's story is familiar to many: originating in Dublin, the group consisted of a group of teenagers who married its own brand of rock with spiritual devotion. When tensions with the church they were attending, the Shalom Fellowship, escalated, the band members seemed to divorce themselves from active Christian fellowship and seemed determined not to use their music to overtly proselytize.

"I do not want to talk about it in terms of music," Bono had remarked early on in his career about his faith. "Anything that has to be said on that personal level is in the music or on stage and I don't want to go through the media. I don't want to talk to the world about it because we will face a situation where people will see us with a banner over our heads. That's not the way U2 is going to work."[1]

"If there is anything in what we have to say," he added, "it will be seen in our lives, in our music, in our performance."[2]

Whether their faith was seen in their lives, music, and performances often depended on who was being asked the questions.

U2's expressions of faith seemed to go in waves and seemed to be linked directly to Bono's individual spiritual journey. Some fellow believers saw U2's faith ebb and flow at various points—ebb around the time of the *Pop* album and flow around the time of the release of *All That You Can't Leave Behind,* which was seen by many as a strong reaffirmation of Bono and the other two members' faith.

On *Pop,* Bono had offered a startlingly frank declaration questioning God: "Jesus, I'm waiting here boss, I know you're looking out for me, but maybe your hands aren't free."[3]

But by the time of the release of *All That You Can't Leave Behind,* he seemed to have undergone a spiritual epiphany. The band, likely at Bono's direction, decided to insert a secret message of sorts into the album's cover art: U2 was photographed in a train station where the sign showing where the train was headed had been deleted and airbrushed over it was this message: J333—which was rumored to be Jeremiah 33:3, the Scripture verse that reads: "Call unto Me and I will answer thee and show thee great and mighty things which thou knowest not."[4]

"It was done like a piece of graffiti," confirmed Bono. "It's known as God's telephone number."[5]

Still more evidence of U2's increasingly ardent behavior came with the group's live shows, which found Bono quoting from the Psalms as he openly worshiped God from the stage. For many fans, Christian and non-Christian alike, it was an unforgettable experience.

Without a doubt, the central figure in the story of U2 was Bono, born Paul Hewson, who thought deeply about spiritual matters from childhood as the son of a Protestant family in a predominantly Catholic nation:

> "I think the Dalai Lama said, 'If you want to consider life, start with death'—the journey toward enlightenment starts with that," said the singer. "And that's what happened to me when my Mother died when I was a kid in school and at my grandfather's funeral. I was this really confident kid, aggro and a freckled face—I looked like a baked bean when I was a kid, I really did. Then a nose started to appear. It was a bit of a shock—out of this baked bean came this nose. I was a little alarmed, and then this chin came, until the two of them finally called it quits. I had the courage of somebody who didn't know anything, who didn't know fear yet

and then came the cold water of your home turning into a house and your relationship to women changing forever. I was 14. But now I see it was a great gift to me. Hopefully most people can avoid that until they're older, but some people have it young."[6]

In 2000, Bono granted a rare interview to the on-line religious journal *Beliefnet.com,* in which he spoke about his beliefs. The singer who had seemed to avoid such talk for fear of being misinterpreted, decided it was time to speak his mind. The resulting interview was both compelling and frustrating. At first glance, Bono seemed to be opening up with the interviewee, a longtime friend.

"I've successfully avoided talking about my faith for 20 years," he said. "But with you, I felt I had to. I said, 'I can't turn this guy down—he's been on every blinkin' boring story!' And I thought to myself, 'it's OK to open up a little bit.' The problem is, when I do these kinds of things, the way it turns out in the tabloid papers here and in England is, 'Bono Pontificates on the Holy Trinity.' And then we're off! But at the same time, I can't let them gag me. These are the uninformed, unfocused thoughts of a student of these things, not a master."[7]

Unfortunately, much as Scott Stapp did with mainstream reporters who were largely unfamiliar with the finer points of Christian doctrine, Bono let slip a line that was then misinterpreted by *Beliefnet* to indicate that the singer was not a Christian at all, something Bono could hardly have intended.

"The most powerful idea that's entered the world in the last few thousand years—the idea of grace—is the reason I would like to be a Christian," he said. "Though, as I said to The Edge one day, I sometimes feel more like a fan, rather than actually in the band. I can't live up to it. But the reason I would like to is the idea of grace. It's really powerful."[8]

With that quote the on-line site was off to the races, claiming that Bono was not a Christian, or not in the band, but rather a fan of the band, an admirer of Christianity who hadn't joined the team. Of course, to anybody who had remotely followed the U2 story, it was a preposterous suggestion that defied all logic and evidence, but it was a common misunderstanding that resulted when Christians in rock tried to explain their faith to reporters who knew more about rock than religion.

Nevertheless, the interview was a fascinating window into Bono's mind and an indication of how far he had come as a man, a Christian, and a rock star who was prepared to throw his weight around a bit more in support of causes and in defense of his faith:

> "I often wonder if religion is the enemy of God. It's almost like religion is what happens when the Spirit has left the building," noted the singer in what had by now become a familiar theme. "God's Spirit moves through us and the world at a pace that can never be constricted by any one religious paradigm. I love that. You know, it says somewhere in the Scriptures that the Spirit moves like a wind—no one knows where it's come from or where it's going. The Spirit is described in the Holy Scriptures as much more anarchic than any established religion credits."[9]

In the past, Bono might have followed up such statements with uncharitable and harsh attacks upon prominent American Christians, especially those who tended to let their religion inform their politics, but the new and improved Bono had begun to change his mind about many prominent Christians—the kind he would have previously been scornful of. In U.S. Senator Jesse Helms, for instance, Bono found not a right-wing ideologue, but a fellow Christian with whom he had much in common:

> I really have had to swallow my own prejudice at times. Because I was suspicious of the traditional Christian church, I tended to tar them all with the same brush. That was a mistake, because there are righteous people working in a whole rainbow of belief systems—from Hasidic Jews to right-wing Bible Belters to charismatic Catholics. We had a meeting in the White House, and President Clinton invited Pat Robertson, who I think had referred to him as a devil and hadn't visited the White House in eight years. I saw him in the room with Andrew Young who said, his voice trembling, that this is the most important thing that's come up for him since the civil rights marches in the '60s. Clinton said, "This is a very odd bunch of people. But if you guys could agree to meet a few more times, you could really change the world."[10]

Meeting men like Helms, Robertson, and others, considered by some in American pop culture to be something of pariahs, gave Bono a sense of respect for those who in their own way seemed to be swimming against the tide of modern American pop culture.

"I'm actually starting to like more and more people who have convictions that are unpopular," said Bono. "Now at what point does an unpopular conviction interfere with your own human rights? Forced female circumcision, for instance . . . the Catholic Church's stance on contraception. The list goes on. You know, God has some really weird kids, and I find it hard to be in their company most of the time."[11]

Finding it hard or not, Bono was increasingly spending time with them in pursuit of what he considered social justice issues and, like Martin Luther King before him, he framed them in starkly religious terms:

> "For all its failings and its perversions over the last 2,000 years—and as much as every exponent of this faith has attempted to dodge this idea—it is unarguably the central tenet of Christianity: that everybody is equal in God's eyes," he said. "So you cannot, as a Christian, walk away from Africa. America will be judged by God if, in its plenty, it crosses the road from 23 million people suffering from HIV, the leprosy of the day. What's up on trial here is Christianity itself. You cannot walk away from this and call yourself a Christian and sit in power. Distance does not decide who is your brother and who is not. The church is going to have to become the conscience of the free market if it's to have any meaning in this world—and stop being its apologist."[12]

By mid 2002, Bono had taken a break from his political activity to finish up another album and spend some well-deserved time with his family, including his newborn son. But his passion for music lived on and his rationale for what he tried to accomplish with U2 seemed clear to him at least, if not to everybody else. Bono seemed to believe that the actual power of music to influence behavior was limited, but that the platform fame had given him on the other hand—the bully pulpit—could be used continually to motivate world leaders and the man on the street alike:

> I love hymns and gospel music, but the idea of turning your music into a tool for evangelism is missing the point. I think carrying

moral baggage is very dangerous for an artist. If you have a duty, it's to be true and not cover up the cracks. Music is the language of the Spirit anyway. Its first function is praise to creation—praise to the beauty of the woman lying next to you, or the woman you would like to lie next to you. It is a natural effusive energy that you shouldn't put to work. When those people get up at the Grammys and say, 'I thank God,' I always imagine God going, "Oh, don't—please don't thank me for that one. Please, oh, that's an awful one! Don't thank me for that—that's a piece of [crap]!'"[13]

With Bono at the helm, U2 had managed to forge a new path through the demilitarized zone that separated rock from religion. Dozens of artists before him with Christian convictions had been consumed by rock & roll. Because of those examples, others that followed had left behind the ugly world of rock. But U2 provided a living example, albeit a messy one, that the road could be navigated successfully:

> "I was never tormented in the way those early rock 'n rollers were between gospel and the blues," Bono once said. "I always saw them as parts of each other. I like the anger of the blues—I think being angry with God is at least a dialogue. You know, [Robert Johnson's] 'Hell Hound on My Trail'—the blues is full of that. And [it runs] right through to Marilyn Manson."[14]

Ultimately, Bono believed all music must ask the important questions and that without those questions rock simply couldn't live up to its promise:

> "These are big questions. If there is a God, it's serious. And if there isn't a God, it's even more serious. Or is it the other way around?" he once joked. "I don't know, but these are the things that, as an artist, are going to cross your mind."[15]

Bono spoke for many in the emerging generation of artists of faith who were breaking out of a religious subculture that had effectively silenced voices of faith in American, and indeed the world's, entertainment culture when he said, "Whenever you see this kind of darkness, there is extraordinary opportunity for the light to burn brighter."[16]

26
Left Behind

As the invasion of mainstream rock by people of faith continued in earnest, elements of the Christian music subculture still
sought to hold on to the separatism that created it to begin with.
The most recent development was the formation of a new sub-
subgenre of music called "praise and worship music."

Typically such music was similar to music in the Psalms, songs
that were written to be sung to God by people who had already
bought the Christian message and didn't need to be convinced
that it was the truth. As such, it was music that could be expected
to be of little interest to those not already convinced of the truth
of that message. While many true believers were enthused by the
emphasis on music that eliminated worldly concerns and focused
on the divine, not all were enthralled, and some even saw it as
just another attempt on the part of people of faith to distance
themselves from those who didn't share their beliefs.

In much the same way that R&B stars who would take a break
from recording R&B music that largely ignored God and instead
make gospel records that suddenly acknowledged His presence,
in Christian music circles it became in vogue to make "worship"
records. Top artists like Third Day, Michael W. Smith, and others who either achieved a degree of success in the mainstream
music world or could have (Smith had a Top Ten record once and

Third Day was once marketed by Jive Records as a mainstream rock band) released praise and worship records, which though musically similar to their usual fare, were simply not made with the general market in mind.

One who strongly criticized this movement was Bob Briner, a respected author and thinker with a large following among Christians, the author of an inspirational tome called *Roaring Lambs,* who passed away in 2000 just before finishing his final book, a sequel called *Final Roar.*

In *Roaring Lambs* Briner had popularized the idea that Christians had been, in American pop cultural terms anyway, like meek little lambs who had had almost no discernable impact on it. Quoting an old Quaker author named Elton Trueblood, Briner suggested that a religion's strength could be gauged by how it had affected the larger culture in which it operated. By that measure, Briner believed, Christians had failed spectacularly.

Briner wasn't the first to call upon Christians to get out of their subculture and into the world. In the early 1980s the impatient, mustachioed son of the late philosopher Francis Schaeffer, Franky, landed with a thud in the Christian world with his books *Addicted to Mediocrity* and *A Time for Anger,* arguing that the lack of spine evangelical Christians had shown in their effect on American culture had rendered them "evan-jellyfish." Schaeffer II quickly burned out and seemed to disappear from the scene. It would be left to others more temperamentally suited for the work to close the deal.

Enter Briner, a then fifty-seven-year-old television executive who in 1993 published *Roaring Lambs,* with a message that was essentially Franky Schaeffer with a smile. If Schaeffer was Nixon, Briner was Ronald Reagan—the sunny optimist who focused his firepower on getting young Christians to retake the country's cultural institutions, promising these would change if they would simply show up and do their jobs excellently. Briner didn't deny that the culture's output was in his view dark, but noted that darkness was merely an absence of light.

Seven years later, Briner was gone, felled by cancer. His last work, *Final Roar,* which was not quite completed when he passed away, hit stores over a year after his death. Briner wanted a different title: *Christians Have Failed America and Some of Us Are Sorry,* but his editor retitled it for wider appeal. In the opening lines, Briner threw bombs no less incendiary than Schaeffer's, but with a dash of humility:

> Rarely in the annals of human history have so many with so much to give to their society given so little and done it so maladroitly as have American Christians over the past 50 years. I feel the need to apologize. I'm sorry.[1]

Later, Briner flashed his righteous anger: "Christians write and publish . . . sing and produce . . . broadcast radio and television programs . . . paint and sculpt . . . carry on often brilliant intellectual discourses . . . operate educational institutions . . . produce and distribute a growing number of newspapers—all for other Christians . . . I personally view this as shameful."[2]

If Briner disliked preaching to the choir, he particularly detested singing to it. In his latter chapters, he managed to get in a few licks against the rise of "praise and worship" music:

> Will all this musical devotion to God in church gatherings lead to devotion out in the workplace, on the campuses, and in our marriages? Or will it simply be a sub-game within a sub-culture that savvy businesspeople capitalize on and exploit for profit all under the convenient guise of praise and worship to God?[3]

In addressing himself to the praise and worship genre, Briner was prescient, sensing that clever marketers would seek to capitalize on what may have started out as a genuine and divine movement. Sure enough, in the wake of the explosion of praise and worship music, some artists who were affiliated with the CCM industry admitted to being pressured by their labels to make "worship" records, in some cases when they really didn't want to.

A young Southern California band with one hit record under its belt faced its label that demanded that they produce a praise and worship record. The band obliged but quietly confided to friends that they only did so under pressure.

Another top band that had hits in both the CCM and mainstream worlds was also pressured, this time by their mainstream label, to make a worship record. No dummies, the executives at their label realized the trend and saw that more money was to be made in creating a worship record. When the band refused and instead proposed making a Christmas record as a compromise, their label turned them down cold. Christmas wasn't hot, but praise and worship was.

The praise and worship paradigm that emerged from the CCM community was really the same struggle that started "Christian music" to begin with and was fraught with the same dangers and theological misunderstandings.

To title a record "praise and worship" was to tacitly admit that one's previous records didn't offer praise or worship to God, a stunning admission for artists who built their reputations on their faith. It also represented an admission that seeking to make music for those who didn't share the faith was too difficult and not worth the effort, whereas making explicit music undecipherable to nonbelievers was ultimately easier and more profitable.

Many observers did indeed acknowledge a need for a portion of those who were involved in the CCM industry to create a subgenre of church music—music that was to be used for the purpose of more explicit corporate worship within the context of the churches, but some suggested that such an effort should be done on a not-for-profit basis and should work under the guidance of existing church denominations. The idea was not a new one.

In an 1876 essay, author R. L. Dabney outlined the importance of such a movement being under the ecclesiastical umbrella of an organized Christian denomination in his warning to a prominent church musician of his day, Ira Sankey, evangelist D. L. Moody's worship leader:

> In order that the church may retain the blessing of good singing, the privilege which Mr. Sankey and his imitators claim, importing their own lyrics into God's worship must be closely watched. If the same license is to be usurped by every self-appointed chorister, we shall in the end have a mass of corrupting religious poetry against which the church will have to wage a sore contest. Our children will then learn, to their cost, how legitimate and valuable was that restriction which we formerly saw in the lyrical liturgies of the old Protestant churches, expressed by the imprimatur of their supreme courts, "appointed to be sung in churches."[4]

Some suggested that executives and "worship leaders" who were interested in promoting church music should instead leave behind the trappings of the record business and ensure that their movement didn't result in enriching and glamorizing its leaders by instead creating not-for-profit organizations in association with existing Christian denominations and placing their groups under ecclesiastical authority. They might also benefit from studying the life of the late singer Keith Green who left the trappings of the record business behind and instead sought to bring his music to fellow believers for as low a cost as possible, sometimes even giving his records away.

For other artists, that vast majority who were devout and sought to communicate their beliefs to both a mainstream audience and fellow believers simultaneously, artists like Jars of Clay provide a useful model of how worshipful music could be incorporated into artists' records without creating separate "worship records," which nonbelievers are unlikely to pick up.

On the band's hit record *Much Afraid*, amidst bridge-building pop/rock numbers like "Crazy Times" and "Five Candles," Jars included an explicit, worshipful song directed to God called "Hymn" that spoke of bringing "worship unto thee."

People of faith—especially those in the black gospel music world—seemed to have a history of making explicit "religious" records for their like-minded fans and "secular" records for their "secular" fans. Aretha Franklin, for instance, would produce "secular" records for the mainstream and albums like *One Lord, One Faith, One Baptism* for her Christian fans. But the new movement of believers into the musical mainstream was clearly indicating that those days of spiritual schizophrenia were being left behind.

Rather, the future appeared to belong to artists like Jars of Clay who refused to live bifurcated lives by releasing one record with one worldview to the home team and another to the unbelieving world, choosing instead to record albums with great songs about love, life, and faith with explicit songs directed to God in their midst. Candid and honest expressions of devotion to God and a refusal to keep those moments of devotion to God away from the unbelieving masses seemed to be the path chosen by many in this new generation of devout rockers.

27

Returning to the Mainstream

Another area of the Christian music subculture that stubbornly resisted change was the Christian-owned radio industry, hundreds of radio stations, which played music that was for all practical purposes solely intended for fellow believers to the exclusion of others.

Instead of creating radio stations that would invite non-Christians to be a part of the listening audience, many of these stations advertised themselves as playing "today's hottest Christian hits" or some variation thereof, telegraphing to most non-believers that their business was not wanted unless they were predisposed toward warm feelings for the Christian faith.

Some stations attempted to reach out to mainstream audiences but quickly gave up in favor of niche marketing to fellow believers, a less difficult and more profitable venture.

In fact, niche marketing to fellow believers usually triumphed over the Great Commission—Christ's admonition to go into all the world and spread his message everywhere. Instead, savvy businessmen often decided that they'd rather target their products at fellow believers with methods that effectively alienated those products from those outside of their community.

Why would followers of a faith who were commanded by their leader to take his message to the highways and byways of the world fall into niche marketing? The answer probably had to do with the fact that it was easier, more profitable (at least in the short term), and consistent with the notion of separatism. Imagining how those outside of their community perceived things and crafting marketing campaigns that appealed to those sensibilities with a product that contained Christian messages while simultaneously assuring fellow believers of the integrity of the product was difficult work. To make narrow, sectarian appeals to fellow believers based on their faith was easier and required less imagination and effort.

While the quality of work of many people of faith in film, television, and music continued to improve, far too many executives who shared that faith still seemed to value niche marketing over the Great Commission. But there were exceptions that proved the rule, and a few had grander designs and intended to get the music heard by a mainstream audience *and* turn a handsome profit.

In March of 2000, veteran radio personality Dave Kirby and producer Josh Foster, both bound by a determination to expand the sphere of influence of artists of faith, teamed up and began what became known as *The Lazerbeam Countdown* radio show.

The duo was armed with research that demonstrated that more than 85 percent of all CDs sold in the general market were sold to twelve- to twenty-four-year-olds and that most born-again Christian young people had nearly identical record collections as their non-Christian counterparts. Translation: Christian kids were listening to Eminem, Korn, Shakira, and Kid Rock.

To fill what the duo saw as an obvious need, *The Lazerbeam Countdown* was born, a weekly mainstream radio show that would mix mainstream hits with hits from the world of Christian-oriented rock. But Kirby and Foster had no intention of embracing the dreaded "Christian music" label, so they avoided the brand entirely, choosing instead to allow the music to offend or inspire on its own.

Walking the fine line between "secular" radio, which played songs with little regard for content, and "Christian" radio, which often played music primarily for its lyrical content, sometimes with little regard to its musical content, *The Lazerbeam* took both into consideration. If the music couldn't compete with the big boys of mainstream rock and pop, it didn't see the light of day. On the other hand, if a mainstream artist created a song that deserved to be heard, it would have a chance to make it onto *The Lazerbeam Countdown*.

In other words, the countdown was content driven, not personality driven: If a song met Kirby and Foster's lyrical and musical criteria, it had a shot at making it to the top—but only if the fans agreed:

> "We add artists from both mainstream and Christian music labels," Foster said. "We are all about engaging the culture, so we can impact it for Christ. From there, listeners go to the website each week and vote, much like MTV's *Total Request Live*."[1]

That mix included artists signed to mainstream labels like Lenny Kravitz, Creed, P.O.D., U2, Mary Mary, Lifehouse, Lauryn Hill, and others, as well as those signed to Nashville-based CCM labels, like tobymac, Out of Eden, and The Benjamin Gate.

The duo produced a demo of the show and aggressively marketed it to hundreds of mainstream Top 40 stations across the country. It took an entire year, but in February of 2001 enough stations signed on to begin production of the first countdown mix, called "Modern CHR." Later, the "Modern AC" version of the countdown was added and, in June 2001, production began on *The Modern Rock* show.

By 2003, *The Lazerbeam* was carried in 40 markets coast-to-coast, with clearance in 32 of the Top 100 markets. According to Arbitron, which monitored radio listenership, the shows had a weekly audience estimate of almost 875,000 in addition to the thousands of listeners who tuned in using the show's website.

Foster's job was to continue to add affiliates—mainstream affiliates, that is, because the countdowns were not available to Christian-oriented radio.

"There are a very limited number of slots for syndication," Foster said. "For a station to carry *The Lazerbeam*, they have to drop Rick Dees, Carson Daly, Hollywood Hamilton, or *Open House Party*. These shows are marketed by major Hollywood syndicators like Premiere Networks and Westwood One. But we

serve a big God. And He gets all the glory. He said He would keep
blessing the effort if we patiently persist and don't give up."[2]

Foster and Kirby saw none other than the famed evangelist
Billy Graham as their role model, and Foster recounted a conversation with one of the stations that carried his show:

> I just got off the line with our new Cincinnati affiliate, Channel
> Z97.3. They carry the *Howard Stern Show* in morning drive. Ap-
> parently, there is a Billy Graham Crusade coming to Cincinnati
> this summer. The program director told me that the Billy Graham
> Evangelistic Association spent a ton of money running commer-
> cials every morning during the *Howard Stern Show*. No wonder
> these brothers and sisters have had such a tremendous impact
> on the culture worldwide, they never miss an opportunity to en-
> gage it. That must sound incredible to listeners: Howard breaks
> for local commercials after a long rap of probably talking about
> some movie star's genitalia and here comes that spot for the Billy
> Graham Crusade again![3]

The Lazerbeam expected to continue its rapid growth by adding new stations in markets where the show was requested and
where mainstream radio stations sensed a growing demand for
the show.

Foster was often a critic of the Christian music industry
and believed that it had used sales of popular artists signed to
mainstream labels, like P.O.D., to show growth in an industry
that, stripped of those sales, would otherwise have shown a
marked decline. And, he believed, because "Christian" record
labels tended to shy away from seriously seeking coverage for
their artists on mainstream outlets like MTV, mainstream radio,
and music magazines and newspapers, artists who were devout
Christians would continue to drift away and find homes with
mainstream labels. Still, he remained passionate about his
dream of exposing artists of deep Christian convictions that he
so admired to mainstream audiences.

"We try to play as many Christian market artists as possible,
but it's not easy," he said. "This music is completely obscure to
our station programmers and hence to their listeners. For that
reason, we have to overcome a sizable audience objection that
Rick Dees and Casey Kasem do not. Because of this, the single
greatest consideration we have in adding a song is whether or not

217

the artist will achieve additional mainstream exposure. There is a big difference between playing an obscure artist that is about to break big, and an obscure artist that will, unfortunately, always remain obscure."[4]

Foster saved his highest praise, however, for P.O.D., whom he largely credited with changing the way rockers of faith were viewed by the mainstream entertainment industry:

> Very few artists have the intestinal fortitude of P.O.D. They took "Rock the Party" door-to-door to every mainstream rock station in the country. It took seven years of tireless effort, but they never gave up. See how God blessed the effort? Now they are headlining Ozzfest—really awesome. That's how you infiltrate the culture for Christ. We pray that our radio shows will one day make the same impact for the Kingdom that P.O.D. is making right now.[5]

Foster's new paradigm was also shared by a two-time Emmy Award–winning television executive who had grown weary of the Christian separation from pop culture and decided to take on MTV. But unlike many fellow Christians, Patrick McGuire didn't have utter contempt for the music channel, but rather respected the accomplishments of MTV CEO Tom Freston who had taken a small startup and turned it into a cultural behemoth that had invaded more than 140 nations.

Rather than boycotting the channel or leading protests outside its studios in New York City, McGuire developed *The Altarnet Experiment*, an alternative music video show that aired weekly on PAX-TV.

McGuire and his associates began producing the first of 580 episodes of their music video show in the autumn of 1999, airing it on the Sky Angel Satellite System, the DISH Network, and in the show's home territory of Colorado Springs, Colorado.

Although *Altarnet* provided a platform for many artists who populated the Christian underground, McGuire was careful not to position it as a religious or Christian music video program, but as a music video program with values that reflected the worldview of its producer.

"*Altarnet* is an alternative to the destructive negative music that seems to get so much airplay these days," stated McGuire.

218

"There is a very hip alternative for the emerging youth culture that is both very attractive to the youth and that parents can be supportive of."[6]

Although McGuire supervised the production, his son Andrew and his twenty-something pals, who already had several years of production experience under their belts, did most of the work.

"We firmly believe that teens know what's cool for teens so we let them make the show," said the senior McGuire. "It's produced and hosted by twenty-somethings and programmed completely by viewer requests."[7]

In many ways, McGuire hoped to achieve in the music video world what the Fox News Channel achieved in news: provide a clear alternative to the primary network, but one that avoided easy labeling from its opponents, thereby allowing it to first reach its core audience and then expand beyond it. Just as the Fox News Channel had, for the most part, dodged the "conservative" label, McGuire's success will most likely hinge on his ability to dodge the tag "Christian entertainment."

In PAX-TV, McGuire had selected the perfect partner, for founder Bud Paxson, the mogul noted for his exclamation "Christian television stinks!" was a devout believer who had managed to avoid having his network labeled "Christian television," while nonetheless producing programming that was reflective of his faith.

McGuire was determined to produce a show that rocked hard but avoided "drug abuse, illicit sex, violence and discrimination." That likely eliminated many artists from consideration, but McGuire held out hope that should such artists reform and come up with content that met his fourfold criteria—and was requested by his audience—he would consider playing it.

McGuire had consistently spurned interest in *Altarnet* from various religious channels, determined to have his show air on a network that was likely to be accessed by those who wouldn't ordinarily tune into "religious" programming.

"The artists we play will not have to sell out their values to get distribution to the youth of America," he said. "We are starting small, a blip on the MTV radar screen. Maybe if we go on every afternoon against *TRL* we can say we are taking them on, but right now we are more like David gathering stones at the brook. We're small, but also very fast."[8]

Still, for most of the radio and television stations around the country owned by people of faith, the situation remained the same and those artists and executives who sought to have their work heard by the primary culture were stuck with broadcasting executives who seemed to value a quick buck over the difficult and tedious work of cultural engagement. But, in so doing, they seemed to ignore the example of One who not only made it a habit to lunch with sinners, but left his followers with the ultimate rejection of niche marketing to the home team when he spoke of setting aside the interests of the ninety-nine sheep who were safely in their pen in order to pursue the one that had wandered away.

28
Getting the Word Out

Despite the gains made by many artists in penetrating the musical mainstream, there were still several key factors that continued to keep music made by people of faith out of the mainstream. One was a lack of understanding of how such music should be marketed, and a key element in that marketing was the work of the publicists who often had the power to make or break artists' careers. When the publicist didn't understand or appreciate either the artist's message or desire to be heard on a mainstream platform, failure almost always followed.

The rap/rock trio dc Talk's record *Supernatural* was a case in point. In 1996 the group signed an agreement with Virgin Records, which for all practical purposes made them Virgin recording artists so far as the mainstream market was concerned.

The band's previous record, *Jesus Freak,* had produced one hit song, "Between You and Me," and the group seemed poised for monumental success as the follow-up record *Supernatural* hit store shelves, with the full corporate power of Virgin Records behind them. But somebody had forgotten to tell Virgin Records' publicist who was charged with promoting dc Talk that the band needed to be pushed to the mainstream rock industry not as a religious act, but as a rock act that would never shy away from its members' faith.

Instead, Virgin's publicist created even more barriers by emphasizing to hard-bitten mainstream rock reporters that dc Talk's roots were in the Christian music market, referring to them as "Christian music artists" in press releases and making it clear to any potential journalist that the band was spending their summer playing Christian rock festivals instead of playing ordinary mainstream venues.

As the person responsible for presenting records to rock journalists—a tough group of people with little love lost for the "Christian rock" genre and who would decide whether or not a record was worth writing about and featuring in their publications—the publicist's job was to minimize those things known to set off such journalists and maximize those things that would cause the artists to be treated in a positive light.

Were a publicist to have Alanis Morissette as a client, for example, they might not want to emphasize to journalists that Morissette was once the Debbie Gibson of Canada, as such information would not endear her to reporters who generally had nothing but contempt for teen heartthrobs. To be sure, a publicist would not be called upon to lie about such a past, and it wouldn't mean that Morissette was necessarily ashamed of her country or her early choice of songs, but a smart publicist would simply refuse to play into the prejudices journalists had about teenybopper stars trying to rehabilitate their careers.

But when it came to presenting dc Talk to the rock journalist community, Virgin's publicist was simply out to lunch.

By contrast, Ken Phillips, the publicist for a band that had origins similar to dc Talk in CCM, Sixpence None The Richer, performed his job masterfully, working to ensure that his artists avoided being marginalized as "Christian rock," but always presented first and foremost as a rock band. By doing so, Phillips gave his artists credibility and legitimacy, allowing their songs and their message to be heard and considered by both critics and the general public.

By contrast, Virgin's publicists contributed to the failure of dc Talk's *Supernatural*—an album loaded with potential hit songs like "Godsend," "Consume Me," and "My Friend (So Long)." Unfortunately, before the music could be heard by a mass audience, dc Talk was sidelined by a publicist who didn't understand the zeitgeist and didn't realize that approaches to any particular culture must be modified to meet the challenges each age poses.

The artists who found themselves within the Christian music industry were also too often ill-served, this time by executives and publicists who didn't seem to share a vision for mainstream penetration and seemed more intent on flying the flag of "Christian music" than in actually winning a hearing for their artists and getting their message out. What they sorely needed were skilled communicators with the wits to navigate around the natural biases of those whose opinions mattered and whose support would be crucial in gaining a hearing for artists with important music to be heard.

29

Doing the Work

Although not fitting the typical profile of the young rock rebel, Eddie Carswell of the pop vocal group Newsong was living proof that no artist in the religious music subculture was beyond hope when it came to adjusting to the new realities and attempting to be relevant to a mainstream audience.

Carswell had been a mainstay of the gospel music circuit for years with his aging boy band, but in the late '90s had come under the influence of *Roaring Lambs* author Bob Briner. Until Carswell's association with Briner, his group had made no apparent effort to break out of the cloistered world of Christian music, but that was all about to change.

Newsong was one of dozens of CCM groups that year after year put out music, some noteworthy some not so, that the CCM machine then marketed to fellow churchgoers. Over time, even the most talented artists fell into the trap of making music that could be appreciated by fellow believers but not so easily by those outside of the camp.

But somewhere on the way to the next Dove Awards ceremony, the parallel religious subculture's version of the Grammys, Carswell seemed to have had a change of heart that in turn changed the history of pop music. For though Carswell was on a CCM market label, it was a label that was owned by Zomba—the mainstream giant that brought the world the hit song "Butterfly Kisses." As such, it was positioned, in theory anyway, to take music that was made in the Christian music market, when it was compelling enough, into the mainstream.

Perhaps realizing that his group had had virtually no discernable impact on the mainstream of American pop music culture, Carswell set to work on a song that would take his message of faith into that culture and connect with listeners by weaving it into a compelling story. Thus the smash holiday hit "The Christmas Shoes" was born.

When it debuted in 2000, "Shoes" was the highest charting new single in the country on *Billboard's* pop singles chart, and by the time Americans took their Christmas trees to the dumpsters it had cracked the Top 40. In 2001, the song charted again, this time accompanied by a companion book of the same title released by a major New York publishing house. The following year the song charted again and was accompanied this time by a CBS TV special based on the book, starring actor Rob Lowe. Carswell and "The Christmas Shoes" were living proof that artists trained in the subculture to be separatists, could instead learn to make music for everybody without compromising their core beliefs or stripping away their beliefs from their music.

The reaction to "The Christmas Shoes" brought to mind the reaction of one of rock's toughest critics, *Rolling Stone* magazine's Dave Marsh, to the newly born-again Donna Summer's 1980 song "I Believe in Jesus." Marsh, not usually a cheerleader of the work of devout Christians, tried to dislike Summer's tribute to her Savior but couldn't.

"Based on the militant fundamentalist hymn 'Onward Christian Soldiers' and the nursery rhyme 'Mary Had a Little Lamb,' the composition escapes being cloying only by the narrowest of margins," Marsh noted. "A chorus sung so perfectly that to deny it is practically inconceivable."[1]

What Summer, Marsh, and now Newsong proved was that contrary to years of woe-is-me propaganda, the work of devout Christians could indeed be lauded by non-Christians with a strong faith-based message intact if the song was compelling enough to overcome the disdain many nonbelievers had for that message, which was exactly what Carswell and Newsong accomplished with "The Christmas Shoes."

Taking the story of a little boy who walked into a store looking to buy his dying mother a pair of shoes to wear on her journey to heaven, who then found himself a few dollars short, Carswell then weaved the key principle of his faith into the song by having the little boy tell the clerk that he needed the shoes "if Mama meets Jesus tonight."

As the song climbed the charts, Newsong was given a unique opportunity to be heard in a culture searching for meaning and truth.

30
A New Path

For several decades the Gospel Music Association (GMA) had given out its Dove Awards to artists who made excellent "Christian" and "gospel" music, recognizing artists who might very well have been honored at the Grammys had they not retreated from mainstream music. To be sure, having such an association and an award may have made sense at one point, but in a post-Christian music culture, where artists of deep Christian faith longed to be heard by everyone in the culture and sought to escape marginalizing terms like "Christian rock," it no longer did.

The only remaining question was whether or not the GMA would have the foresight to adjust to the new realities that were rushing upon it: a generation of artists, executives, and fans who were tired of being marginalized and pushed into the religious section of popular music.

Some suggested a new role for groups like the GMA, perhaps adding two letters to its title, making it the Gospel *in* Music Association and honoring those songs and artists who most ably articulated the gospel message in each genre of music. Some hoped that such a move might crush the outdated notion that music written by Christians should *ipso facto* be categorized as "Christian" or "gospel." Instead, they hoped that a revamped organization could encourage artists who shared a Christian commitment to be full participants in the genre that reflected their musical style, be it jazz, rock, pop, or hip-hop, and provide pastoral care for such artists on and off the road. Others saw a role for a GIMA to help facilitate the analysis and evaluation of lyrics to aid discerning young people in figuring out the world-view of various artists' songs. This would be done in addition to working with existing religious denominations to encourage the creation of a not-for-profit association to help provide funds for artists who were focused on serving the needs of churches.

The strategy would be a departure to be sure, requiring the association to move out of the *business* of "gospel music" and instead into the ministry of supporting the majority of artists who belonged in the mainstream of American music, as well as the smaller group who should get out of the music business and into a ministry catering to the needs of fellow believers in church settings without the temptations of the commercial music industry.

31
Affirmative Action for People of Faith

Many in the Christian music business were still a long way from embracing a mentality that saw their artists as full participants in the mainstream entertainment industry. Regularly nominated by their labels in the so-called "Gospel" category at the Grammys were artists like Jennifer Knapp, Jars of Clay, and Third Day, despite the fact that these artists didn't play gospel music—a unique genre of music characterized typically by African-American artists singing en masse and sometimes wearing robes. Rather, Jars of Clay played alternative pop/rock, Third Day's style was straight ahead roots rock, and Knapp played the type of rock one might hear on the Lilith Fair tour.

Still, the Christian market labels, along with the National Academy of Recording Arts and Sciences (NARAS), the same organization that showed fans how out of touch it was with the music scene by giving dinosaur rockers Jethro Tull a nomination in the Best Hard Rock category a decade ago, persisted in refusing to mainstream these and other worthy artists, by continuing to grant Grammy "Gospel" nominations and awards to artists who happened to have a deep Christian faith but who had signed with record labels that were aligned with the Contemporary

Christian Music industry. In doing so, NARAS confused musicians who proclaimed the gospel in their music with a style of music called gospel.

But two powerful forces—those who seemed to care more about enlarging their artificial genre than allowing their artists to be heard by the mainstream culture and those militant secularists in the mainstream musical community who were only too happy to keep the obnoxious religious types out of circulation—seemed to form an unlikely alliance, which resulted in artists with Christian convictions being kept out of mainstream circulation.

For the religious, it allowed their genre to grow and got the word out to more true believers, who just didn't buy enough of their records. Apparently they didn't mind that their artists and their message were thereby buried at the bottom of Grammy newspaper coverage, off of prime-time TV, and generally in the basement of pop culture.

It was a tidy arrangement, but it didn't serve fans, who may not have been Christians but may have found the music interesting nonetheless, or artists who wanted to be heard by non-churchgoers. In short, it was clearly a lousy arrangement that needed to change.

Until such change came, NARAS continued to look as it did during the Jethro Tull fiasco, for the organization seemed to single out Christians for the special Grammys, never sorting out other worldviews or religious beliefs for separate awards. Thus, "Buddhist Music" Grammys weren't given to artists like the Beastie Boys, Courtney Love, and Herbie Hancock, "Satanic Music" Grammys to Marilyn Manson, or "Mormon Music" Grammys to the Osmonds in the '70s.

But NARAS wasn't the only cultural outpost that had a hard time adjusting to the new realities, for the American Music Awards, Dick Clark's direct competition to the Grammys, took a step backward in 2001 when it added a religious category to their awards ceremony, despite the fact that it had long been open to artists of faith who won the traditional way: winning fans in the mainstream arena.

In 1990 Michael W. Smith had won an American Music Award for Best New Artist the hard way—he earned it. Geffen Records had distributed his records to the mainstream market, and the singer scored big with his Top Ten pop hit "Place in This World," which hit #6 on the pop charts.

Smith didn't win a "Best New Christian Artist" award—he was the Best New Artist of 1990 bar none. Unfortunately, the days of an artist like Smith winning Best New Artist of the year were now over if the decision to create a religious category were to stand. While Clark and the AMAs should be commended for realizing that they had far too often ignored music emerging from that community, the cure was worse than the disease. Instead of bringing artists of faith out of the ghetto, it sentenced them to further cultural obscurity and reinforced the misimpression that music created by devout performers should be categorized as "gospel" or "religious" music.

Those within the Christian music business who lobbied for the creation of such a category seemed to be sending the wider culture a message: "You are normal. Your music is normal. Ours is odd because it doesn't ignore the Creator of the universe. Your artists can win the 'normal' award. We'll take home the 'religious' award."

Creating a special award that recognized only "Christian" artists not only cheapened the award but also served to keep future Michael W. Smiths from winning in the "normal" categories. In fact, it was probably a safe bet that had the award been in place in 1990, Smith wouldn't have been honored as Best New Artist, but as Best New Inspirational Artist. But, fortunately for Smith, the American Music Awards didn't have that category in 1990, and he won the hard way. Still, for a new generation of artists of faith, the bar was lowered, and instead of following Smith's worthy example of getting the culture's attention, artists would be tempted to lower their sights and strive for Best New Inspirational Artist, and the broader culture would be deprived of another voice of faith.

Until artists and music industry people who happened to be devout Christians stopped seeing themselves as a persecuted minority deserving of special categories because they couldn't win in the established ones, they would carry on in the cultural gulag they had created for themselves and their message would continue to stay out of mass circulation.

Still, some suggested that they should look to the historical example of African-Americans, who showed how a minority

231

could successfully emerge to affect the wider culture. Jackie
Robinson, the famed African-American baseball player who
broke the color barrier in baseball, was not content to play
in the Negro Leagues but insisted on breaking into the Major
Leagues, despite the racists who didn't want him there. Once
in the big leagues, African-American ball players like Sammy
Sosa never lobbied for, nor likely would have accepted, demean-
ing awards like "most home runs by a black man," when Sosa
came up short in his race for the home run crown against Mark
McGuire. Rather, they understood that the key to their having
an effect on the cultural mainstream was to stay planted in that
mainstream and competing.

32

Beyond the Male Nurse Syndrome

By constantly marginalizing or allowing themselves to be marginalized, many who populated the Christian music subculture were not unlike other groups in our society who found themselves saddled with terms that demeaned the value of their contributions.

Terms like "male flight attendant," "male nurse," and "female police officer" were all used to indicate that the presence of that particular gender in that particular position was in some way inappropriate or unexpected. The need to qualify the occupations with the gender meant that somewhere in the collective conscience of most Americans there persisted a feeling that nurses should be women, police officers men, and flight attendants women.

Terms like "Christian rock" and "Christian artist" had much in common with those, for the need to add "Christian" before "rock" or "music" was also an indication that the culture somehow viewed rock music that ignored God and the really important issues of life as ordinary and undeserving of a qualifier.

On the other hand, by implication the culture seemed to have decided that those artists who had life-changing spiritual experiences with the Creator of the universe and refused to keep those experiences out of their music were viewed as strange and in need of a qualifier. Hence the term "Christian music."

To be sure, there were progressive forces within the Christian music business who understood that, ironically enough, the success of the introduction of their ideas into the culture via rock music hinged on their ability to drop the label "Christian rock" and move away from terms that trivialized what they did. Still others seemed to stubbornly cling to the past, embracing their own marginalization. In fact, there appeared to be something of a battle going on for the soul of the future of the Christian music industry, and that battle was on display when lobbying by that industry caused the Target retail chain to create a separate religious section in their stores.

It was also seen in the recent tug-of-war between the band Jars of Clay and its label. Amazingly, just as Jars was contacting retail stores asking that its record be moved into the "ordinary" record bins in these stores, its label appeared to be contacting the same retailers and asking that the record be moved to the gospel section.

One side understood that labeling music "Christian" drove away non-Christians in the same way that labeling Duncan Sheik's music "Buddhist rock" would probably have driven away non-Buddhists who may otherwise have liked his music. The other side didn't seem to fully grasp the reality that most Americans lived in a post-Christian culture populated by people who were refusing to even go near certain artists because they had been labeled "Christian music."

One side wanted their CDs racked in mainstream retail outlets the way all artists were—alphabetically, where most music fans browsed—the other side in a separate section.

One side was content to be in its niche—just as for years African-Americans were happy to sit at the back of the bus. The other side understood that riding in the bus was not enough, that the only solution was full integration for those who wanted to have their ideas heard by the wider culture.

In an article in the trade publication *Radio & Records,* one CCM industry official noted hopefully: "People of faith have broken out of their subculture. They've decided that they can speak about their faith when not in a house of worship."[1]

Beyond the Male Nurse Syndrome

But another said: "We don't need to get out of our culture, we need to expand our culture. There are about 100 million people who define themselves as Christians in America. What other genre of music can claim 100 million potential customers?"[2]

Those were the two competing visions in a nutshell.

Still, at many of these Christian market labels change was in the air, especially among lower-level staffers who were quietly rebelling against their superiors by building bridges into mainstream radio, music channels, and publications. Even traditional mainstream outlets like *Billboard* magazine had made tremendous strides in mainstreaming such artists, bringing them to the attention of the *Billboard* readership without marginalizing terms and outside of the "gospel" section where artists of faith had been relegated for years.

235

33

Rock and Religion: A Potent Mix

For years, devout Christians had complained about the output of Hollywood, arguing that popular media failed to reflect their values and beliefs. But amazingly enough, in spite of that history, instead of celebrating the presence of artists like P.O.D. in the mainstream entertainment culture and the real possibility that a Christian worldview might actually be introduced to a group of otherwise disinterested individuals, some in the Christian community resisted the idea of cultural penetration and engagement.

A book by former Nixon aide Chuck Colson, who went on to become a thinker and writer deeply respected in Christian circles, and philosopher Nancy Pearcey, a disciple of the late philosopher Francis Schaeffer, questioned the very notion that serious Christians could participate in certain corners of popular music. Perhaps unwittingly, the duo was creating a climate which, were it to remain unanswered, would spook young people of faith out of popular music, returning to a time when MTV and American radio were dominated by groups like 2 Live Crew and songs like "Sympathy for the Devil."

In *How Now Shall We Live?* the duo included these lines:

The sheer energy of rock—the pounding beat, the screams, the spectacle—is intended to bypass the mind and appeal directly to the sensations and feelings. Thus rock music by its very form encourages a mentality that is subjective, emotional, and sensual—*no matter what the lyrics may say.*[1] (italics added)

To be sure, the authors did argue in other parts of their book for a more responsible and enlightened approach to popular culture, indicating that people of faith must not "ignore our responsibility to redeem the surrounding culture," and later added that "turning our backs on the culture is a betrayal of our biblical mandate and our own heritage." They also cleverly noted the need to embrace "the cultural commission" and not just "the great commission."[2]

But in promoting the questionable view that rock couldn't and/or shouldn't be a conduit for Christian values, the authors seemed to throw cold water on the efforts of courageous artists like P.O.D. who had clawed their way out of the cultural gulag of "Christian Rock" and finally made their way onto the map of American pop culture.

Those in the rock music world who preferred that faith-based ideas stay off the airwaves found unlikely allies in the authors, for in essence they were telling Creed, Sixpence None The Richer, P.O.D., Lifehouse, and dozens of other artists that whatever they sang about simply didn't matter—it was inexorably overpowered by the "devil's beat."

The long march of people of faith out of the subculture and into the center of the marketplace of ideas—including popular music—would likely continue with or without the support of these important thinkers. As orthodox Christian ideas increasingly become a staple on cultural outposts like MTV, the evening news, and on mainstream radio and in print, people of faith would be forced to decide which they preferred: the good old days when their ideas were kept out of mass circulation, or a new world where their ideas were up for consideration because of courageous young artists who rejected arguments of cultural isolation.

By late 2002, the pace of Christian-oriented bands joining mainstream music had considerably accelerated. Chevelle withdrew from their deal with Squint and surfaced at Epic with a record that opened at #14 on the album charts. Swedish rockers Blindside saw their U.S. record debut on P.O.D.'s label, distributed through Atlantic. Switchfoot surfaced with a stunning record, *The Beautiful Letdown*, on Columbia Records. Pillar signed with Universal and rereleased a record that had previously only serviced the CCM market. Seventeen-year-old singer Stacie Orrico signed with Virgin Records and rocked *TRL* with her song "Stuck." And Evanescence, an Arkansas-based rock band, made a strong debut when its song was used in the *Daredevil* soundtrack.

The unusual turn of events was a victory for those believers who embraced the vision of cultural engagement over withdrawal, a fulfillment of the declaration by the old Dutch Prime Minister and thinker Abraham Kuyper who once said: "There is not one square inch of the entire creation about which Jesus Christ does not cry out: 'This is mine. This belongs to me.'"[3]

Still, for people of faith who had always had an uneasy relationship with the mass media culture and were fearful (sometimes with cause) that their fellow believers simply couldn't maintain their faith in the crazy world of rock & roll, the experience of '70s rocker Mylon Lefevre would serve as a haunting reminder of the dangers they would face. Lefevre, who had gotten his start in music as a member of his family's gospel group, had earned millions as a teenager when Elvis recorded his song "Without Him," and gone on to a respectable solo career in rock, working closely with stars like Eric Clapton, George Harrison, and many others. There were clearly dangers along the path of attempting to marry rock and religion, and Lefevre had been an early casualty of the effort. His experience would serve as a constant reminder that rock and religion were potent and powerful forces that could destroy one another if they weren't carefully synthesized:

> "We were a rock 'n' roll band who believed that Jesus was the son of God," the singer remembered. "We didn't know the Word very well, we prayed before we went on stage, but we also smoked marijuana. Naturally it was just a matter of time until the Gospel was taken over by the rock 'n' roll. I got away from my family and I got away from my church. If anybody had come backstage and

talked to me he would have decided that he didn't want any part of the life I was leading. I could not live for Jesus and be around rock 'n'roll. I didn't have the faith or guts to do that."[4]

With or without the support of separatist Christians or militant secularists who both seemed to long for the good old days when rock was synonymous with sex and drugs and not God, it was clear that a new generation was intent on marrying rock music with rather orthodox notions of spirituality. The novelist Jan Karon, who herself, though a devout believer, operated in the literary mainstream, seemed to speak for many of this new crop of artists when she said of her own work:

> Even if I never mentioned the name of Jesus Christ, I can't hide from you who I am. In truth, the work that has no faith is for me not a whole work. It may be an amusing or credible or clever work, but not a whole work. Faith is a critical and urgent and necessary component of human wholeness.[5]

For the first time, on a mass scale and in the middle of the popular entertainment culture, rock was getting religion—understanding its power to transform, engage, and illuminate a generation hungering for spiritual renewal, enlightenment, and ultimate meaning.

Notes

Chapter 1: You Say You Want a Revolution

1. Interview on the *Howard Stern Radio Show,* 18 March 2000.
2. Ibid.
3. Interview on *The Late Show with David Letterman,* www.CBS.com, 6 July 1999.
4. Jann S. Wenner, "Goddess in the Doorway," *Rolling Stone,* 21 November 2001.
5. Ibid.
6. Ibid.
7. Ben Forrest, "God Shows Up at the Grammy's," www.Christrock.com/html_ article_god_at_the_grammys.shtml.
8. "Dig In" lyrics, http://display.lyrics.astraweb.com:2000/display.cgi?lenny_ kravitz..lenny..dig_in.
9. "Get Right with God" lyrics.
10. Forrest, "God Shows Up at the Grammy's."
11. Keith Cartwright, www.ent-today.com/9-7/pod-feature.htm.
12. www.christianitytoday.com/ct/2002/104/22.0.html.
13. Philip E. Johnson, *Reason in the Balance: The Case Against Naturalism in Science, Law, and Education,* Intervarsity Press, 1995.

Chapter 2: One Man's Creed

1. www.teenmusic.about.com/library/weekly/aa120400a.htm.
2. Elysa Gardner, "Creed Stays the Course. *Weathered* Lyrics Now Seem Prescient," *USA Today.*
3. Ibid.
4. Ibid.

5. Kevin A. Miller, *Rock's Real Rebels: Christians (And the God-Hunted) Make Inroads into New Territory.*

6. Gardner, "Creed Stays the Course."

7. Pat Angelo, "Rock's Roll Creed," www.Christianity.com.

8. MXTV Creed interview.

9. Ibid.

10. Ibid.

11. Edna Gunderson, "Forecast for Creed's *Weathered:* Hard-Rock Hooks, Soft-Focus," *USA Today.*

12. MXTV Creed interview.

13. Ibid.

14. Ibid.

15. Featured interview from VH-1 *Behind the Music.*

Chapter 3: Payable on Death

1. "P.O.D. Doesn't Bless Religious Label," www.almenconi.com/news/feb02/020702.html, 7 February 2002.

2. "Rock the Party (Off the Hook)," www.lyrics.jp/lyrics/P004900010002.asp.

3. Andy Argyrakis, "Spins: P.O.D.'s Satellite," *Illinois Entertainer.*

4. Brian Quincy Newcomb, "P.O.D. launched its positive energy-laden statement of hope and thanksgiving on the musical world from CCM.com," www.almenconi.com/news/feb02/020802.html, 8 February 2002.

5. "P.O.D. Doesn't Bless Religious Label."

6. Sarah Rodman, *Boston Herald,* "P.O.D. Sends Up a Spiritual Satellite," www.almenconi.com/news/jan02/011502, 15 January 2002.

7. Keith Ryan Cartwright, www.ent-today.com/9-7/pod-feature.htm.

8. Ibid.

9. Ibid.

10. Ibid.

11. "P.O.D. Doesn't Bless Religious Label."

12. Cartwright, www.ent-today.com/9-7/pod-feature.htm.

13. Argyrakis, "Spins: P.O.D.'s Satellite."

Chapter 4: Building (a) Lifehouse

1. David Wild, "The Rock and Roll Gospel According to Lifehouse," www.rollingstone.com.

2. Ibid.

3. Ibid.

4. Mike Ross, "Crossed Wires," www.canoe.ca/jammusicartistsL/lifehouse.html, 4 May 2001.

5. Wild, "The Rock and Roll Gospel According to Lifehouse."

6. Ross, "Crossed Wires."

7. Ibid.

8. Jonathan Mensink, "Lifehouse Rocks Calvin," Calvin Chimes, www-stu.calvin.edu/chimes/2001.09.21/fro4.html.

9. Wild, "The Rock and Roll Gospel According to Lifehouse."

10. Sarah Aldridge-McNeece, www.ccmupdate.com.

11. Ibid.

12. Edna Gunderson, www.usatoday.com/life/music/2001-07-11-lifehouse.htm#more.

13. Wild, "The Rock and Roll Gospel According to Lifehouse."

14. Erin K. McCormick, "Currently Known as Lifehouse," www.breakpoint.org.

Chapter 5: Daly Impact

1. "Carson Daly," *Teen People*, February 1999.

2. Mark Schwed, "Carson Daly: Mom, Memories, and MTV," *TV Guide*.

3. Mike Janke, "Feeling Disillusioned?" www.cmcentral.com/features/4.html, 27 June 2001.

4. www.geocities.com/lildevil124/bio.html.

5. Schwed, "Carson Daly: Mom, Memories, and MTV."

6. www.geocities.com/lildevil124/bio.html.

7. Ibid.

8. Ibid.

9. Ibid.

10. Ibid.

11. Carson Daly interview on 20/20, www.abcnews.go.com/onair/2020/transcripts/2020_000728_daly_trans.html.

12. Ibid.

13. Ibid.

14. Ibid.

15. Ibid.

16. Ibid.

17. www.geocities.com/lildevil124/bio.html.

18. Ibid.

19. Ibid.

20. "Carson Daly," *Teen People*, February 1999.

Chapter 6: Magnified Plaid

1. "The Ever Passing Moment," www.mtv.com/news/articles/1440435/20010223/mxpx.jhtml, 23 February 2001.

2. "Meet MxPx," www.mtv.com/news/articles/1432466/19970926/mxpx.jhtml, 26 September 1997.

3. www.math.ukans.edu/~parker/billpint.html.

4. Mark Heard lyrics, "Stuck in the Middle."

5. Andrea Scratch, "Mike from MxPx and the Wonderful Andrea Scratch," www.decapolis.com/musicreviews/interviews/mxpxinterview.shtml.

6. Ibid.

7. Ibid.

8. Ibid.

9. Ibid.

10. Ibid.

11. Ibid.

12. "Meet MxPx."

13. Ibid.

14. Ibid.

15. Scratch, "Mike from MxPx and the Wonderful Andrea Scratch."

Chapter 7: The Minister's Daughter

1. www.allpop.com interview.
2. www.fox.com interview, 14 August 2002.
3. *YM*'s March 2002 issue, interview with Carson Daly.
4. Elysa Gardner, "Simpson Cites Her 'Abstinence' as Crucial," *USA Today*.
5. Erin Boyle, www.caneltdian.com/non/artists/s/jessicasimpson/biography.html.
6. Gardner, "Simpson Cites Her 'Abstinence' as Crucial."
7. Ibid.
8. Ibid.
9. Ibid.
10. Arlene Vigoda, "Simpson, Lachey Play Love Match," *USA Today*.
11. Gardner, "Simpson Cites Her 'Abstinence' as Crucial."
12. Ibid.
13. Vigoda, "Simpson, Lachey Play Love Match."
14. Rachel Hoskins Lioi, "Pure and Single," *The Washington Times*.
15. www.allpop.com interview.
16. Hoskins Lioi, "Pure and Single."
17. Chuck Taylor, "Fans Find Jessica Simpson *Irresistible*," www.billboard.com.
18. Ibid.
19. www.allpop.com interview.
20. Taylor, "Fans Find Jessica Simpson *Irresistible*."
21. Ibid.
22. Ibid.
23. www.allpop.com interview.
24. Gardner, "Simpson Cites Her 'Abstinence' as Crucial."
25. Ibid.

Chapter 8: Rockin' the Sabbath

1. Kevin Raub, "Two for One. Evan and Jaron: Not from Concentrate," www.rollingstone.com.
2. Ibid.
3. Ibid.
4. Ibid.
5. Ibid.
6. Ibid.
7. www.usaweekend.com/01_issues/010826/010826evan_jaron.html.
8. Chelsea J. Carter, "Teen Magazines Take Note: Twins Evan and Jaron Don't Want the 'Boy Band' Label," www.evanandjaronnewsletter.com/article13.html, 13 August 2001.
9. Ibid.
10. Ibid.
11. Raub, "Two for One. Evan and Jaron: Not from Concentrate."
12. www.usaweekend.com/01_issues/010826/010826evan_jaron.html.
13. Ibid.
14. Raub, "Two for One. Evan and Jaron: Not from Concentrate."
15. www.usaweekend.com/01_issues/010826/010826evan_jaron.html.
16. Raub, "Two for One. Evan and Jaron: Not from Concentrate."
17. Ibid.

18. www.usaweekend.com/01_issues/010826/010826evan_jaron.html.
19. Ibid.
20. Carter, "Teen Magazines Take Note: Twins Evan and Jaron Don't Want the 'Boy Band' Label."
21. Raub, "Two for One. Evan and Jaron: Not from Concentrate."

Chapter 9: Manifest Destiny

1. Geoff Boucher, "Destiny, Manifest," www.latimes.com.
2. Teresa Hairston, "Women of Divine Destiny," *Gospel Today*.
3. Sharon Tubbs, "And God Made the World . . . 'Bootylicious,'" *St. Petersburg Times*.
4. Boucher, "Destiny, Manifest."
5. Ibid.
6. Ibid.
7. Ibid.
8. Ibid.
9. Jancee Dunn, "A Date with Destiny," www.rollingstone.com.
10. Bob Smithouser, "The Art Reflects the Heart," www.briomag.com/briomagazine/music/a0002595.html.
11. Tubbs, "And God Made the World . . . 'Bootylicious.'"
12. Hairston, "Women of Divine Destiny."
13. Dunn, "A Date with Destiny."
14. Hairston, "Women of Divine Destiny."
15. Ibid.
16. Tubbs, "And God Made The World . . . 'Bootylicious.'"
17. Dunn, "A Date with Destiny."
18. Hairston, "Women of Divine Destiny."

Chapter 10: Reinventing Alice

1. Brian McCollum, from Knight-Ridder Newspapers, published in *The Kansas City Star*, 22 August 1997.
2. Rich Black, interview with Alice Cooper.
3. Ibid.
4. Lonn Friend, "Exclusive Interview! Alice Cooper: Prince of Darkness/Lord of Light," www.knac.com.
5. Ibid.
6. Ibid.
7. Black, interview with Alice Cooper.
8. Friend, "Exclusive Interview! Alice Cooper: Prince of Darkness/Lord of Light."
9. Ibid.
10. Black, interview with Alice Cooper.
11. Friend, "Exclusive Interview! Alice Cooper: Prince of Darkness/Lord of Light."
12. Michael Dwyer, "Shock Rock's Pious Prophet," www.theage.com.au/entertainment/2001/04/17/FFX6RJX3LLC.html, 17 April 2001.
13. Friend, "Exclusive Interview! Alice Cooper: Prince of Darkness/Lord of Light."
14. Black, interview with Alice Cooper.
15. Friend, "Exclusive Interview! Alice Cooper: Prince of Darkness/Lord of Light."

Notes

Chapter 11: Cherone's Pulpit

1. "What Extreme Sez," www.fortunecity.co.uk/madchester/trance/648/17hm.htm.
2. Ibid.
3. Ibid.
4. Ibid.
5. Ibid.
6. Ibid.
7. Author interview with Chris Sernel.
8. Ibid.
9. "What Extreme Sez," www.fortunecity.co.uk/madchester/trance/648/17hm.htm.
10. Ibid.
11. Ibid.
12. Ibid.
13. Ibid.

Chapter 12: After the Flood

1. Gregory Rumberg, "The Other Side of the Tracks," *CCM*, July 1996, 40.
2. Brian Mansfield, "Jars of Clay: After the Flood," www.jarchives.com.
3. Ibid.
4. Peter Cooper, "Jars of Clay Kick Off Their New Tour Tonight at Lipscomb University."
5. Mansfield, "Jars of Clay: After the Flood."
6. Ibid.
7. Ibid.
8. Ibid.
9. Ibid.
10. Ibid.
11. "Jar-Head-Jars of Clay Dan Haseltine Pushes to the Front," www.nationalreview.com/comment/comment-joseph071202.asp.
12. Ibid.
13. Matt Odmark, liner notes from *The Eleventh Hour*, prerelease CD.
14. "Old School Jars Carries Timeless Message," *CCM*, June 2002.
15. Cooper, "Jars of Clay Kick Off Their New Tour Tonight at Lipscomb University."

Chapter 13: God's Troubadour

1. James Jensen, "Listening for the Song—David Wilcox Discovers the Songs Waiting in His Guitar," www.solidairrecords.com/AMR_interviews/wilcox.html, 7 June 1994.
2. TC Smythe, www.empirezine.com, September 1989.
3. Jensen, "Listening for the Song—David Wilcox Discovers the Songs Waiting in His Guitar."
4. Ibid.
5. Smythe, www.empirezine.com, September 1989.
6. Jensen, "Listening for the Song—David Wilcox Discovers the Songs Waiting in His Guitar."

7. Ibid.

8. Ibid.

9. David Trotter and Spencer Burke, "Going Deeper: An Interview with David Wilcox," http://www.theooze.com/articles/article.cfm?id=57.

10. Ibid.

11. Ibid.

12. Ibid.

13. Ibid.

14. Ibid.

15. Ibid.

16. Ibid.

17. Bill DeMain, "David Wilcox Biography," www.concertedefforts.com/artists_wilc.asp.

18. Ibid.

Chapter 14: A Creek Runs through It

1. www.cmt.com/comm/20quest/nickel.creek2.jhtml.

2. Ibid.

3. Ibid.

4. Randy Lewis, "Nickel Creek Builds Bridges Between Genres," www.latimes.com.

5. www.cmt.com/comm/20quest/nickel.creek2.jhtml.

6. Ibid.

7. Ibid.

8. Ibid.

9. Ibid.

10. Ibid.

11. Ibid.

12. Ibid.

13. Ibid.

14. Ibid.

15. Ibid.

16. Ibid.

17. Ibid.

18. Ibid.

19. Ibid.

20. P. W. Miller, "Up Nickel Creek without a Banjo," www.boulderweekly.com/archive/032201/buzzlead.html.

21. Ibid.

22. www.cmt.com/comm/20quest/nickel.creek2.jhtml.

23. Ibid.

24. Ibid.

25. Ibid.

26. Shelly Fabian, www.countrymusic.about.com/library/blnickelcreekrev.htm.

27. www.cmt.com/comm/20quest/nickel.creek2.jhtml.

Chapter 15: Roxie's Boy

1. Tracey Pepper, "Deep Joy" interview, www.findarticles.com/cf_0/m1285/n7_v28/20870216/p1/article.jhtml.

2. Ibid.

3. William Shaw, "Are You There God?" *Details* magazine, November 1995, 158.
4. Pepper, "Deep Joy" interview.
5. Ibid.
6. Ibid.
7. www.vivamusic.com/events/u_lennykravitz2.htm.
8. Dan Neer, "Lenny Kravitz Interview," www.vivamusic.com/events/u_lennykravitz.htm.
9. "Kravitz Proves Rock 'n' Roll Isn't Dead," *Toronto Paper*, 3 February 1996.
10. "Lenny Kravitz: Greatest Hits," by Center for Faith and Culture Staff, http://216.239.51.100/search?q=cache:LtrCfWMcNAQC:leninanworld.iespana.es/leninanworld/entrev2.htm+lenny+kravitz+i+was+taught+by+my+grandfather+that+your+mind+&hl=en&ie=UTF-8.
11. www.vivamusic.com/events/u_lennykravitz3.htm.
12. Pepper, "Deep Joy" interview.
13. Neer, "Lenny Kravitz Interview."
14. Pepper, "Deep Joy" interview.
15. Neer, "Lenny Kravitz Interview."
16. Ibid.
17. Pepper, "Deep Joy" interview, and "Kravitz Proves Rock 'n' Roll Isn't Dead."
18. Ibid.
19. Pepper, "Deep Joy" interview.
20. Neer, "Lenny Kravitz Interview."
21. Lyrics from "You Were in My Heart," Lenny Kravitz.

Chapter 16: Much the Richer

1. Jay S. Jacobs, "Sixpence None The Richer," www.popentertainment.com/sixpence.htm.
2. Interview transcripts, www.christianteens.about.com/library/weekly/aa11267.html.
3. Ibid.
4. Jacobs, "Sixpence None The Richer."
5. "Matt Slocum of Sixpence None The Richer," www.tollbooth.org/features/6pence.html.
6. Jacobs, "Sixpence None The Richer."
7. Ibid.
8. Ibid.
9. Ibid.
10. Charlie Craine, www.hiponline.com/artist/music/s/sixpence_none_the_richer/interview/100007.html.
11. Interview transcripts, www.christianteens.about.com/library/weekly/aa11267.html.
12. Interview by Rachel Haring, Kohli and Elizabeth Crepeau, "Sixpence None The Richer," http://members.tripod.com/swizzlestickzine/features/sixpence.htm.
13. Ibid.
14. Interview transcripts, www.christianteens.about.com/library/weekly/aa11267.html.
15. Michael Johns, "Faith in Tough Times," www.christianitytoday.com/cl/8c2/8c2030.html.
16. Ibid.

17. Interview transcripts, www.christianteens.about.com/library/weekly/aa11267.html.

18. Johns, "Faith in Tough Times."

19. Jacobs, "Sixpence None The Richer."

Chapter 17: Mary²

1. Robin Parrish, "Mary Mary Interview," www.cmcentral.com/interviews/15.html.

2. Melanie Clark, "Why 'Mary Mary'?" www.tbn.org, original TBN live broadcast on 22 March 2001.

3. Chris Mugan, Mary Mary Interview, www.virgin.net/music/features/feature_4903.html+mary-mary+interview&hl=en.

4. Ibid.

5. Ibid.

6. Interview, www.google.com/search?hl=en&q=mary-mary+interview.

7. Ibid.

8. "Being Who They Are," www.gospelflava.com/articles/marymary2.html.

9. Parrish, "Mary Mary Interview."

10. Claire Duesbury, "Hail Mary!" www.mobo.net/features/marymary.shtml.

11. Mugan, "Mary Mary Interview."

12. Ibid.

13. "Being Who They Are," www.gospelflava.com/articles/marymary2.html.

14. Interview, www.google.com/search?hl=en&q=mary-mary+interview.

15. Ibid.

16. "Being Who They Are."

17. Matthew Turner, Crosswalk.com Entertainment Channel—Part 2.

18. Duesbury, "Hail Mary!"

19. Ibid.

20. "Being Who They Are."

21. Duesbury, "Hail Mary!"

22. "Being Who They Are."

23. Clark, "Why 'Mary Mary'?"

24. "Being Who They Are."

Chapter 18: Jordan's Sister

1. Biography, Kendall Payne, www.hiponline.com/artist/music/p/payne_kendall.

2. Ibid.

3. Ibid.

4. Ibid.

5. Michael Herman, "Kendall Payne: Got Depth?," www.christianitytoday.com/music/interviews/kpayne-0701.html.

6. Biography, Kendall Payne.

7. "Kendall Payne: Jams Line Biography," www.jamsline.com/b_payne.htm.

8. Biography, Kendall Payne, www.hiponline.com/artist/music/p/payne_kendall.

9. Herman, "Kendall Payne: Got Depth?"

10. Sarah Sharpe, www.popmatters.com.

11. Herman, "Kendall Payne: Got Depth?"

12. Martin Cockroft, www.christianitytoday.com from Campus Life, Sept/Oct 2000.

13. "Kendall Payne: Jams Line Biography."

14. Herman, "Kendall Payne: Got Depth?"
15. Ibid.
16. Cockroft, www.christianitytoday.com from Campus Life, Sept./Oct. 2000.
17. www.cmcentral.com/artists/27.html.
18. "Kendall Payne: Jams Line Biography."
19. Ibid.

Chapter 19: Supergirl

1. David Lindquist, "Path to Stardom. Moral Compass Guides Newcomer Krystal as She Takes the Stage," *The Indianapolis Star,* 4 March 2001.
2. Greg Webb, Krystal Harris interview, www.cmcentral.com/interviews/30.html, 5 June 2002.
3. Lindquist, "Path to Stardom. Moral Compass Guides Newcomer Krystal as She Takes the Stage."
4. Webb, Krystal Harris interview.
5. Ibid.
6. Ibid.
7. Lindquist, "Path to Stardom. Moral Compass Guides Newcomer Krystal as She Takes the Stage."
8. Ibid.
9. Ibid.
10. Ibid.
11. Ibid.
12. Ibid.
13. Ibid.
14. Webb, Krystal Harris interview.
15. Ibid.
16. Ibid.
17. Ibid.
18. Ibid.
19. "Krystal: The Super Girl Returns!" www.popmusicfan.com/interviews/krystal2.html.
20. www.efanguide.com/~kharris/hoja.html.
21. "Krystal: The Super Girl Returns!"
22. Webb, Krystal Harris interview.
23. Ibid.

Chapter 20: The Stones

1. www.iconomusic.com/it/2002/12s/index.shtml.
2. Ibid.
3. Mike Parker, "The Fast and the Furious," www.webrock.net.
4. Sam Bello, "Paul McCoy of 12 Stones," interview, www.rockrage.com/rockrage_interview/paul_mccoy/paulmccoy_interview2.html.
5. www.iconomusic.com/it/2002/12s/index.shtml.
6. www.relevantmagazine.com.
7. www.iconomusic.com/it/2002/12s/index.shtml.
8. Parker, "The Fast and the Furious."
9. www.iconomusic.com/it/2002/12s/index.shtml.
10. Bello, "Paul McCoy of 12 Stones," interview.

11. Lyrics to "Broken," 12 Stones, www.relevantmagazine.com.
12. www.iconomusic.com/it/2002/12s/index.shtml.
13. Bello, "Paul McCoy of 12 Stones," interview.
14. Ibid.
15. www.relevantmagazine.com.
16. Ibid.
17. www.iconomusic.com/it/2002/12s/index.shtml.
18. Ibid.
19. Ibid.
20. Parker, "The Fast and the Furious."
21. www.iconomusic.com/it/2002/12s/index.shtml.
22. www.relevantmagazine.com.
23. www.iconomusic.com/it/2002/12s/index.shtml.
24. Ibid.
25. Parker, "The Fast and the Furious."
26. www.iconomusic.com/it/2002/12s/index.shtml.
27. Parker, "The Fast and the Furious."
28. www.relevantmagazine.com.

Chapter 21: A New Hill

1. Kevin Powell, www.horizonmag.com/1/hill.htm.
2. Gabriella, "Lauryn Hill: How Sweet It Is," www.insidecx.com/interviews/archive/laurynhill.html.
3. Ibid.
4. Ibid.
5. Ibid.
6. www.mtv.com/bands/h/hill_lauryn/NewsFeature_080401/feature2.jhtml.
7. Ibid.
8. Ibid.
9. Ibid.
10. Ibid.
11. Ibid.
12. Cameron Strang, "The Light Has Enough Light," *Relevant* magazine.
13. http://billboard.com/billboard/hotprod/index.jsp.
14. Robert Hilburn, "On Lauryn Hill's New Album, Less Would Have Been More," *Los Angeles Times.*
15. Jewly Hight, "Unplugged and Unprogrammed," www.relevantmagazine.com.
16. www.mtv.com/bands/h/hill_lauryn/NewsFeature_080401/feature2.jhtml.
17. Powell, www.horizonmag.com/1/hill.htm.
18. www.mtv.com/bands/h/hill_lauryn/NewsFeature_080401/feature2.jhtml.

Chapter 22: A Lion's Roar

1. Tom Chandler, interview with Pedro's David Bazan, www.rasputins.com/manifesto/archives/pedro0900.html.
2. Pedro the Lion interview, www.citypromotions.net/ibellevue/arts/music/pedro.html.
3. Robbie Mackey, "Pedro the Lion" interview, www.carolinabeacon.net/04.20.02/01.shtml.
4. Chandler, interview with Pedro's David Bazan.

251

5. "Pedro the Lion" interview, www.citypromotions.net/ibellevue/arts/music/pedro.html.

6. Ibid.

7. Tom and Scott Hatch, interview, www.decapolis.com/musicreviews/interviews/pedrointerview.shtml.

8. Tim McMahan, "David the Lion," www.timmcmahan.com/pedrothelion.htm.

9. Tom and Scott Hatch, interview.

10. McMahan, "David the Lion."

11. Ibid.

12. Ibid.

13. Mackey, "Pedro the Lion" interview.

14. McMahan, "David the Lion."

15. Interview with "Pedro the Lion," by Michael, Tom Fest 1996, www.geocities.com/athens/olympus/9682/pedro.html.

16. Ibid.

17. McMahan, "David the Lion."

18. "Pedro the Lion" interview.

Chapter 23: Church Boy

1. Brad England and Adam Woodroof, "Ten Questions with Kirk Franklin," www.ccmcom.com/archives/fullstory.asp?id=1629.

2. Susan Brill, "The Curtain Never Falls—Kirk Franklin on Living in the Spotlight," www.somethingtosingabout.com/kirk.asp.

3. www.cogop.org/youth/vickirk.html.

4. Ibid.

5. Ibid.

6. Ibid.

7. Ibid.

8. Ibid.

9. Melissa Riddle, "The Revolution of a Broken Man," www.ccmcom.com/archives/fullstory_cont2.asp?id=2020.

10. Brill, "The Curtain Never Falls—Kirk Franklin on Living in the Spotlight."

11. England and Woodroof, "Ten Questions with Kirk Franklin."

12. Riddle, "The Revolution of a Broken Man."

13. Ibid.

14. Ibid.

15. Ibid.

16. Ibid.

17. Brill, "The Curtain Never Falls—Kirk Franklin on Living in the Spotlight."

18. Interview, www.cogop.org/youth/vickirk.html.

19. Brill, "The Curtain Never Falls—Kirk Franklin on Living in the Spotlight."

Chapter 24: Carrabba's Confession

1. Dashboard Confessional Chris Carrabba interview, by Conrad and Julia Zulia, www.decapolis.com.

2. Ibid.

3. Ibid.

4. Ibid.

5. Josh Spencer, www.strangerthingsmag.com/fsf.html, 24 September 2000.

6. Ibid.

Notes

7. Ibid.

8. Tricia Gallagher, www.altarnative.com/2001/may/features/dashboard.shtml.

9. Interview, www.angelfire.com, 8 July 2001.

10. Spencer, www.strangerthingsmag.com/fsf.html, 24 September 2000.

11. Dashboard Confessional Chris Carrabba interview, by Conrad and Julia Zulia.

12. www.angelfire.com/geek/nca/dashboardconfessional.html.

13. Spencer, www.strangerthingsmag.com/fsf.html, 24 September 2000.

14. Dashboard Confessional Chris Carrabba interview, by Conrad and Julia Zulia.

15. Ibid.

16. Gallagher, www.altarnative.com/2001/may/features/dashboard.shtml.

17. Ibid.

18. Interview, www.angelfire.com, 8 July 2001.

19. Spencer, www.strangerthingsmag.com/fsf.html, 24 September 2000.

20. Dashboard Confessional Chris Carrabba interview, by Conrad and Julia Zulia.

Chapter 25: Under the Radar

1. http://atu2.com.

2. "Direct Quotes From U2," www.mindspring.com/~twhite21/band/U2dquotes.html, January 1987.

3. "Wake Up Dead Man," www.geocities.com/sunsetstrip/backstage/7715/lyrics/pop.html#wake%20Up%20Dead.

4. King James Bible, www.godrules.net/library/kjv/kjvjer33.htm.

5. *Rolling Stone* magazine, 18 January 2001.

6. Alan Light, "Unbreakable Heart," www.atu2.com/news/article.src?ID=1778.

7. Anthony DeCurtis, "Bono: the beliefnet interview, www.beliefnet.com.

8. Ibid.

9. Ibid.

10. Ibid.

11. Ibid.

12. Ibid.

13. Ibid.

14. Ibid.

15. Ibid.

16. Light, "Unbreakable Heart."

Chapter 26: Left Behind

1. Bob Briner, *Final Roar*, Broadman & Holman, 2001.

2. Ibid.

3. Quoted in ibid.

4. www.capo.org/premise/95/april/payton.html.

Chapter 27: Returning to the Mainstream

1. Author interview with Josh Foster, 2002.

2. Ibid.

3. Ibid.

8. Ibid.

4. Ibid.

5. Ibid.

6. Author interview with Patrick McGuire.

7. Ibid.

8. Ibid.

Chapter 29: Doing the Work

1. Quoted in Mark Joseph, *The Rock & Roll Rebellion: Why People of Faith Abandoned Rock Music and Why They're Coming Back* (Nashville: Broadman & Holman, 1999).

Chapter 32: Beyond the Male Nurse Syndrome

1. *Radio & Records* magazine, 19 April 2002, "State of the Industry: Where Are We, And Where Are We Going?—A Conversation with Four Industry Leaders."

2. Ibid.

Chapter 33: Rock and Religion: A Potent Mix

1. Chuck Colson and Nancy Pearcey, *How Now Shall We Live?* (Grand Rapids: Zondervan, 2000).

2. Ibid.

3. Quoted in Os Guinness, *The Call* (Waco, Tex.: Word, 1988).

4. Mark Joseph, *The Rock & Roll Rebellion: Why People of Faith Abandoned Rock Music and Why They're Coming Back* (Nashville: Broadman & Holman, 1999).

5. Terry Mattingly, "Yes, There Is a Mitford," www.tmatt.net.

To keep up with daily news on these and many other artists, go to www.rockrebel.com.